Determinants and Systemic Consequences of International Capital Flows

HG
3891
.D47
1991

A Study by the Research Department of the International Monetary Fund

INTERNATIONAL MONETARY FUND

Washington DC

March 1991

Library of Congress Cataloging-in-Publication Data

Determinants and systemic consequences of international capital flows :
  a study / by the Research Department of the International Monetary
  Fund.
    p. cm. — (Occasional paper / International Monetary Fund,
ISSN 0251-6365 ; no. 77)
    "March 1991."
    Includes bibliographical references
    ISBN 1-55775-205-2
    1. Capital movements. 2. International finance. 3. Balance of
payments—Developing countries. I. International Monetary Fund. Research Dept. II. Series: Occasional paper (International Monetary
Fund) ; no. 77.
HG3891.D47 1991
332'.042—dc20   91-2289
                                                CIP

Price: US$10.00
(US$7.50 to full-time faculty members and
students at universities and colleges)

Please send orders to:
International Monetary Fund, Publication Services
700 19th Street, N.W., Washington, D.C. 20431, U.S.A
Tel.: (202) 623-7430   Telefax: (202) 623-7201

Contents

The following symbols have been used throughout this paper:

... to indicate that data are not available;

— to indicate that the figure is zero or less than half the final digit shown, or that the item does not exist;

– between years or months (e.g., 1990–91 or January–June to indicate the years or months covered, including the beginning and ending years or months;

/ between years (e.g., 1990/91) to indicate a crop or fiscal (financial) year.

"Billion" means a thousand million.

Minor discrepancies between constituent figures and totals are due to rounding.

Preface

This study was prepared in the Research Department of the International Monetary Fund. Its authors are Morris Goldstein, Deputy Director of the Research Department; Donald J. Mathieson, Chief of the Financial Studies Division; David Folkerts-Landau, Deputy Chief of the Financial Studies Division; and Timothy Lane, J. Saúl Lizondo, and Liliana Rojas-Suárez, Economists of the Financial Studies Division. A number of colleagues in the Fund greatly facilitated the preparation of this study by their willingness to exchange views and provide information. The authors are also grateful to Kellett Hannah and Rosita Vera-Bunge for their excellent research assistance, to the editor Elin Knotter, of the External Relations Department, and to Gail Campbell and Rosalind Oliver, for their excellent word processing services. The authors alone are responsible for the study; the opinions expressed are theirs and do not necessarily reflect the views of the Fund.

I

Determinants and Systemic Consequences of International Capital Flows

Morris Goldstein, Donald J. Mathieson, and Timothy Lane

In its communiqué of September 25, 1989, the Interim Committee "encouraged the Executive Board to continue improving the analytical and empirical framework underlying multilateral surveillance, including the measurement, determinants, and systemic consequences of international capital flows." This study addresses the determinants and systemic consequences of international capital flows. A study on the measurement of international capital flows is under preparation.

The first section identifies four of the main trends in capital flows during the 1970s and 1980s. First, there has been a sharp expansion in the scale of net and gross capital flows among the industrial countries, as well as a much increased participation by foreign investors and by foreign financial institutions in the major domestic financial markets. Available indicators suggest that this expansion has been significantly greater than that of international trade flows over the same period. Second, the easing of capital controls and the broader liberalization of financial markets in industrial countries have stimulated competition and brought about a growing integration of domestic and offshore markets—which in turn has generated important efficiency gains. The degree of integration of international capital markets is captured better by rate-of-return differentials (appropriately defined) between markets than by the scale of capital flows themselves. Third, private rather than official capital flows have been the principal source of financing the historically large current account and fiscal imbalances of the industrial countries in the 1970s and 1980s, and within these private flows, flows of securities have increasingly dominated banking flows. Private flows accounted for approximately 75 percent of the financing of the cumulative U.S. current account deficit during 1983–88. Fourth, after borrowing heavily from international banks in the 1970s, many indebted developing countries found their access to international financial markets sharply curtailed in the 1980s, resulting in a pattern of official and private capital flows to them in the late 1980s that was similar to that of the early 1970s. Net nondebt-creating flows nearly matched the cumulative current account deficit of indebted developing countries over the period 1987–89.

The second section examines the determinants of net and gross capital flows. Net capital flows, which serve as the financial counterpart to the transfer of real resources through a trade or current account imbalance, arise only when saving and investment are imbalanced within countries. Gross capital flows, which allow individuals and firms to adjust the form of financial claims issued and held, can be important in improving the liquidity of portfolios and in diversifying risks. Since gross capital flows can be mutually offsetting across countries, they need not involve a transfer of real resources.

Over the past two decades, net and gross capital flows have responded to economic fundamentals, official policies, and market distortions. These economic fundamentals included the global investment opportunities available, the covariances between expected returns on various investments, the growth of wealth in different countries, and differences across economic agents in their willingness to assume risk and in rates of time preference. The relevant official policies include tax policies; official guarantees; capital controls; limitations on the entry of foreign firms into domestic markets; restrictions on the domestic activities, products, locations, and interest rates charged by financial institutions; misaligned real exchange rates; restrictive trade policies; debt-servicing arrears and reschedulings; and unstable macroeconomic policies. Distortions or imperfections inherent in the operation of private markets, such as transaction costs and asymmetric information among market participants, can also limit portfolio diversification and sometimes even distort asset prices.

It has proved difficult to obtain stable empirical relationships between (gross or net) capital flows and their underlying determinants. A key reason is that capital markets can respond to a shock either through capital flows, or through a change in asset prices, or through some combination of the two. Most econometric models have by now forsaken traditional capital flow equations in favor of modeling financial linkages via (arbitrage-type) interest rate parity relationships. Nevertheless, the experience of the past two decades highlights particular fundamentals and/or distortions as playing an important role in explaining particular capital flow developments. It would be hard, for example, to understand the large-scale capital outflows from Germany[1] in 1987–89 without reference to the planned withholding tax on interest income; or the large capital inflow into the United States during 1981–85 without reference to the sharp differences in the monetary/fiscal policy mix between the United States on the one hand and Japan and Germany on the other; or the large-scale capital flight from many developing countries during 1977–84 without reference to uncompetitive interest and exchange rates, large fiscal deficits, and high external debt burdens in these countries.

The third section discusses the systemic consequences of international capital flows for both industrial and developing countries. While it is widely recognized that the closer integration of major domestic and offshore financial markets has yielded important efficiency benefits, structural changes in these financial markets may have reduced the effectiveness of monetary and fiscal policy, may have created new systemic risks associated with increased asset price variability, and may have made more uncertain the access by many developing countries to these markets.

Financial innovation and liberalization provide market participants with "safety valve" sources of credit (whenever domestic credit conditions tighten) and with alternatives for the placement of funds that offer market-related rates of return. This process generally weakens the predictability of the relationship between the authorities' operating instruments, monetary aggregates, and nominal income; reduces the effect of a change in the level of interest rates on the substitution between money and nonmonetary assets; and implies that monetary policy now works more through changes in interest rates and exchange rates than through liquidity or credit constraints. However, the track record of industrial countries in the 1980s does not suggest that the ability of monetary policy to promote price stability has been impaired.

The increased availability of external funding for financing fiscal imbalances raises the issue of whether "fiscal discipline" has been weakened. One answer is that private markets will impose

such discipline progressively on errant borrowers by first charging a widening interest rate differential and then, only if this warning is ignored, by excluding the borrower from the market. But if market discipline is to operate in such a progressive manner, the following four conditions need to be satisfied: (1) there must not be any explicit or implicit guarantee of a bailout by the central or regional authorities; (2) there must not be a "monetization" of the borrower's debts by central bank purchases of these debts; (3) market participants must be fully aware of the debtor's obligations so that an accurate assessment can be made of its debt-servicing obligation and capacity; and (4) the financial system must be strong enough that no single borrower is regarded as "too large to fail." Experience suggests that these conditions have often not been fulfilled.

The growing integration of international capital markets has also increased the incentives and pressures for greater coordination of macroeconomic and financial policies. The increased incentives come partly from the potentially larger "spillover effects" of domestic macroeconomic policy actions when linkages among financial markets are stronger. Given the speed with which major financial shocks can now spread across global markets (as in the equity market crash of October 1987), the case for coordinated crisis management policies, especially among central banks, seems to have been strengthened. In addition, official measures in industrial countries to limit contagion effects in international financial markets have centered on strengthening the structures of major financial institutions and of payments, clearance, and settlement systems as well as on developing better techniques of crisis management.

Official capital flows represent yet another mechanism by which asset prices and the geographical distribution of global saving and investment can be influenced. Except for military assistance, the dominant official capital flows among industrial countries have reflected exchange market intervention. The usefulness and limits of sterilized intervention are by now well known. The key implication of conducting intervention in an environment of potentially large private capital flows is that it will be more difficult for authorities in a single country to achieve their objectives by "going it alone"; if anything, the case for concerted intervention (rather than unilateral intervention) would seem to be strengthened.

Official capital flows from industrial to developing countries encompass a broad range of economic, humanitarian, and military assistance and have been supplied under highly heterogeneous terms and conditions. The availability of official

---

[1] All references to Germany in this paper are to the Federal Republic of Germany as it existed before October 3, 1990 when unification took place.

flows helped cushion the sharply reduced access to private international financial markets by many developing countries since 1982. The 1980s suggest that re-establishing creditworthiness can be a lengthy process, even for countries taking strong adjustment measures, and that official flows can make a valuable contribution during the transition.

This section also reviews more broadly the extent to which developing countries can benefit from a more integrated international financial system. It is argued that the outcome depends largely on whether perceptions of creditworthiness are subject to "contagion effects," on how adept developing countries become in utilizing financial instruments and markets most suitable to their needs, on how successful developing country policy reforms are in both attracting greater private inflows and stemming capital flight, and on whether external resources are put to productive uses.

Private capital flows to developing countries in the 1970s were dominated by commercial bank lending. Flows of securities, including the use of market-based hedging instruments, and direct foreign investment are likely to play a relatively larger role in the 1990s. During the late nineteenth century and the 1920s, long-term bond financing was the principal vehicle for resource transfer between industrial and developing countries. Such bonds can be used to match the maturity of a long-term investment with its financing. At present, considerations of creditworthiness limit the number of developing countries that can tap this market; as creditworthiness is restored, bond markets should become a more prominent source of external finance. Equally promising are equity-related capital flows, namely, foreign direct investment and portfolio investment in equities. One constraint is that only a small number of developing countries presently offer foreign investors free and unrestricted repatriation of capital and of income from shares.

International capital markets can also be used to advantage by developing countries to manage their foreign asset and liability positions. Short-term hedging operations can be carried out using financial and commodities futures and options, and medium-term hedges can be constructed with interest rate caps and forward agreements for major exchange rates and commodity prices. Despite some nontrivial costs and constraints associated with using these hedging instruments, developing country recourse to them has expanded in recent years.

Although the measurement of capital flight raises difficult conceptual and measurement issues, empirical analyses have generally concluded that the domestic residents of many developing countries sharply increased their holdings of external assets during the 1970s and 1980s. While this increase has in part reflected the desire of residents to hold internationally diversified portfolios, it has also been a response to the perceived risks of holding domestic financial instruments. Sound macroeconomic policies, financial liberalizations, and other structural reforms are likely to be key elements in creating incentives for the residents of developing countries to hold their savings in domestic rather than external financial markets.

Studies dealing with systemic risks in payments, clearance, and settlement systems, the determinants of foreign direct investment, and the pricing of risk in securities markets comprise the other chapters in this Occasional Paper.

Trends in International Capital Flows

This section reviews trends in international capital flows among industrial and developing countries during the 1970s and 1980s. The discussion is based on the data presented in the IMF's *Balance of Payments Yearbook*, *International Financial Statistics*, and International Banking Statistics, which reflect the conceptual framework for the capital account described in the Fund's *Balance of Payments Manual* (1977).

Measurement of Capital Flows

A comprehensive examination of the problems associated with measuring international capital flows will be made in a forthcoming report of the Working Party on the Study of the Measurement of International Capital Flows. The measurement of capital account transactions raises the fundamental issues of defining what constitutes a cross-border financial transaction[2] and of deciding how to treat changes in the value of holdings of foreign financial instruments that do not arise as a result of transactions with a nonresident.[3] If all countries[4] adopted

---

[2]Since not all transactions involve an exchange of financial instruments for money (for example, the reinvestment of earnings in an enterprise owned by a foreign direct investor), balance of payments accounting focuses on transactions involving an exchange of value between two parties rather than payments.

[3]Valuation changes arising from exchange rate or asset price movements present a special problem. By convention, realized capital gains or losses that occur with a change of ownership are included in the balance of payments, whereas valuation changes on instruments that are not exchanged are excluded from the balance of payments. Write-offs and write-downs can also change the value of financial assets without a change of ownership.

[4]It should be noted that the term "country" used in this paper does not in all cases refer to a territorial entity that is a state as understood by international law and practice. The term also covers some territorial entities that are not states but for which statistical data are maintained and provided internationally on a separate and independent basis.

Table 1. Global Balances on Capital Account, 1982–88
(In billions of SDRs)

	1982	1983	1984	1985	1986	1987	1988
Capital account balance	56.7	63.8	47.6	38.2	7.2	4.9	27.3
Direct investment	26.9	14.2	13.0	–14.1	–19.6	–28.5	–9.7
Abroad	–21.6	–31.4	–39.0	–61.5	–83.7	–112.8	–109.4
In the reporting economy	48.6	45.5	52.0	47.4	64.1	84.3	99.8
Portfolio investment	–12.0	15.0	27.0	36.2	–7.3	–19.2	–32.2
Assets	–60.2	–42.9	–53.5	–115.1	–158.7	–99.3	–156.8
Liabilities	48.1	57.9	80.5	151.3	151.4	80.0	124.6
Other long-term capital	23.9	14.3	1.1	22.7	–3.1	–7.3	–7.0
Assets	–85.8	–82.8	–69.0	–57.8	–62.8	–74.5	–45.3
Liabilities	109.7	97.1	70.1	80.4	59.7	67.2	38.3
Other short-term capital	–14.8	24.8	24.2	10.1	33.5	123.0	76.2
Assets	–203.5	–101.7	–146.5	–201.5	–375.9	–359.1	–258.8
Liabilities	188.7	126.5	170.7	211.5	409.4	482.1	335.0
Reserves	30.4	–19.9	–33.1	–15.4	–21.0	–119.5	–30.9
Liabilities constituting foreign authorities' reserves	2.3	15.5	15.4	–1.3	24.7	56.4	30.8
Memorandum items:							
Current account balance[1]	–85.9	–64.1	–69.5	–62.9	–36.1	–12.2	–41.3
Net errors and omissions	29.1	0.1	21.5	23.9	28.3	6.9	13.8

Source: International Monetary Fund, *Balance of Payments Statistics,* Vol. 40, Part 2.
[1]Including exceptional financing transactions.

symmetrical accounting treatments of cross-border transactions, the reported capital outflows and inflows of all countries would, in principle, just match. However, discrepancies can arise if a transaction is not recorded or recorded asymmetrically in the accounts of the capital exporting and capital importing countries.[5] Moreover, the scale of capital flows may be understated if a transaction is missed in both sets of accounts. These measurement difficulties are reflected in the global capital account discrepancy, which averaged SDR 35 billion a year during 1982–88 (Table 1).[6]

New financial instruments and institutional arrangements in major domestic and offshore financial markets have contributed to these measure-

ment problems.[7] New instruments, such as interest rate and exchange rate swaps, required that new reporting channels be developed. More generally, changes in computer and telecommunication technologies have increased the ability of domestic institutions to undertake transactions with nonresidents that are beyond the reach of existing domestic reporting requirements. The extent to which these structural changes have led to an underreporting of capital flows is not yet known. In what follows, it is assumed that measurement problems are not severe enough to invalidate the broad trends evident in existing data.

Major Trends

Four key trends have characterized capital flows during the 1970s and 1980s.

---

[5]In the presence of capital controls, overinvoicing and underinvoicing of exports and imports can also create confusion between current and capital account transactions.

[6]This discrepancy implies a growing stock of cross-border assets recognized by the issuing countries but not reflected in the statistics of countries whose residents have acquired these instruments.

[7]The structural changes in international markets were examined in "Innovations and Institutional Changes in Major Financial Markets—A Ten-Year Perspective," Section III in Watson and others (1988).

Sharp Expansion in Scale of Net and Gross Capital Flows in Major Industrial Countries

The sharp upswing in the level of *net capital flows* among the major industrial countries has been the counterpart to the historically large current account imbalances during the 1970s and 1980s (Table 2). Although large current account imbalances were evident in 1973–75 and in 1979–81, net capital flows between the industrial countries expanded most rapidly after 1982. Germany had an average annual net capital outflow of $1 billion (equivalent to 0.5 percent of GNP) in 1970–72; in 1985–88, this outflow had grown to an average of $38 billion a year (equal to nearly 4 percent of GNP). Over the same period, Japan's capital outflow rose from $5 billion a year to $75 billion a year (3.6 percent of GNP). The net capital inflow into the United States accelerated from an average of $2 billion a year (0.1 percent of GNP) in 1970–72 to an average of $129 billion a year (3 percent of GNP) in 1985–88.

An even more rapid expansion has occurred in the scale of *gross capital flows* (Table 3), which has been reflected in increased cross-border banking and flows of securities, the development of the off-shore (Eurocurrency) markets, and the entry of foreign institutions into domestic markets. For example, the stock of international loans (net of re-depositing by banks) rose from $175 billion at the end of December 1973 (5 percent of industrial countries' GNP) to $2,490 billion at the end of September 1989 (17 percent of industrial countries'

GNP). The stock of Eurocurrency and foreign bonds also increased from $259 billion at the end of 1982 (3 percent of industrial countries' GNP) to $1,085 billion at the end of 1988 (8 percent of industrial countries' GNP). Moreover, between 1979 and 1988, the volume of international equity transactions increased on average by 18 percent a year; and reached $1.2 trillion in 1988.

The "foreign" presence in major domestic financial markets has also increased as the need to finance large fiscal and current account balances in the industrial countries has created pressures for the breakdown of restrictions on domestic and external financial transactions. Data on the residency of the holders of industrial countries' bonds are notoriously poor; nonetheless the United States reported that, while foreign and international entities held 7 percent of the Federal Government's outstanding securities at the end of 1970, the proportion reached nearly 17 percent at the end of 1988. In Germany, central government debt held by foreigners was reported to have increased from 5 percent at the end of 1974 to 34 percent at the end of 1988. As cross-border holdings of equity have expanded, Salomon Brothers (1989) have estimated, for example, that the average correlation between U.S. stock prices and those in other major markets has increased from 0.35 in 1975–79 to 0.62 in 1985–88. In any case, it has become evident that large shocks can be quickly transmitted across these markets (such as in October 1987 and October 1989). Competitive pressures in major domestic

Table 2. Net International Capital Flows of Major Industrial Countries, 1970–88
(Period averages)

	Germany			Japan			United States		
	1970–72	1979–81	1985–88	1970–72	1979–81	1985–88	1970–72	1979–81	1985–88
Capital account balance[1] (in billions of U.S. dollars)	–0.98	7.57	–37.57	–4.79	4.77	–75.12	1.63	–2.36	128.71
Capital account balance (in billions of U.S. dollars deflated by U.S. GNP deflator (1985 = 100))	–2.45	9.76	–35.95	–12.00	6.15	–71.88	4.08	–3.04	123.15
Capital account balance as percent of GNP	–0.45	0.96	–3.77	–1.88	0.48	–3.59	0.13	–0.08	2.93

Source: International Monetary Fund, *Balance of Payments Statistics.*
[1]This is taken as the counterpart to the current account imbalance. A positive value indicates a capital account surplus (inflow).

Table 3. International Bank Lending and International Bonds, 1973–First Three Quarters of 1989[1]
(In billions of U.S. dollars)

	1973	1974	1975	1976	1977	1978	1979	1980	1981	1982	1983	1984	1985	1986	1987	1988	First Three Quarters 1989[2]
International bank lending																	
BIS data (net of redepositing: stocks)	175	230	265	340	435	530	665	810	945	1,020	1,085	1,285	1,485	1,790	2,225	2,380	2,490
Growth rate (in percent)		31	15	28	28	22	25	22	17	8	6	18	16	21	24	7	12
BIS data (net of redepositing: flows)		45	50	70	55	85	125	160	165	95	85	90	105	180	300	225	235
Growth rate (in percent)		26	22	26	16	20	24	24	20	10	8	8	8	12	17	10	11
BIS data (gross: flows)		57	88	97	89	180	206	241	265	181	106	124	234	512	598	425	410
Growth rate (in percent)		18	22	22	16	27	24	22	20	12	7	6	11	20	18	10	9
IMF data (gross: flows)							347	414	404	186	166	180	276	532	798	557	506
Growth rate (in percent)							27	24	20	8	7	7	10	17	20	11	...
International bonds																	
BIS data (outstanding stock)										259	...	...	557	773	991	1,085	...
OECD data (net of redemptions: flows)										58	59	90	132	163	105	144	133

Sources: Bank for International Settlements (BIS); Organization for Economic Cooperation and Development (OECD); International Monetary Fund, International Banking Statistics (IBS); and IMF staff estimates.

[1] IMF-based bank lending data on cross-border changes in bank claims are derived from the Fund's International Banking Statistics (cross-border interbank accounts by residence of borrowing bank plus international bank credits to nonbanks by residence of borrower), excluding changes attributed to exchange rate movements. BIS-based data are derived from quarterly statistics contained in the BIS's *International Banking Developments*; the figures shown are adjusted for the effects of exchange rate movements. Differences between the IMF data and the BIS data are mainly accounted for by the different coverages. The BIS data are derived from geographical analyses provided by banks in the BIS reporting area. The IMF data derive cross-border interbank positions from the regular money and banking data supplied by member countries, while the IMF analysis of transactions with nonbanks is based on data from geographical breakdowns provided by the BIS reporting countries and additional banking centers. Neither the IBS nor the BIS series are fully comparable over time because of the expansion of coverage.

[2] Provisional data.

Table 4. Bid-Ask Spreads on Eurocurrency Deposits[1]
(Average of daily spreads)

	1980–82	1987–89
Six-month deposits		
U.S. dollar	12.21	12.56
Pound sterling	66.94	12.12
French franc	47.92	13.46
Deutsche mark	12.96	12.61
Japanese yen	16.89	11.54
Three-month deposits		
U.S. dollar	12.58	12.61
Pound sterling	66.74	12.00
French franc	48.96	13.36
Deutsche mark	12.82	12.88
Japanese yen	16.95	11.75

Source: Data Resources, Incorporated.
[1] Measured in basis points.

financial markets have also been increased by the entry of foreign institutions. Between 1970 and 1985 the number of foreign banking offices in the United States rose from about 50 to over 780, whereas in Germany, foreign banking offices rose from 77 to 287.

Increased competition has also generated important efficiency gains in major domestic and offshore markets, which have been reflected in a sharp decline in bid-ask spreads.[8] In the Eurocurrency markets, for example, bid-ask spreads for three- and six-month time deposits denominated in some currencies had declined by the late 1980s to only one fifth of the levels evident in the early 1980s (Table 4). These spreads are now relatively uniform across currencies.

Globalization and Integration of Offshore and Major Domestic Financial Markets

The progressive relaxation of capital controls as well as the broader financial liberalization in the industrial countries has brought about a growing integration and globalization of major offshore and domestic financial markets. Indeed, the integration of global financial markets has proceeded much more rapidly than that of goods markets—in part because the latter has been inhibited by protection-

ism. As discussed in the final section, this growing integration of financial markets has important implications for the effectiveness of macroeconomic policies and systemic risks.

There are several different approaches to measuring the degree of integration of financial markets. A high degree of integration can be present even without a large volume of capital flows. For example, trading of some benchmark U.S. Government securities often takes place simultaneously on markets both inside and outside the United States. The announcement of an unanticipated event (such as an increase in the Federal Reserve's discount rate) can trigger an immediate adjustment of the prices of these securities in the markets in all countries without any capital flows or even any transactions occurring. Capital flows between countries are likely to occur only if participants in the different markets have conflicting views on the effects of the unanticipated event. This suggests that other measures besides the scale of capital flows must be examined when attempting to gauge the degree of integration between financial markets.

One measure of the integration of major domestic and offshore markets is the interest differential between the cost of interbank funds denominated in the same currency in the two markets.[9] As indicated in Chart 1, these differentials have been reduced dramatically during the 1980s, especially for countries such as France, which have relaxed their capital controls.

Another measure of interest rate relationships is the covered interest rate differential. It can be defined as the difference between the interest rates on instruments issued by comparable borrowers but denominated in different currencies, adjusted for the cost of cover in the forward exchange market.[10] Covered interest rate parity (CIP) is achieved when this difference is arbitraged to zero. Recent empirical studies[11] have concluded that the removal or weakening of exchange controls in the industrial countries has helped establish CIP in many short-term markets. Such arbitrage has been most clearly evident in the relationship between interest rates on Eurocurrency deposits (Chart 2)

---

[8] The bid price reflects an offer to buy an instrument, whereas the ask price reflects an offer to sell.

[9] As capital controls have been relaxed and financial liberalizations have occurred in the major industrial countries, the cost and regulatory incentives for operating in the offshore markets have diminished (see Folkerts-Landau and Mathieson (1988)).

[10] If F is the forward exchange rate for the delivery of foreign exchange in n periods, and S is the current spot exchange rate (in units of domestic currency per unit of foreign currency), then the forward premium (if positive) or discount (if negative) on the foreign currency will be $\delta = (F-S)/S$. Moreover, if i is the nominal interest rate in the domestic country (with an asterisk indicating the foreign country) on an instrument maturing in n periods, then the covered interest rate differential is $i - i^* - \delta$.

[11] For a summary of available evidence, see Frankel (1991).

Chart 1. Domestic and Offshore Interest Rates: United States and France, June 1973–December 1989
(In percent)

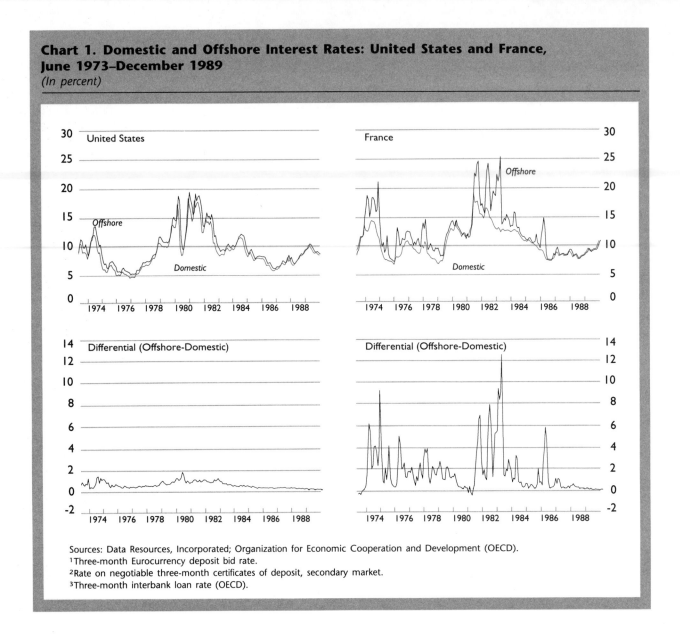

Sources: Data Resources, Incorporated; Organization for Economic Cooperation and Development (OECD).
[1]Three-month Eurocurrency deposit bid rate.
[2]Rate on negotiable three-month certificates of deposit, secondary market.
[3]Three-month interbank loan rate (OECD).

and between onshore and offshore interest rates for comparable monetary instruments.[12]

Yet a third indicator is provided by deviations from uncovered interest parity (UIP), where the interest rate differential is adjusted for the expected rate of depreciation of the domestic currency rather than for the cost of forward cover. This concept is more general in the sense that it can be applied to even long-maturity instruments where forward cover is not available. However, judging whether UIP has been satisfied requires estimating the expected rate of depreciation, which is not directly observable. Empirical analyses[13] suggest that departures from UIP could therefore reflect either a lack of integration, or errors in measuring expected exchange rate depreciation, or a risk premium.[14]

---

[12]However, the arbitrage of covered interest rate differentials in medium- and long-term securities tends to be less exact, since the availability of forward cover for maturities beyond two years is limited. The rapid growth of the markets for interest rate and foreign exchange swaps has helped fill this gap. Nonetheless, most swaps still have an average maturity of only five years.

[13]Boughton (1988) surveys this work.

[14]The increased volatility of exchange rates in the 1980s may have made exchange rate forecasting more difficult and inhibited the establishment of UIP for longer-maturity instruments.

**Chart 2. Covered and Uncovered Interest Rate Differentials:[1]
U.S. Dollar Versus Other Currencies**

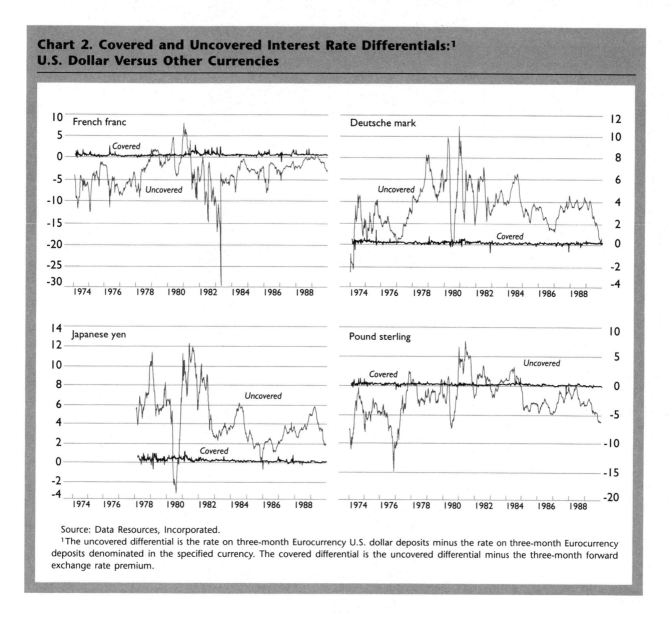

Source: Data Resources, Incorporated.
[1]The uncovered differential is the rate on three-month Eurocurrency U.S. dollar deposits minus the rate on three-month Eurocurrency deposits denominated in the specified currency. The covered differential is the uncovered differential minus the three-month forward exchange rate premium.

Capital market integration can also be measured in terms of departures from real interest rate parity.[15] Such deviations can reflect the failure of either UIP or purchasing power parity (PPP). Since the expected change in the exchange rate and in price levels at home and abroad are not directly observable, it has proved difficult to identify the most important sources of real interest rate spreads. On an ex post basis, real interest rate spreads, especially on longer-term instruments, have remained significantly large (Chart 3).[16]

[15]The real interest rate spread can be measured as the sum of the uncovered interest rate spread and the expected real exchange rate depreciation. If r is the real interest rate, the real interest rate differential can be written as $r - r^* = (i - \pi_p) - (i^* - \pi_p^*) = (i - i^*) - (\pi_p - \pi_p^*)$, where i is the nominal interest rate, π_p is the expected rate of inflation, and asterisks represent foreign variables. By adding and subtracting the expected depreciation of the home currency π^e, then

$$r - r^* = (i - i^* - \pi^e) + (\pi^e - \pi_p + \pi_p^*)$$

uncovered interest rate spread	expected real exchange rate depreciation

[16]While Frankel and MacArthur (1988) concluded that expected real exchange rate depreciation has been the principal source of real interest rate spreads, Adler and Lehmann (1983) argued that PPP holds on an ex ante, if not ex post basis, which suggests that deviations from UIP would be the primary source of real interest rate spreads. Such deviations could reflect uncertainties about country risks (for example, owing to the imposition of capital controls, taxes, or other country-specific restrictions on capital flows) and default risks (especially on private securities).

Chart 3. Real Interest Rate Differentials[1]

(In percent per annum)

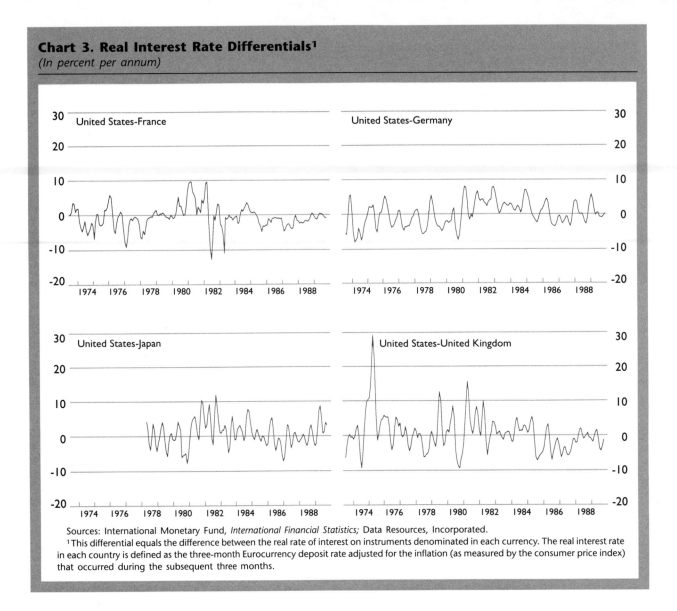

Sources: International Monetary Fund, *International Financial Statistics;* Data Resources, Incorporated.

[1] This differential equals the difference between the real rate of interest on instruments denominated in each currency. The real interest rate in each country is defined as the three-month Eurocurrency deposit rate adjusted for the inflation (as measured by the consumer price index) that occurred during the subsequent three months.

To sum up, recent studies of interest rate differentials suggest that integration in major financial markets has proceeded quite far for short-term instruments. In contrast, the presence of exchange risk still limits the degree of financial integration for longer-term markets—although returns on longer-term debt and equity instruments have recently shown a greater tendency to move together—especially during periods of turbulence, such as October 1987.

In a world characterized by highly integrated capital markets, domestic saving and investment need not be tightly linked, since domestic investors can rely on external financing. However, starting with work by Feldstein and Horioka (1980), it has generally been found that the ratios of investment to income and saving to income have in practice been highly correlated, and this holds for both industrial and developing countries.[17]

This apparent conflict between high correlations of national saving and investment (which suggest low capital mobility) and the shrinking of cross-border interest rate differentials (which suggest high capital mobility) has in turn brought forth several explanations, ranging from government policy responses to current account developments, to

---

[17]Dooley, Frankel, and Mathieson (1987) examined the correlations for both industrial countries and various groups of developing countries. The only group where there was *not* a high correlation between domestic saving and investment was for the developing countries that were large recipients of official transfers.

barriers that inhibit net wealth transfers, to differences between private and official behavior.[18] At this point, the evidence needed to discriminate among these alternative hypotheses is not yet available.[19]

Dominant Role of Private Flows in Financing Fiscal and Current Account Imbalances

Private capital flows provided most of the cross-country financing of fiscal and current account imbalances for the developing countries in the 1970s and for the industrial countries in the 1970s and 1980s. Moreover, while banking flows were the dominant source of private financing to developing countries in the 1970s, transactions in securities became an increasingly important element in private capital flows among the industrial countries throughout the 1970s and 1980s.

A hallmark of the period 1973–81 was that the financing of the current account imbalances of the non-oil developing countries (Tables 5 and 6) and of the oil exporting developing countries[20] (Tables 7 and 8) relied much more than in earlier periods on the use of indirect finance (through financial intermediaries) and less on direct finance (through bond issuance or foreign direct investment).[21] The large current account surpluses of the oil exporting

developing countries initially led to the placement of funds in bank deposits and short-term government securities in the industrial countries and offshore markets; only later was a large proportion of these surpluses invested in long-term securities and other less liquid assets.[22] By the same token, nearly three fourths of the current account deficits for the non-oil developing countries were financed by other net external borrowing.[23]

Any description of capital flows of developing countries should also pay attention to the development of capital flight. Notwithstanding the considerable conceptual and measurement problems involved, previous *World Economic Outlook* studies[24] have estimated the scale of capital flight from developing countries as $165–200 billion in 1975–85. The pace of capital flight was uneven—with about $5 billion a year occurring during 1975–78, and $25–30 billion a year during 1979–82. Since both net lending by foreign creditors to developing countries and capital flight increased sharply during the second half of the 1970s, the intermediation between domestic savings and investment in some developing countries was essentially internationalized: a portion of domestic savings was placed offshore, and this portion was offset by increased bank claims on national governments and private corporations. With the onset of debt-servicing difficulties for many developing countries in the 1980s, this intermediation process stopped. At this point, capital flight involved a net real resource transfer in the sense that the residents of the indebted developing countries could obtain net external claims only through larger net exports of goods and services to the rest of the world.

---

[18]Fiscal policy changes that are undertaken to limit current account imbalances could imply, for example, a high measured correlation between national saving and investment even in the presence of high capital mobility. Alternatively, the small interest rate differentials could imply high capital mobility only for short-term financial instruments but not for claims on physical capital. Financial liberalization may have only a relatively limited impact on physical capital mobility, which would be more influenced by uncertainties regarding country risk factors such as future taxes, capital controls, and political and economic instability.

[19]Frankel (1991) and Feldstein and Bacchetta (1991) have argued that the high correlation between saving and investment in the industrial countries began to break down in the 1980s. Bayoumi (1990) has also indicated that the relationship between saving, investment, and current account imbalances has varied with the nature of the exchange rate regime. Using long-term data on the United Kingdom, he found that there was little correlation between U.K. saving and investment during the gold standard period but a high correlation in the postwar period up to 1980. In the 1980s, the relationship appears to be reverting to that evident in the gold standard period.

[20]The oil exporting developing countries included Algeria, Indonesia, the Islamic Republic of Iran, Iraq, Kuwait, Libyan Arab Jamahiriya, Nigeria, Oman, Qatar, Saudi Arabia, United Arab Emirates, and Venezuela.

[21]Yeager (1976) noted that the current account deficits of the United States and Latin America in the late 1800s were primarily financed by bond purchases by European (particularly British) investors.

Much of this indirect finance was conducted through institutions located in offshore rather than domestic markets, in part reflecting the desire of financial intermediaries to operate in a less regulated environment. In addition, savers in both industrial

and developing countries indicated a preference for holding indirect (deposit) claims on financial institutions based in the industrial countries rather than direct claims (either through holding external debt or domestic financial instruments) on developing countries. This portfolio preference presumably reflected the perception that indirect deposit claims offered higher risk-adjusted returns than holding direct claims, the presence of explicit (or implicit) official deposit insurance in some industrial countries, and the desire to hold relatively liquid short-term instruments. For a discussion of these factors, see Folkerts-Landau (1985).

[22]Since some oil exporting countries also borrowed from abroad, their cash surplus exceeded their current account surplus. The *World Economic Outlook* estimated that the cumulative cash surplus available for disposition during 1974–81 amounted to approximately $475 billion.

[23]Other net external borrowing included borrowing from private creditors and short-term official flows. As a result of this borrowing, total external debt of the net debtor developing countries rose from $164 billion at the end of 1974 to $781 billion at the end of 1982.

[24]For example, see Deppler and Williamson (1987). These studies have been based on a "derived" measure, which estimated that part of a country's stock of foreign assets that did not yield a recorded inflow of investment income credits (see Dooley (1986)).

Table 5. Non-Oil Developing Countries: External Financing, 1969–79
(In billions of U.S. dollars)

	1969	1970	1971	1972	1973	1974	1975	1976	1977	1978	1979
Deficit on goods, services, and private transfers[1]	5.99	11.46	14.82	8.41	9.54	37.12	45.29	31.92	28.15	39.62	58.57
Nondebt-creating flows, net	4.98	5.93	7.15	6.85	10.33	14.76	12.21	12.15	14.64	16.66	21.97
Official transfers	2.75	2.91	3.39	3.79	5.77	9.26	7.86	7.77	8.67	8.57	11.42
Direct investment, net	2.07	2.27	2.66	2.71	4.22	4.83	4.92	4.49	5.14	6.41	8.63
SDR allocation, gold monetization, and valuation changes	0.16	0.75	1.10	0.35	0.33	0.68	–0.57	–0.11	0.83	1.68	1.91
Asset transactions, net[2]	–1.31	–0.90	–1.11	–3.18	–4.34	–2.95	–2.31	–5.33	–6.48	–5.58	–7.98
Net errors and omissions[3]	–0.93	0.50	0.49	–0.36	–0.75	–1.66	–3.96	–5.89	–4.91	–6.51	–1.67
Use of reserves	–4.12	–4.07	–4.47	–11.35	–12.75	–4.28	–2.12	–15.61	–14.14	–20.13	–13.16
Net external borrowing	7.38	9.99	12.76	16.45	17.05	31.25	41.48	46.59	39.04	55.17	59.41
Reserve-related liabilities	–0.15	–0.49	0.12	0.29	0.22	1.58	2.08	3.97	1.07	1.96	1.45
Net credit from IMF[4]	–0.18	–0.50	0.10	0.28	0.12	1.49	1.98	2.97	0.09	0.53	0.97
Liabilities constituting foreign authorities' reserves[5]	0.03	0.01	0.02	—	0.09	0.09	0.10	1.00	0.99	1.43	0.47
Long-term borrowing from official creditors, net[6]	...	—	3.43	5.05	4.52	8.08	13.06	12.78	11.92	12.31	28.95
Other net external borrowing[7]	...	10.48	9.21	11.12	12.31	21.59	26.34	29.84	26.04	40.90	29.01
Memorandum items:											
Net borrowing from commercial banks[8]	...	...	...	...	...	...	...	...	...	...	...
Exceptional financing	–0.02	0.24	0.30	0.70	0.45	1.51	3.29	2.76	2.63	1.19	1.82
Of which:											
Arrears	0.04	—	0.02	0.09	–0.04	0.31	0.16	0.29	1.89	0.74	0.04
Reschedulings	—	—	—	—	—	—	—	—	0.01	0.01	0.52

Source: International Monetary Fund, *World Economic Outlook*, various issues.

Note: Except where otherwise footnoted, estimates shown here are based on national balance of payments statistics. These flows are not always easily reconcilable with year-to-year changes in either debtor- or creditor-reported debt statistics, in part because the latter are affected by changes in valuation.

[1] Equivalent to current account deficit less official transfers. In this table, official transfers are treated as external financing.

[2] Pertains primarily to export credit.

[3] Positioned here on the presumption that estimates reflect primarily unrecorded capital outflows.

[4] Includes use of Fund credit under General Resources Account, Trust Fund, structural adjustment facility, and enhanced structural adjustment facility. The impact of prospective programs is incorporated.

[5] Comprises short-term borrowing by monetary authorities from other monetary authorities.

[6] Estimates of net disbursements by official creditors (other than monetary authorities) derived from debt statistics. Official net disbursements include the increase in official claims caused by the transfer of officially guaranteed claims to the guarantor agency in the creditor country, usually in the context of debt reschedulings.

[7] Residually calculated. Except for discrepancies in coverage, amounts shown reflect net external borrowing from private creditors and short-term official flows (primarily interest arrears on official debt).

[8] Based on changes in cross-border bank claims reported in the Fund's International Banking Statistics, adjusted for valuation changes attributed to exchange rate movements. Excludes six offshore banking centers covered by the *World Economic Outlook* (The Bahamas, Bahrain, Hong Kong, Netherlands Antilles, Panama, and Singapore).

Table 6. Non-Oil Developing Countries: External Financing, 1980–89
(In billions of U.S. dollars)

	1980	1981	1982	1983	1984	1985	1986	1987	1988	1989
Deficit on goods, services, and private transfers[1]	81.35	104.82	82.64	49.84	35.22	39.83	31.30	8.11	12.69	23.48
Nondebt-creating flows, net	22.13	26.29	23.43	21.21	21.26	30.44	28.05	36.27	31.70	28.71
Official transfers	12.32	13.23	12.56	12.99	13.22	15.96	16.83	16.67	17.25	17.23
Direct investment, net	8.39	12.76	11.75	8.33	9.43	8.73	8.41	11.52	12.61	11.59
SDR allocation, gold monetization, and valuation changes	1.42	0.30	–0.88	–0.10	–1.39	5.76	2.82	8.08	1.84	–0.11
Asset transactions, net[2]	–8.22	–12.88	–8.84	–7.05	–10.86	–12.78	–13.25	–13.34	–15.86	–9.51
Net errors and omissions[3]	–10.18	–14.67	–20.18	–13.69	–6.07	–1.94	7.77	–1.58	–1.58	—
Use of reserves	–8.67	–5.75	4.50	–10.78	–16.18	–8.26	–26.45	–47.83	–12.71	–23.87
Net external borrowing	86.30	111.83	83.73	60.15	47.08	32.37	35.19	34.58	11.15	28.16
Reserve-related liabilities	4.55	7.07	10.69	7.15	4.56	–0.08	–3.27	–6.06	–4.44	–2.25
Net credit from IMF[4]	3.04	6.64	6.95	10.56	4.73	0.34	–2.73	–6.45	–4.94	–1.75
Liabilities constituting foreign authorities' reserves[5]	1.51	0.42	3.75	–3.40	–0.16	–0.42	–0.54	0.39	0.51	–0.49
Long-term borrowing from offical creditors, net[6]	23.14	27.28	29.38	30.17	29.92	17.99	24.56	16.58	14.90	23.79
Other net external borrowing[7]	58.62	77.49	43.66	22.82	12.60	14.46	13.89	24.06	0.69	6.61
Memorandum items:										
Net borrowing from commercial banks[8]	59.29	84.59	42.76	22.20	16.78	4.31	2.02	17.15	–10.36	4.17
Exceptional financing	5.94	11.95	20.29	32.30	39.28	32.26	40.58	46.76	46.64	46.80
Of which:										
Arrears	–1.22	5.52	9.90	7.41	2.92	–9.61	9.27	5.51	8.62	9.21
Reschedulings	3.38	3.65	5.50	22.78	33.10	38.54	27.83	40.78	36.69	33.93

Source: International Monetary Fund, *World Economic Outlook*, various issues.

Note: Except where otherwise footnoted, estimates shown here are based on national balance of payments statistics. These flows are not always easily reconcilable with year-to-year changes in either debtor- or creditor-reported debt statistics, in part because the latter are affected by changes in valuation.

[1] Equivalent to current account deficit less official transfers. In this table, official transfers are treated as external financing.

[2] Pertains primarily to export credit.

[3] Positioned here on the presumption that estimates reflect primarily unrecorded capital outflows.

[4] Includes use of Fund credit under General Resources Account, Trust Fund, structural adjustment facility, and enhanced structural adjustment facility. The impact of prospective programs is incorporated.

[5] Comprises short-term borrowing by monetary authorities from other monetary authorities.

[6] Estimates of net disbursements by official creditors (other than monetary authorities) derived from debt statistics. Official net disbursements include the increase in official claims caused by the transfer of officially guaranteed claims to the guarantor agency in the creditor country, usually in the context of debt reschedulings.

[7] Residually calculated. Except for discrepancies in coverage, amounts shown reflect net external borrowing from private creditors and short-term official flows (primarily interest arrears on official debt).

[8] Based on changes in cross-border bank claims reported in the Fund's International Banking Statistics, adjusted for valuation changes attributed to exchange rate movements. Excludes six offshore banking centers covered by the *World Economic Outlook* (The Bahamas, Bahrain, Hong Kong, Netherlands Antilles, Panama, and Singapore).

Table 7. Oil Exporting Developing Countries: External Financing, 1969–79
(In billions of U.S. dollars)

	1969	1970	1971	1972	1973	1974	1975	1976	1977	1978	1979
Deficit on goods, services, and private transfers[1]	1.47	0.62	−1.63	−1.68	−6.14	−69.64	−36.51	−39.46	−28.81	−5.03	−65.84
Nondebt-creating flows, net	0.60	0.55	0.94	−0.75	−0.62	−16.08	−2.86	−6.19	−3.97	−5.57	−4.40
Official transfers	−0.11	−0.05	0.10	−0.14	−0.74	−2.16	−4.34	−3.51	−4.16	−5.84	−5.12
Direct investment, net	0.64	0.52	0.45	−0.46	0.14	−6.33	1.19	−2.57	−0.60	0.54	−0.37
SDR allocation, gold monetization, and valuation changes	0.07	0.08	0.38	−0.15	−0.02	−7.60	0.29	−0.10	0.79	−0.27	1.09
Asset transactions, net[2]	−0.02	−0.33	−0.35	−2.00	−3.45	−23.78	−20.18	−26.82	−19.63	−16.63	−39.10
Net errors and omissions[3]	−0.33	−0.24	−0.50	0.61	−2.62	−2.16	−2.30	0.28	−3.51	−0.26	−6.33
Use of reserves	0.63	−0.04	−3.07	−2.04	−4.44	−38.21	−9.57	−9.86	−11.49	4.37	−27.10
Net external borrowing	0.59	0.68	1.36	2.51	4.98	10.58	−1.60	3.13	9.79	13.06	11.09
Reserve-related liabilities	0.05	0.12	0.12	−0.31	−0.02	0.08	−0.21	—	0.02	−0.12	—
Net credit from IMF[4]	0.05	0.03	−0.01	−0.02	−0.10	−0.02	—	—	—	—	—
Liabilities constituting foreign authorities' reserves[5]	—	0.09	0.13	−0.29	0.09	0.10	−0.21	—	0.02	−0.12	—
Long-term borrowing from official creditors, net[6]	...	—	0.93	0.60	0.99	0.46	0.88	1.73	2.56	3.82	1.77
Other net external borrowing[7]	...	0.56	0.31	2.22	4.01	10.05	−2.26	1.40	7.21	9.37	9.31
Memorandum items:											
Net borrowing from commercial banks[8]	...	...	...	...	...	...	...	...	...	...	...
Exceptional financing	—	—	—	—	—	—	1.20	0.28	—	—	—
Of which:											
Arrears	—	—	—	—	—	—	—	—	—	—	—
Reschedulings	—	—	—	—	—	—	—	—	—	—	—

Source: International Monetary Fund, World Economic Outlook, various issues.

Note: Except where otherwise footnoted, estimates shown here are based on national balance of payments statistics. These flows are not always easily reconcilable with year-to-year changes in either debtor- or creditor-reported debt statistics, in part because the latter are affected by changes in valuation.

[1]Equivalent to current account deficit less official transfers. In this table, official transfers are treated as external financing.

[2]Pertains primarily to export credit.

[3]Positioned here on the presumption that estimates reflect primarily unrecorded capital outflows.

[4]Includes use of Fund credit under General Resources Account, Trust Fund, structural adjustment facility, and enhanced structural adjustment facility. The impact of prospective programs is incorporated.

[5]Comprises short-term borrowing by monetary authorities from other monetary authorities.

[6]Estimates of net disbursements by official creditors (other than monetary authorities) derived from debt statistics. Official net disbursements include the increase in official claims caused by the transfer of officially guaranteed claims to the guarantor agency in the creditor country, usually in the context of debt reschedulings.

[7]Residually calculated. Except for discrepancies in coverage, amounts shown reflect net external borrowing from private creditors and short-term official flows (primarily interest arrears on official debt).

[8]Based on changes in cross-border bank claims reported in the Fund's International Banking Statistics, adjusted for valuation changes attributed to exchange rate movements. Excludes six offshore banking centers covered by the World Economic Outlook (The Bahamas, Bahrain, Hong Kong, Netherlands Antilles, Panama, and Singapore).

Table 8. Oil Exporting Developing Countries: External Financing, 1980–89
(In billions of U.S. dollars)

	1980	1981	1982	1983	1984	1985	1986	1987	1988	1989
Deficit on goods, services, and private transfers[1]	−109.79	−54.51	2.35	16.92	2.41	−5.03	24.79	1.63	11.37	−1.09
Nondebt-creating flows, net	−10.71	−4.86	2.59	−2.50	−1.52	1.53	−0.40	−0.27	−1.21	−0.52
Official transfers	−6.99	−6.21	−4.65	−3.85	−3.10	−2.97	−2.01	−2.79	−2.28	−2.16
Direct investment, net	−4.68	4.88	8.06	4.39	4.22	1.85	1.09	0.88	0.91	1.46
SDR allocation, gold monetization, and valuation changes	0.96	−3.52	−0.83	−3.04	−2.64	2.64	0.52	1.64	0.16	0.17
Asset transactions, net[2]	−68.21	−65.57	−40.60	4.40	−4.92	1.99	−4.72	2.73	−3.13	−2.08
Net errors and omissions[3]	−3.13	−5.74	−5.53	−5.28	1.16	−0.97	−0.80	−2.58	−1.33	—
Use of reserves	−30.49	12.49	31.26	8.34	5.23	−10.12	22.34	−7.21	12.42	−7.52
Net external borrowing	2.76	9.18	14.64	11.95	2.45	2.55	8.37	8.95	4.62	9.03
Reserve-related liabilities	−0.19	−0.15	−0.12	0.69	−0.08	−0.62	—	0.80	0.77	2.90
Net credit from IMF[4]	—	—	—	0.45	—	−0.39	—	0.60	−0.06	2.80
Liabilities constituting foreign authorities' reserves[5]	−0.19	−0.15	−0.12	0.23	−0.08	−0.23	—	0.20	0.83	0.10
Long-term borrowing from official creditors, net[6]	1.35	3.28	5.36	3.47	4.03	6.10	4.30	5.40	3.38	5.42
Other net external borrowing[7]	1.60	6.05	9.40	7.80	−1.50	−2.94	4.06	2.75	0.47	0.72
Memorandum items:										
Net borrowing from commercial banks[8]	14.04	16.71	8.76	7.01	−2.61	0.59	−0.33	0.31	4.89	2.65
Exceptional financing	—	—	3.35	7.99	1.18	1.59	8.32	3.56	4.20	4.88
Of which:										
Arrears	—	—	3.35	6.06	0.93	−1.72	−1.29	−4.80	3.14	−5.14
Reschedulings	—	—	—	1.94	0.26	3.31	9.61	8.36	0.95	9.02

Source: International Monetary Fund, *World Economic Outlook*, various issues.

Note: Except where otherwise footnoted, estimates shown here are based on national balance of payments statistics. These flows are not always easily reconcilable with year-to-year changes in either debtor- or creditor-reported debt statistics, in part because the latter are affected by changes in valuation.

[1] Equivalent to current account deficit less official transfers. In this table, official transfers are treated as external financing.
[2] Pertains primarily to export credit.
[3] Positioned here on the presumption that estimates reflect primarily unrecorded capital outflows.
[4] Includes use of Fund credit under General Resources Account, Trust Fund, structural adjustment facility, and enhanced structural adjustment facility. The impact of prospective programs is incorporated.
[5] Comprises short-term borrowing by monetary authorities from other monetary authorities.
[6] Estimates of net disbursements by official creditors (other than monetary authorities) derived from debt statistics. Official net disbursements include the increase in official claims caused by the transfer of officially guaranteed claims to the guarantor agency in the creditor country, usually in the context of debt reschedulings.
[7] Residually calculated. Except for discrepancies in coverage, amounts shown reflect net external borrowing from private creditors and short-term official flows (primarily interest arrears on official debt).
[8] Based on changes in cross-border bank claims reported in the Fund's International Banking Statistics, adjusted for valuation changes attributed to exchange rate movements. Excludes six offshore banking centers covered by the *World Economic Outlook* (The Bahamas, Bahrain, Hong Kong, Netherlands Antilles, Panama, and Singapore).

In many of the industrial countries during the 1970s and 1980s, large fiscal deficits were financed primarily through bond issuance;[25] domestic bond markets therefore expanded sharply,[26] with foreigners purchasing an increasing share of these bonds. In addition, cross-border transactions in private securities and foreign direct investment expanded sharply. Perhaps the most striking feature was the surge in cross-border portfolio investment flows. While the United States experienced an average portfolio capital inflow of $0.1 billion in 1970–82, this inflow increased to an average of $40 billion in 1983–88. For Japan, an average annual inflow of $1 billion of portfolio investment in 1970–82 changed to an average annual outflow of $52 billion in 1983–88.

This pattern of private flows was most evident in the capital accounts of the United States, Germany, and Japan. Between 1983 and 1988, when the United States ran a cumulative current account deficit of $664 billion, inflows of portfolio investment, other private short-term capital, and net foreign direct investment financed about 75 percent of the external deficit.[27]

One counterpart to the large U.S. current account deficits was current account surpluses in Germany and Japan. Over the period 1983–88, for example, Germany and Japan had cumulative current account surpluses of $165 billion and $357 billion, respectively. However, the composition of their capital flows differed. While cumulative foreign direct investment abroad was equivalent to about 22 percent of the cumulative current account surplus for both countries during 1983–88, cumulative net portfolio investment abroad amounted to $314 billion for Japan (88 percent of its cumulative current account surplus) versus $16 billion for Germany (10 percent of its cumulative current account sur-

plus). In Japan, moreover, other long-term capital outflows equaled $118 billion (33 percent of the cumulative current account surplus) and reserve holdings increased by $64 billion (18 percent of the cumulative current account surplus). In contrast, other long-term capital outflows from Germany amounted to only $11 billion (6 percent of the cumulative current account surplus) and reserve accumulation was $8 billion (5 percent of the cumulative current account surplus). The most significant difference in the pattern of capital flows was in short-term flows. While Germany experienced a short-term *outflow* of $112 billion in 1983–88, Japan experienced an *inflow* of $219 billion.[28]

Similarities Between Early 1970s and Late 1980s in Pattern of Official and Private Capital Flows to Developing Countries

By the late 1980s, the pattern of official and private capital flows to net debtor developing countries was similar in a number of respects to that in the early 1970s. In both periods, limited access to international financial markets[29] resulted in nondebt-creating capital flows, especially from official sources, providing most of the financing for the current account deficits of the indebted developing countries (Tables 9 and 10 and Chart 4). For example, nondebt-creating flows, which represented 58 percent of the net debtors' current account imbalances in 1971–72, amounted to only 33 percent of their current account deficits in 1973–82. However, in 1987–89, such flows provided 98 percent of the financing of this group's current account deficits.[30] Moreover, the sum of official transfers and net long-term borrowing from official creditors represented an even larger proportion of the net debtors' current account deficit in 1987–89 (115 percent) than in 1971–72 (69 percent).[31] These official transfers and loans were also equivalent to

---

[25]Fiscal positions in the industrial countries deteriorated sharply in 1974–75, and central government borrowing requirements reached nearly 5 percent of their GNP in 1975 (compared with only 1.5 percent in 1972). Central government fiscal deficits also rose from 3.6 percent of GNP in 1981 to 5.3 percent in 1983 and remained above 3 percent of GNP until 1989.

[26]Salomon Brothers (1989) reported that outstanding central government bond issues in 1975 and 1988 were as follows:

	Billions of local currency (end of year)	
	1975	1988
France	14	617
Germany	34	347
Japan	13,911	154,482
United Kingdom	34	137
United States	206	1,426

[27]U.S. liabilities constituting the foreign exchange reserves of other countries also expanded by $127 billion between 1983 and 1988, with most of the expansion taking place in 1986–88.

[28]As noted in International Monetary Fund (1989), the short-term capital inflow into Japan reflected the preference of Japanese financial institutions to undertake many of their money market operations in offshore rather than domestic markets.

[29]Other net external borrowing, which reflects net external borrowing from private creditors and short-term official flows (primarily interest arrears on official debt), fell from an average of $64 billion in 1981–82 to an average of $11 billion in 1985–89 (Table 10). Much of this net external borrowing in 1985–89 reflected the accumulation of arrears and reschedulings.

[30]In 1987–89 and in 1969–72, the current account deficits of the indebted developing countries were equivalent to 1–2 percent of their GNP. During 1981–82, the current account deficits of these countries exceeded 5 percent of their combined GNPs. Since indebted developing countries also accumulated reserves during 1987–89, the sum of official transfers and net long-term borrowing from official creditors represented 79 percent of cumulative current account deficits and reserve accumulation.

[31]These official flows had represented only 53 percent of the net debtors' current account imbalance in 1973–82.

Table 9. Net Debtor Developing Countries: External Financing, 1969–79
(In billions of U.S. dollars)

	1969	1970	1971	1972	1973	1974	1975	1976	1977	1978	1979
Deficit on goods, services, and private transfers[1]	6.78	12.15	15.46	9.57	9.40	20.40	41.85	30.58	32.20	51.10	47.68
Nondebt-creating flows, net	5.34	6.45	7.95	6.61	10.94	14.14	13.15	12.00	15.31	17.31	23.14
Official transfers	2.86	3.05	3.68	3.90	5.81	8.61	7.60	7.75	8.62	8.40	11.23
Direct investment, net	2.45	2.54	2.97	2.06	4.81	4.75	6.29	4.40	5.80	6.94	9.10
SDR allocation, gold monetization, and valuation changes	0.03	0.86	1.30	0.65	0.32	0.78	−0.74	−0.14	0.90	1.97	2.81
Asset transactions, net[2]	−1.20	−0.98	−1.10	−3.34	−4.39	−4.68	−5.55	−7.13	−7.72	−9.32	−11.97
Net errors and omissions[3]	−1.12	0.52	0.35	0.23	−1.41	−2.29	−4.30	−6.45	−6.85	−5.08	−3.32
Use of reserves	−4.26	−4.28	−5.74	−11.55	−15.10	−17.80	−3.38	−18.21	−16.21	−20.63	−31.96
Net external borrowing	8.02	10.45	14.01	17.62	19.36	31.03	41.92	50.36	47.67	68.81	71.79
Reserve-related liabilities	−0.10	−0.47	0.22	0.17	0.20	1.66	1.86	3.97	1.09	1.94	1.45
Net credit from IMF[4]	−0.13	−0.47	0.09	0.26	0.02	1.47	1.98	2.97	0.09	0.53	0.97
Liabilities constituting foreign authorities' reserves[5]	0.03	—	0.13	−0.09	0.18	0.20	−0.12	1.00	1.01	1.41	0.47
Long-term borrowing from official creditors, net[6]	...	—	4.22	5.48	4.89	8.75	13.75	13.61	12.72	13.62	30.27
Other net external borrowing[7]	...	10.92	9.56	11.97	14.27	20.61	26.31	32.79	33.86	53.25	40.07
Memorandum items:											
Net borrowing from commercial banks[8]	...	...	...	...	...	...	...	...	...	...	...
Exceptional financing	−0.02	0.24	0.30	0.70	0.45	1.51	4.49	3.04	2.63	1.19	1.82
Of which:											
Arrears	0.04	—	0.02	0.09	−0.04	0.31	0.16	0.29	1.89	0.74	0.04
Reschedulings	—	—	—	—	—	—	—	—	0.01	0.01	0.52

Source: International Monetary Fund, *World Economic Outlook*, various issues.

Note: Except where otherwise footnoted, estimates shown here are based on national balance of payments statistics. These flows are not always easily reconcilable with year-to-year changes in either debtor- or creditor-reported debt statistics, in part because the latter are affected by changes in valuation.

[1] Equivalent to current account deficit less official transfers. In this table, official transfers are treated as external financing.

[2] Pertains primarily to export credit.

[3] Positioned here on the presumption that estimates reflect primarily unrecorded capital outflows.

[4] Includes use of Fund credit under General Resources Account, Trust Fund, structural adjustment facility, and enhanced structural adjustment facility. The impact of prospective programs is incorporated.

[5] Comprises short-term borrowing by monetary authorities from other monetary authorities.

[6] Estimates of net disbursements by official creditors (other than monetary authorities) derived from debt statistics. Official net disbursements include the increase in official claims caused by the transfer of officially guaranteed claims to the guarantor agency in the creditor country, usually in the context of debt reschedulings.

[7] Residually calculated. Except for discrepancies in coverage, amounts shown reflect net external borrowing from private creditors and short-term official flows (primarily interest arrears on official debt).

[8] Based on changes in cross-border bank claims reported in the Fund's International Banking Statistics, adjusted for valuation changes attributed to exchange rate movements. Excludes six offshore banking centers covered by the *World Economic Outlook* (The Bahamas, Bahrain, Hong Kong, Netherlands Antilles, Panama, and Singapore).

Table 10. Net Debtor Developing Countries: External Financing, 1980–89

(In billions of U.S. dollars)

	1980	1981	1982	1983	1984	1985	1986	1987	1988	1989
Deficit on goods, services, and private transfers[1]	57.09	120.96	118.44	69.51	44.13	50.57	66.61	30.89	33.67	40.20
Nondebt-creating flows, net	21.79	24.62	24.02	21.44	21.18	31.60	29.16	34.35	35.44	32.98
Official transfers	12.11	13.14	12.42	12.87	13.11	16.03	17.45	16.82	17.41	17.41
Direct investment, net	8.09	13.15	12.52	8.93	9.74	9.11	8.88	12.34	17.28	15.50
SDR allocation, gold monetization, and valuation changes	1.60	−1.67	−0.92	−0.36	−1.67	6.46	2.83	5.19	0.75	0.06
Asset transactions, net[2]	−10.50	−17.95	−13.33	−6.44	−11.44	−13.41	−11.01	−14.80	−13.75	−8.91
Net errors and omissions[3]	−10.61	−16.81	−26.60	−12.59	−4.07	−1.08	5.36	−1.62	−1.06	—
Use of reserves	−33.79	18.52	37.95	−5.01	−15.79	−5.17	6.64	−18.33	−7.11	−23.30
Net external borrowing	90.20	112.57	96.40	72.12	54.24	38.63	36.46	31.28	20.15	39.44
Reserve-related liabilities	4.36	6.93	10.58	7.85	4.48	−0.69	−3.26	−5.25	−3.66	0.65
Net credit from IMF[4]	3.04	6.64	6.95	11.01	4.72	−0.04	−2.73	−5.85	−5.00	1.05
Liabilities constituting foreign authorities' reserves[5]	1.32	0.28	3.64	−3.16	−0.24	−0.65	−0.54	0.60	1.34	−0.40
Long-term borrowing from official creditors, net[6]	24.38	29.35	33.73	35.47	34.09	24.56	28.81	22.50	17.84	28.85
Other net external borrowing[7]	61.46	76.30	52.08	28.81	15.67	14.77	10.92	14.03	5.98	9.93
Memorandum items:										
Net borrowing from commercial banks[8]	69.60	91.49	49.43	28.26	13.46	5.94	−3.00	4.64	−9.27	8.80
Exceptional financing	5.94	11.95	23.64	40.29	40.46	33.85	48.89	50.32	50.84	51.68
Of which:										
Arrears	−1.22	5.52	13.26	13.47	3.85	−11.33	7.98	0.71	11.76	4.07
Reschedulings	3.38	3.65	5.50	24.71	33.36	41.85	37.44	49.14	37.64	42.95

Source: International Monetary Fund, World Economic Outlook, various issues.

Note: Except where otherwise footnoted, estimates shown here are based on national balance of payments statistics. These flows are not always easily reconcilable with year-to-year changes in either debtor- or creditor-reported debt statistics, in part because the latter are affected by changes in valuation.

[1] Equivalent to current account deficit less official transfers. In this table, official transfers are treated as external financing.

[2] Pertains primarily to export credit.

[3] Positioned here on the presumption that estimates reflect primarily unrecorded capital outflows.

[4] Includes use of Fund credit under General Resources Account, Trust Fund, structural adjustment facility, and enhanced structural adjustment facility. The impact of prospective programs is incorporated.

[5] Comprises short-term borrowing by monetary authorities from other monetary authorities.

[6] Estimates of net disbursements by official creditors (other than monetary authorities) derived from debt statistics. Official net disbursements include the increase in official claims caused by the transfer of officially guaranteed claims to the guarantor agency in the creditor country, usually in the context of debt reschedulings.

[7] Residually calculated. Except for discrepancies in coverage, amounts shown reflect net external borrowing from private creditors and short-term official flows (primarily interest arrears on official debt).

[8] Based on changes in cross-border bank claims reported in the Fund's International Banking Statistics, adjusted for valuation changes attributed to exchange rate movements. Excludes six offshore banking centers covered by the World Economic Outlook (The Bahamas, Bahrain, Hong Kong, Netherlands Antilles, Panama, and Singapore).

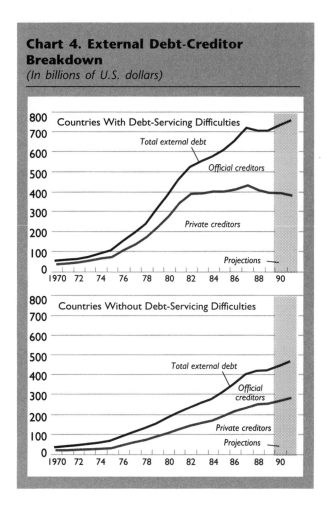

Chart 4. External Debt-Creditor Breakdown
(In billions of U.S. dollars)

developing countries with recent debt-servicing difficulties between 1971–72 and 1987–89; but, during the same period, they fell from the equivalent of 1.8 percent to 1.0 percent of the combined GNPs of those countries without debt-servicing difficulties.[32]

One difference in the position of the net debtor developing countries in the early 1970s and the late 1980s, however, was that exceptional financing (including arrears and reschedulings with both private and official creditors) was equivalent to only 4 percent of their current account imbalances in 1971–72 but to nearly 145 percent in 1987–89. In addition, as discussed in the final section, the residents of these countries also held a much larger stock of external assets at the end of the 1980s than at the beginning of the 1970s.

Determinants of International Capital Flows

The sharp changes in the pattern of net and gross international capital flows during the 1970s and 1980s raise the issues of what factors motivated these flows and of how they affected the performance of the international economy. As noted in the previous section, the private component of these flows has reflected both the reallocation of global savings across countries and the international diversification of portfolios. This section examines how cross-border transactions have responded to economic fundamentals, official policies, and capital market distortions.

Role of Financial Markets and the Fundamental Determinants of Capital Flows

The primary function of domestic and international financial markets is to channel resources from surplus units—households, firms, or governments—that are spending less than their revenues, or saving, to deficit units—that are spending more than their revenues, or dissaving. Such financial market transactions can help overcome the limitations imposed by self-financing investment expenditures and, by directing savings toward the most productive investments, can raise the overall productivity of investment. As a result, savers can realize a higher average yield from

about 1.3 percent of the net debtors' GNPs in both 1971–72 and 1987–89.

Official flows were important for financing the current account deficits of both the net debtor developing countries that experienced debt-servicing difficulties and those that did not. For example, official transfers and net long-term loans from official creditors to the net debtor developing countries with recent debt-servicing problems rose from the equivalent of 46 percent of this group's current account deficit in 1971–72 to 101 percent in 1987–89, whereas for the net debtor developing countries without debt-servicing difficulties the corresponding proportion rose from 114 percent to 154 percent. However, this overstates the importance of these official flows to the countries without debt-servicing difficulties, since their current account deficits were smaller than those of the countries with debt-servicing difficulties in both the early 1970s and the late 1980s. An alternative perspective is provided by the fact that these official flows increased from the equivalent of 1.2 percent to 1.6 percent of the combined GNPs of the net debtor

---

[32]The relative importance of other net external borrowing has also differed for the two groups. While such borrowing corresponded to 81 percent of the current account deficits of the net debtor developing countries with debt-servicing difficulties in 1973–82, this proportion fell to –0.3 percent in 1987–89. In contrast, such borrowing increased from 71 percent of the current account deficits of the net debtor countries without debt-servicing difficulties in 1973–82 to 106 percent in 1987–89.

postponing consumption. This function of financial markets gives rise to net flows of funds among economic units. Net international capital flows are the financial counterpart to a real transfer of resources through a trade or current account imbalance, which occurs only when saving and investment are unbalanced across countries.

Channeling resources from surplus to deficit units is clearly not the only function of international financial markets. Many economic units are simultaneously borrowers and lenders: most financial intermediaries borrow in one form and lend in another. In addition, both households and firms diversify their portfolio holdings to reduce risks. Gross capital flows between countries, which may be mutually offsetting, can be important in improving the liquidity of a portfolio and in diversifying risks. Diversifying across assets located in different countries may be particularly useful in reducing country-specific risk: for example, cocoa production in Côte d'Ivoire is affected by very different events than is cadmium production in Canada, so the returns to these activities have low covariance. A portfolio combining shares in these two activities would be less risky than a portfolio limited to one or the other.[33]

In contrast to net capital flows, gross capital flows do not necessarily correspond to a transfer of real resources across countries. Indeed, most gross capital flows arise as portfolio managers attempt to improve the *composition* of their existing portfolios (to diversify risks or minimize tax burdens) rather than the *scale* of their portfolios.

Gross international flows of capital have risen sharply over the last two decades as investors (often institutional investors such as insurance companies and pension funds) have sought to diversify their portfolios internationally.[34] This diversification has been facilitated by new computer and telecommunications technologies that have allowed investors to examine a broader range of investments in many countries and to manage more effectively the risks inherent in their global portfolios.

While international capital flows can potentially play an important role in improving economic efficiency, this contribution can be realized only if fi-

nancial markets evaluate correctly the portfolio preferences of savers; identify and fund the most productive investments; establish asset prices that appropriately reflect the underlying risks and returns; and help overcome limitations introduced by uncertainty and incomplete information.[35] By now, an extensive literature has developed on how financial markets incorporate risks and returns into the prices of financial claims.[36] In the absence of distortions, assets would be priced so that the more risky assets offered higher rates of return. Moreover, while overall risk could be reduced to some minimum level by holding a diversified portfolio, some nondiversifiable (*systematic*) risk would remain and would have to be reflected in the prices of the risky assets. In addition, since an asset's contribution to the riskiness of the portfolio would depend not only on its own riskiness but also on the *covariance* of its return with the returns on other assets in the market portfolio,[37] investors would have to be compensated, via higher returns, for a higher covariance. These considerations imply that the fundamental determinants of capital flows in the absence of distortions would include the set of investment opportunities available throughout the

---

[33]In addition to flows of securities, such diversification can also be achieved through foreign direct investment, which allows the investor greater control over the use of the resources placed in another country.

[34]For example, gross international equity investments of residents of Germany, Japan, the United Kingdom, and the United States increased from an annual rate of $800 billion in 1986 to $1,213 billion in 1988, and, by 1988, one ninth of all the equity transactions involved either a buyer or a seller that was a nonresident.

[35]On an international level, these functions are performed by complex financial systems based on both direct and indirect finance. With direct finance, a surplus unit in one country acquires a claim on a deficit unit in another country (such as in the markets for corporate bonds or equity); with indirect finance, a surplus unit in a particular country acquires a claim on an international financial intermediary, which in turn holds claims on deficit units in a second country. In addition, some flows reflect self finance (such as a multinational corporation that finances a foreign direct investment out of retained earnings). Financial intermediaries generally provide the most efficient sources of financing when there are high fixed costs involved in starting up certain activities, where specialization reduces costs (such as in administering activities), when intermediaries can issue liabilities that are more liquid than direct claims, and when the intermediaries can reduce risks by holding a diversified portfolio of claims.

[36]Following early work by Markowitz (1959) and Tobin (1958), which focused on the issue of the relationship between the return on a single risk asset relative to that on some risk-free asset, Sharpe (1964) and Lintner (1965) examined the relative pricing of heterogeneous capital assets with interdependent risks. Black and Scholes (1973) extended the analysis of the market pricing of risk to contingent claims. See Friedman (1989) for a review of this literature.

[37]Each asset in a market portfolio would be held in the same proportion as the proportion in which each asset exists in the economy. In the absence of distortions, differentials between the rates of return on different assets would compensate for differences between their contributions to the riskiness of the market portfolio. If this was not true, residents of *all* countries would have excess demand for assets whose returns were unusually attractive in relation to their riskiness, but this excess demand, because it would be general, could not be resolved through capital flows; it could only be resolved through a rise in the prices of assets for which there is excess demand, which would result in a reduction in the rate of return of these assets.

global economy, the covariances between the expected returns on various investment projects, and the growth of wealth in different countries; the preferences of households in different countries for present and future consumption; and their willingness to assume risks.

A problem of attempting to measure empirically the relative influence of these fundamental factors on capital flows is that international capital markets can respond to a shock in one country either through capital flows or through changes in the prices of the country's financial claims, or through some combination of capital flows and asset price changes. As noted in the previous section, there can be a trade-off between asset price adjustment and net capital flows in helping to restore capital market equilibrium. As markets become more highly integrated and portfolios become more internationally diversified, asset price changes are likely to substitute increasingly for net capital flows to restore market equilibrium. This again illustrates one of the dangers of using the volume of capital flows to measure the degree of integration.

This trade-off between asset price changes and capital flows also helps to explain why most studies have had difficulties in obtaining stable empirical relationships between measures of gross and net capital flows and the fundamental determinants of capital flows. Since changes in the fundamentals impinge on both capital flows and international rate-of-return differentials, and since the direction of influence depends on the source of the shock, it is even in principle difficult to trace a stable relationship between interest differentials and capital flows.

Early empirical studies attempted to trace a relationship between international capital flows and their determinants, with particular attention to the role of international interest rate differentials.[38] For example, Branson (1968) started with a portfolio framework in which desired holdings of foreign assets depended on total wealth, domestic and foreign interest rates, and risk considerations. Gross capital flows were then explained in terms of changes in domestic and foreign interest rates, as well as in other factors reflecting changes in wealth and risk.

Kouri and Porter (1974) pointed out that, because capital flows themselves affect interest rates, Branson's approach could yield biased estimates,

leading to an underestimate of the effect of interest differentials on capital flows; the bias could be particularly serious in economies that were highly open to capital movements. Kouri and Porter also focused on the role of net capital movements in adapting to other portfolio shifts, arguing that for instance an increase in desired holdings of money may lead wealth-holders to draw down their holdings of both domestic and foreign bonds, leading to a net inflow of capital. Accordingly, they examined the effects on capital flows of changes in the determinants of demand for money and in domestic credit, and also estimated offset coefficients representing the role of net capital flows in offsetting domestic monetary policy. This focus on net capital flows, along with the development of the monetary approach to the balance of payments, also spawned a large body of empirical literature.

The search for an appropriate empirical model of the determination of capital flows was exemplified by successive versions of the Multicountry Model (MCM) developed at the Board of Governors of the U.S. Federal Reserve System.[39] The early versions of the MCM incorporated the effects of interest rate differentials on gross capital flows, but the estimated empirical relationships had poor explanatory power and yielded implausible results in policy simulations. Later versions of the model sought to explain net flows of capital, either by specifying net liabilities to foreigners as a function of domestic and foreign wealth and the covered interest rate differential, or by trying to explain exchange rate movements rather than the flows of capital themselves. Neither approach proved successful in explaining capital movements. Such lackluster results have typified the empirical literature on capital flows in general; even when stable empirical relationships have been identified within a given period, they have often turned out to provide poor forecasts in subsequent periods. As a result, most econometric models now incorporate financial linkage across countries in terms of interest rate parity relationships that link domestic interest rates through arbitrage to foreign interest rates and to anticipated exchange rate movements. In essence, it has been found easier to specify the asset price linkages that are the *outcome* of arbitrage between markets—rather than the capital flows that are part of the arbitrage process.

Official Policies, Market Imperfections, and Capital Flows

In addition to the "fundamentals," government policies and capital market imperfections inherent

---

[38]Both stock and flow models of capital flows were employed in these studies. Flow models attempted to identify stable empirical relationships between capital flows and such variables as the levels of interest rate differentials. Stock models assumed stable demands for holdings of foreign assets and attempted to link changes in these holdings (that is, capital flows) to changes in variables such as interest rate differentials and wealth.

[39]See Stevens and others (1984).

in the functioning of private markets also affected international capital flows during the 1970s and 1980s. It is difficult, however, to quantify the impact of these policies and distortions on the levels and pattern of capital flows. In part, this reflects the fact that, while many of these policies and imperfections created barriers to cross-border financial transactions, others (such as those created by tax policies) stimulated gross capital flows. Moreover, the effects of such policies and distortions on net capital flows depend ultimately on their impact on saving and investment relationships across countries; these impacts in turn are difficult to gauge with the present lack of empirical evidence. Nonetheless, it is possible to identify some of the qualitative effects of official policies and other factors on capital flows and asset prices.

Influence of Official Policies

Capital controls, which have been the most important impediments to market access, have seldom completely eliminated all flows, but they have made international transactions more costly and have eliminated certain types of flows. As a result, although foreign assets account for a growing proportion of portfolios, international diversification is far from complete.[40]

Capital controls have often been supplemented by restrictions on the entry of foreign financial firms into domestic markets. While such restrictions have typically been designed to limit foreign ownership of domestic financial institutions, they have reduced competition both within domestic financial systems and in the provision of financial services across countries. As these restrictions have been removed in the industrial countries, the presence of foreign financial institutions in major domestic markets has sharply expanded; for example, in 1960, only 8 U.S. banks had foreign branches, but by the late 1980s the tally had increased to over 200.[41] To some extent, the entry of foreign financial institutions has led to a reduction in measured capital flows even though the provision of financial services by foreign institutions may have increased.

Restrictions on the domestic activities, interest rates, products, and location of financial institutions—which have been used to minimize the risks assumed by certain financial institutions and to separate commercial and investment banking activities—have also influenced international capital flows. Financial institutions often responded to these regulations by providing restricted financial services to domestic enterprises through offshore subsidiaries or branches. The resulting gross international capital flows in reality represented the intermediation of domestic saving and investment. Indeed, the periods of most rapid growth in the Eurocurrency markets in the 1970s often occurred either when Eurocurrency deposit interest rates rose above administered interest rates in major countries or when financial institutions were able to introduce new instruments or services that were not available in domestic markets.

While official guarantees (such as deposit insurance) and the availability of a lender of last resort have enhanced the stability of the financial system in times of crises, they can also lead to a mispricing of risk. In particular, a moral hazard can be created if the managers of large financial institutions, their depositors, and their creditors take the view that some institutions are "too large to fail," and, as a result, will receive emergency assistance during any period of market disturbance. Such official guarantees can then create a "veil" between the risks assumed by the financial institutions and the perceived risks that depositors or creditors believe they are assuming when making funds available to these institutions. This moral hazard can result in excessive risk being taken by some institutions and in savings being directed to excessively risky investments both within and across countries.[42]

Taxation may also affect the pattern and scale of capital flows. Holdings of foreign assets are sometimes subject to double taxation, while sometimes they can be used to avoid (or evade) taxation altogether. Divergent tax withholding rates have at times caused capital flows into countries or offshore markets where tax is not withheld.[43] Turnover and other taxes on transactions in securities have tended to shift such transactions to other countries or offshore markets.

---

[40]In some cases the capital controls that limited the degree of international portfolio diversification may have had the paradoxical effect of increasing net capital flows. With incomplete international portfolio diversification, shocks are borne disproportionately by residents of the country where the shocks occur, and thus are more likely to lead its residents' expenditures to differ from their income. As a result, current and capital account imbalances could actually be exacerbated by restrictions on capital movements.

[41]The role of foreign financial institutions in the major industrial countries is discussed in Folkerts-Landau and Mathieson (1988).

[42]This problem is addressed in the next section.

[43]Even the announcement of a planned (or proposed) tax can induce substantial capital flows. For example, in October 1987 the authorities in Germany announced that a 10 percent withholding tax on interest income would be introduced as of January 1, 1989. This led many German investors to purchase deutsche mark Eurobonds and other offshore assets, and many German financial firms set up offshore investment funds in Luxembourg to facilitate such capital outflows. The abolition of the withholding tax was announced in April 1989 to be effective on July 1, 1989. See International Monetary Fund (1990).

Since most financial claims are denominated in national currencies,[44] domestic monetary policies can induce changes in domestic interest rates, exchange rates, and inflation, which alter the expected relative returns to assets denominated in different currencies. The perception that the monetary policies of the major industrial countries were at times pursuing conflicting or inconsistent objectives led to abrupt adjustments in exchange rates and other asset prices. In developing countries, monetary and exchange rate policies that have created expectations of exchange rate movements have often given rise to currency substitution (that is, shifts between holding foreign and domestic currency) even if they have caused no other capital flows. This phenomenon appears to have been particularly important when the combination of high inflation and ceilings on domestic interest rates has resulted in highly negative real rates of return on domestic bank deposits.

The use of money, and the resulting potential for governments to levy an inflation tax, also implies that a country's reputation for financial stability may have an important effect on capital flows. Assets denominated in currencies issued by governments with a reputation for sound finance tend to bear lower rates of return than assets denominated in other currencies. Differences in credibility may lead primarily to differences in asset returns, but may also lead to actual gross flows of capital. Another issue associated with the credibility of the government is sovereign risk, which arises because the enforcement of contracts made by the government or residents of a country depends on the cooperation of that government itself. The occurrence of debt-servicing arrears, reschedulings, and default can create barriers to capital mobility and have direct and indirect effects on capital flows.

The role of fiscal imbalances in generating net flows of capital has been emphasized in the *World Economic Outlook* reports of the 1980s. An excess of government expenditures over revenues must be financed through a net inflow of capital, unless it is offset by an excess of domestic private saving over investment. In an economy closed to capital movements, the increase in net private saving required by an increased fiscal deficit would have to be brought about through an increase in interest rates. Opening an economy to capital flows removes the necessity for interest rates to rise in response to an increased fiscal imbalance, unless the country in question is very large; capital flows can thus be a short-run substitute for interest rate increases and the resulting private sector adjustments.[45]

It has been evident during the 1980s that the cross-country mix of monetary and fiscal policies can affect the pattern of capital flows. For example, the combination of large fiscal deficits and a relatively restrictive monetary policy in the United States was at times associated with both an appreciation of its currency and a large capital inflow, as well as higher domestic interest rates. Such inflows were often intensified when other major countries simultaneously pursued less restrictive monetary policies and less expansionary fiscal policies.

Exchange rate arrangements can influence both the scale and the direction of capital flows, especially where there is significant overvaluation or undervaluation of exchange rates. For example, Makin (1974) argued that during the late 1960s and early 1970s, an overvaluation of the U.S. dollar, which increased the costs of producing in the United States relative to abroad, distorted the pattern of foreign direct investment flows between the industrial countries. While Makin was concerned with the distortions created by a system of fixed exchange rates, more flexible exchange rate systems could also potentially experience currency misalignments which, although transitory, could be sufficiently long-lived to distort capital flows. If bandwagon effects or speculative "bubbles" drive exchange rates away from values consistent with economic fundamentals, capital flows may be inhibited by increased exchange rate risk and rapidly changing asset prices. Some have also argued (Feldstein (1990), for example) that attempts by the authorities to stabilize exchange rates when inflation rates differ can lead to persistent trade imbalances, unwarranted exchange rate trends, and rising interest rates. If the authorities succeed in creating the expectation that exchange rates will be stable, investors will then purchase the bonds with the highest nominal yields, which tend to occur in countries with the highest rates of inflation. Such portfolio shifts could lead interest rates in the low-inflation countries to rise and the exchange rates of the high-inflation countries to appreciate.

---

[44]Some international bond issues have been denominated in "composite" currencies such as the European currency unit or the SDR.

[45]Private savings may still be affected, if private households take into account the additional future taxes they will have to pay to service the resulting national debt; in the extreme case, characterized as Ricardian equivalence, the additional private sector savings will be just sufficient to cover the additional public sector borrowing, and neither an additional net international flow of capital nor any change in interest rates need occur. There has been far from universal agreement on the empirical relevance of the Ricardian equivalence proposition, or even of the less extreme proposition that private savings adjust to some extent to offset a public sector deficit. See for instance Barro (1974) and Tobin (1980), Chapter III.

Market Imperfections

In practice, significant costs are entailed in carrying out transactions in financial assets. These costs reflect the bringing together of buyers and sellers, setting prices at which assets can be bought and sold, and undertaking the actual transfers of funds and assets. Such costs are responsible in part for international differentials in rates of return on otherwise similar assets.[46] They likewise help to explain attempts to economize on the costs of trading through the standardization of financial assets, the existence of financial centers in which trading activity is concentrated, and the establishment of accompanying specialized firms providing financial services as brokers, dealers, and specialist traders. Transaction costs also figure in the failure of many individuals to hold portfolios of assets that are diversified, especially across countries: the transaction costs of buying, and gradually adding to, a diversified portfolio of assets may exceed the benefits for many individuals of limited wealth. Indeed, transaction costs are the principal reason why much of the international diversification of portfolios in the industrial countries during the 1980s has been carried out by large institutional investors (pension funds, insurance companies, and mutual funds). Unlike individual investors, they have been able to reduce significantly their per unit transaction cost by pooling transactions, by negotiating commission charges, and by using the private placement markets.

While transaction costs are inevitable, their magnitude and the nature of the barriers they erect are not; more specifically, these costs and barriers are affected by the regulatory, technological, and tax structure. The liberalization of major financial markets (which has increased competition in the provision of financial services) and new computer technologies have reduced transaction costs and allowed residents to hold a wider range of financial assets.

Obtaining the information needed to evaluate and to monitor a borrower's investment activities can be quite costly. As a result, financial market participants often are faced with asymmetrical information, a problem that can be made more serious as a result of different national systems for accounting standards, disclosure requirements, and the commercial codes governing the enforcement of contracts. The absence of adequate information increases the uncertainty that economic agents face, and can lead savers to demand that a large risk premium be incorporated into yields on securities issued by entities whose creditworthiness is doubtful.

Asymmetrical information also provides a clue as to why lending and deposit taking by financial intermediaries and direct foreign investment have been such important components of international capital flows. Since information is costly and subject to economies of scale, financial intermediaries can gather information, monitor the activities of borrowers, and diversify at lower cost than can most individuals. This advantage is one of the principal reasons why cross-border bank lending expanded by 19 percent a year during 1973–88. However, the development of new computer and telecommunication technologies, the expanded global role of credit rating agencies, the increased importance of institutional investors, and improved disclosure of corporate financial information have combined to erode the informational advantages of intermediaries such as commercial banks. As a result, the international role of banks has changed from one of simply extending credit to one of facilitating transactions,[47] and transactions in securities have become an increasingly important element in international capital flows.

In an international context, asymmetrical information also provides a rationale for the existence of multinational corporations, which allow for direct supervision of foreign investments.[48] Direct investment is also, in some respects, a solution to the problem of transaction costs and barriers to capital flows: a multinational corporation, with a broad network of transactions in goods and assets, can frequently find a means, inaccessible to private individuals, of circumventing these barriers.

Since savers and investors seldom deal with each other directly, especially in cross-border transactions, competitive financial arrangements work well only if they ensure that the savers' *agents* act in the interest of savers (the *principals*). While complex institutional and supervisory frameworks have evolved in most countries to meet this requirement, the extension of this protection to international transactions has raised intricate legal, regulatory, and supervisory issues. As discussed in the final section, progress has been made in the international coordination of the supervision of bank

---

[46]The role of transaction costs in accounting for international interest rate differentials was examined, for instance, by Frenkel and Levich (1977).

[47]In particular, banks have increasingly focused on off-balance-sheet activities that involve packaging assets normally not traded (such as bank loans, corporate receivables, and credit card receivables) into tradable securities, offering backup lines of credit or guarantees, and providing risk-management services. Greenspan (1990) noted that this change has also been motivated by a desire by at least U.S. banks to economize on costly equity capital.

[48]The determinants of foreign direct investment and the activities of multinational corporations are discussed in the study by Lizondo in Chapter III below.

branches and subsidiaries or foreign branches of securities houses, and of legal codes governing international capital flows. Nonetheless, many legal, accounting, and disclosure requirements (as well as taxes) have not been harmonized across countries, creating incentives for "regulatory arbitrage"—the shifting of financial activities to locations with the fewest restrictive financial regulations, the least comprehensive supervision, or the lowest taxes. Such regulatory and tax arbitrage has created pressures on the authorities to harmonize tax and regulatory systems; it has also raised concerns that "competitive" deregulation could eventually lead to a structure of supervision and regulation that does not adequately protect savers and investors.

Systemic Consequences and Policy Issues

Although the closer integration of major capital markets has generated significant efficiency gains, there are concerns that the rapid integration of capital markets could subject the world economy to various systemic strains. In part, these concerns reflect the experience with increased variability of asset prices and the demonstrated speed with which major financial shocks can be transmitted across global markets. In addition, major domestic and offshore financial markets have undergone extensive structural changes that have created uncertainty about the nature of not only financial market linkages between countries but also the environment in which monetary and fiscal policies must be implemented. This section examines some of the risks created by the rapid integration of global financial markets and the policy options for managing these risks.

Financial Integration and Innovation, Macroeconomic Policy Effectiveness, and Policy Coordination

As the linkages between major domestic and offshore financial markets have increased, the environment in which monetary and fiscal policies are implemented has changed dramatically. Financial innovation and the availability of credit from offshore markets have forced the monetary authorities to move away from quantitative restrictions on domestic lending toward instruments that operate more through "market prices," namely, exchange rates and interest rates. In addition, the availability of external savings has allowed creditworthy countries to finance larger fiscal and current account deficits longer than previously. Moreover, as the "spillover effects" of macroeconomic policies have increased, financial market participants have come to respond more rapidly to cross-country policy uncertainties and conflicts. This has underscored the importance of credible and coordinated macroeconomic and financial policies for a system of stable exchange rates and asset prices.

Effectiveness of Monetary Policy

During the 1950s and 1960s, financial institutions and regulatory structures in each of the major industrial countries evolved in relative isolation from external developments, in part reflecting the comprehensive systems of capital and exchange controls in some industrial countries (such as France, Japan, and the United Kingdom). These diverse financial structures naturally led the monetary authorities to employ quite different operational techniques. While some authorities (such as in France) relied heavily on direct controls on domestic credit expansion by financial institutions, other countries (such as the United States) relied more heavily on indirect money market instruments (such as open market operations). Moreover, the channels by which monetary policy influenced economic activity were often affected by domestic financial regulations. Even where direct credit controls were not employed, liquidity and credit constraints were often key elements in transmitting monetary policy effects. A rise in market interest rates could reduce the volume of credit as financial institutions lost deposits when market interest rates rose relative to regulated interest rates on deposits. The resulting credit rationing often induced an abrupt reduction in spending in certain sectors of the economy (such as housing investment) that had few alternative sources of credit.

During the 1970s, institutional structures and monetary policy operating procedures were forced to adapt to greater macroeconomic instability, to the need to finance large fiscal and current account imbalances, and to the expansion of offshore markets. The latter in particular provided large enterprises and financial institutions with a "safety valve" source of credit (whenever domestic credit conditions were tightened) and an alternative for the placement of funds that offered market-related rates of return.

To allow institutional structures to adjust to these new macroeconomic conditions, the authorities in the major industrial countries removed or relaxed capital controls and eliminated a variety of restrictions on domestic financial market activities, instruments, and interest rates. Increased use was made of market-based instruments (such as open market operations), and greater emphasis was placed on controlling the growth of monetary aggregates as part of a medium-term strategy for bringing down inflation.

The potential contribution of intermediate monetary aggregate targets to a successful anti-inflation program depended on a predictable relationship between the central bank's instruments and the intermediate targets, and a stable relationship between the intermediate targets and nominal demand or inflation. In some countries, however, financial liberalization and changes in computer and telecommunication technologies resulted in institutional changes and financial innovations that created difficulties for (1) measuring monetary aggregates; (2) controlling the expansion of the aggregates; and (3) maintaining the stability of the velocity relationships between the aggregates and nominal demand. For example, abrupt changes in the rate of expansion of key monetary aggregates sometimes occurred as households and firms substituted holdings of new interest-bearing deposit accounts and instruments (such as money market mutual funds) for traditional transaction balances, which often bore no interest.[49] For broader monetary aggregates, which typically encompassed both interest-bearing and noninterest-bearing deposits, this type of substitution was less of a problem in some countries;[50] but the ability of major enterprises and financial institutions to hold deposits in offshore banks stimulated the development of comparable domestic instruments (such as negotiable certificates of deposit) that required the redefinition of some broader aggregates. Moreover, foreign holdings of domestic currency at times had a strong influence on the behavior of narrow aggregates.[51]

Since the financial liberalizations typically involved the removal of interest rate ceilings, they also affected the predictability of the relationship between monetary aggregates and the authorities' operating instruments (usually short-term money market interest rates).[52] As the yields on bank deposits became increasingly governed by market forces, a change in the level of interest rates no longer induced as large a portfolio substitution between money and nonmonetary assets. This weakened one channel through which the behavior of

monetary aggregates had been influenced, and it also implied that monetary policy would have to rely more on its effects on the level of interest rates than on its effects on the spread between money and nonmonetary assets.

Even if financial innovation has made short-run control over monetary aggregates less precise, broad objectives for monetary aggregates can still be important medium-term guides for anti-inflation policies if there is a relatively predictable long-run velocity relationship between monetary aggregates and nominal income. However, while velocity relationships in Germany and Japan were relatively stable during the late 1970s and early 1980s, other countries experienced considerable variability throughout the period.[53]

The difficulties with monetary targeting and direct credit controls have led the authorities in a number of industrial countries toward a more "eclectic" approach to monetary policy. While this approach has continued to involve the announcement of targets for certain monetary aggregates, a broader range of indicators of monetary conditions has also been monitored. The focus is mainly on nominal variables (such as nominal spending), since experience suggests that relying on real variables alone puts inflation too much at risk. However, there is no consensus on what variables should receive the most weight.

Price data from centralized auction markets such as bond, foreign exchange, and commodity markets are nonetheless increasingly viewed as providing useful "summaries of or aggregators of information embodying the knowledge and expectations of large numbers of buyers and sellers who have incentives to make informed decisions in an uncertain world."[54] Since such asset market prices embody expectations about future developments, they can contain information about inflation expectations and can be a much better indicator of market conditions during a crisis than most forms of monetary or reserve aggregates.[55]

As a result of these structural changes, the effects of monetary policy are increasingly transmitted through induced changes in interest rates and exchange rates rather than through liquidity or credit constraints. Consumption is influenced through wealth effects, income effects, and intertemporal substitution effects as purchases are either brought forward or delayed depending on the

---

[49]Such substitution was most evident in growth of the M1 (currency and noninterest-bearing demand deposits) aggregates in the United States and Canada in the 1980s.

[50]Even with the broader aggregates, however, the relaxation of constraints on competition for deposits by banks could destabilize demand for money relationships. An example is the experience of the United Kingdom following the reform known as "competition and credit control" in the early 1970s (see Hacche (1974)).

[51]The German authorities cited this as one factor influencing their decision to switch their target from central bank money to M3 in 1988.

[52]For a recent description and analysis of these operating procedures, see Batten and others (1990).

[53]See Isard and Rojas-Suarez (1986) for a discussion of this experience. The M2 velocity in the United States has also remained relatively stable.

[54]Johnson (1990), p. 12.

[55]Johnson (1990) notes that during a crisis the demand for liquidity can change quickly and dramatically.

real cost of credit and the real return on saving.[56] Business investment can be affected through current income/cash flow effects in the short run and the user cost of capital in the long run.[57]

The scope that the authorities have for pursuing an eclectic independent monetary policy is naturally influenced by the country's exchange rate arrangements. While an increase in the degree of capital mobility will affect the channels by which monetary policy is transmitted under any exchange rate regime, the loss of monetary policy effectiveness will be greatest with a fixed exchange rate.[58] Indeed, there is the question of whether the degree of capital mobility is currently so high as to have eliminated all vestiges of domestic monetary policy independence for countries with no capital controls and a fixed exchange rate such as those in the European Monetary System (EMS). Any elements of independence would have to reflect the existence of a subset of domestic borrowers and intermediaries that have only limited ties to international markets.[59] This could allow the authorities to influence the cost and availability of credit from local intermediaries, through the use of reserve requirements, credit ceilings, direct credit surveillance, or through deposit interest rate ceilings (to the extent that such ceilings still exist). A problem with such controls is that they create strong incentives, even for smaller firms, to develop linkages with external financial institutions; and they put local intermediaries at a cost disadvantage relative to foreign intermediaries, which could threaten their longer-term survival.[60]

Fiscal Policy

During the 1970s and 1980s, the fiscal authorities in the major industrial countries used a variety of financial instruments to attract new domestic and foreign creditors and to add flexibility to their debt management operations. In addition, withholding taxes on foreign holdings of government securities have generally been removed, and turnover taxes that inhibited domestic trading of government (and private) securities have been progressively eliminated. The result has been a sharp increase in foreign holdings of government securities (see above).

The increased availability of external funding to finance fiscal imbalances has raised the issue of whether "fiscal discipline" has been weakened in the major industrial countries. Since fiscal deficits in the industrial countries have been primarily financed through bond issuance, the degree of fiscal discipline has increasingly reflected the discipline that private markets impose on a borrower whose creditworthiness deteriorates.[61]

The ultimate form of market discipline for any borrower is the complete denial of credit at any interest rate. If such discipline is applied abruptly, it necessitates a sharp adjustment of the borrower's spending activity unless an alternative nonmarket source of finance is available. An important question is whether private financial markets will only impose discipline abruptly or whether they indicate earlier that such discipline will be imposed unless the borrower acts to improve its debt or debt-servicing position.

---

[56]Monetary policy will affect the households' net interest payments, but because the household sector is a net creditor in some countries, higher interest rates actually increase household income. A rise in interest rates also lowers perceptions of permanent income if it increases the discount rate on future labor and nonlabor income. In addition, induced exchange rate changes can alter the relative attractiveness of domestic versus foreign goods.

[57]During the 1980s, securitization, note issuance facilities, and noninvestment grade ("junk") bonds have increased corporate access to capital markets and reduced their reliance on financial intermediaries as a source of funding. In normal circumstances, credit is therefore available to large firms even when monetary policy is tight—albeit at a higher price. However, new and/or small firms with limited access to securities markets and without a firm relationship to large banks may still be liquidity constrained when monetary policy is tightened.

[58]For a small country, a fixed exchange rate regime would generally imply a loss of *long-term* monetary control regardless of the degree of capital mobility.

[59]Branson (1990) addresses this issue within the context of the EMS.

[60]The experience in the Netherlands in the late 1980s provides an example of how the authorities have adapted their instruments to make the most of diminishing opportunities for monetary independence. The authorities focused both on keeping the exchange rate within its EMS bands and on achieving long-run monetary expansion consistent with domestic price sta-

bility. When the lending operations of commercial and savings banks produced an expansion of credit and monetary aggregates that exceeded an acceptable growth rate for a prolonged period, the authorities imposed limitations on how rapidly such lending could grow. For example, a substantial outflow of capital in 1986 resulted in an informal agreement between the central bank and banks to limit the expansion of the banks' net money-creating operations to an annual rate of 11–12 percent during 1986–87. Although this target rate of growth was exceeded, domestic capital market conditions tightened and the interest rate differential with Germany widened. The capital outflow was reversed in part because enterprises borrowed (net) abroad about f. 3 billion in 1986–87 compared with about f. 1 billion in 1983–85. However, this created difficulties for certain banks, especially for small foreign banks operating in the domestic market that had short-term loans funded by short-term liabilities that they could not expand because of the informal agreement. While some special relief was allowed for a number of hardship institutions, the authorities moved to establish a cash reserve system that required banks to hold a noninterest-bearing cash reserve at the central bank if their net money-creating operations exceeded some specified rate. Although this allowed all banks to expand at different rates, it still put them at a competitive disadvantage relative to banks abroad. This experience is discussed by Wellink (1989) and van der Werff and Sluijter (1989).

[61]It has been suggested that the integration of major capital markets has created a double-edged sword for fiscal discipline: greater availability of external resources with sound policies, but increased capital flight with questionable policies.

Market discipline is said to operate in stages. At first, there should be a widening differential between the interest rate paid by the private or public sector debtor whose creditworthiness is deteriorating and that paid by creditworthy borrowers. Only if this warning is ignored should the market apply the ultimate sanction of exclusion from the market.[62] For markets to operate in such a progressive manner, four fundamental conditions need to be fulfilled. First, there must not be any explicit or implicit guarantee that the borrower will be bailed out by the government or, if it is a central government, by a regional government body. If such a guarantee existed, the interest rate charged to the borrower would reflect the creditworthiness of the guarantor rather than the borrower. Second, market participants must be aware of the full magnitude of the debtor's obligations to make an assessment of its debt-servicing obligations and capacity. In evaluating the obligations of the central government, the position of commercial trading or financial entities owned or guaranteed by the state would also have to be considered. Third, the financial system must be strong enough that no single borrower is regarded as too large to fail. If a borrower were too large, it might be able to force the domestic authorities (or, if the borrower was the central government, other governments or regional authorities) to provide emergency assistance to prevent the bankruptcy (or default) of not only the borrower but other financial institutions that are large holders of the borrower's obligations.[63] A final condition is that the borrower's debts are not "monetized" through central bank purchases. Such purchases could lead to inflation or exchange rate depreciation that would erode the real value of debts denominated in the borrower's currency, making it difficult for private markets to price appropriately the risk of holding such debt.

In practice, it is unlikely that all of these conditions will be fully satisfied. Many borrowers are in fact viewed as carrying explicit or implicit guarantees either from some government entity or, if government units, from the central government or regional government bodies. The perception that the authorities consider some financial institutions too large to fail is hard to dispel, short of actually allowing some large institutions to fail. Moreover, it

could prove difficult to establish credibility that large sovereign borrowers would not be assisted if the failure to rescue could lead to fragmentation of regional institutions in which members have already invested high political stakes.

Most institutional investors also find it too costly to undertake their own analysis of each borrower's creditworthiness. Instead, they hold instruments of a certain minimum credit standing as defined by major credit rating agencies. While the ratings of these agencies are widely accepted and play a key role in pricing securities, problems can arise about the timing and accuracy of the credit evaluations, the uncertainties created by the evaluation process, and the evaluation of new factors or events.

One concern has been that the ratings of borrowers tend to be relatively "sticky," reflecting changes in a borrower's debt-servicing capacity only with a considerable lag. Credit agencies face the problem that an adverse change in a borrower's credit rating may become a self-fulfilling prophecy if creditors quickly withdraw funding from the borrower. Moreover, it may be difficult for the agencies to obtain complete information about a borrower, especially in the early stages of a deterioration of debt-servicing capacity, since management may not have an incentive to reveal relevant information before officially mandated reporting dates. In addition, in an era when a growing number of state enterprises are being privatized, it may be unclear what "residual" government guarantees still apply to the enterprises.

When a significant unanticipated event occurs, the credit agencies often indicate that the borrower's rating will be reviewed (the "credit watch" period). Since the extent of any change in the borrower's credit rating may be uncertain, a new element of risk enters into the pricing of the borrower's debt obligations. Moreover, the evaluation of new events or factors can present a particular problem. For example, since the position of the existing senior debt of a corporation can be eroded during leveraged buyouts (LBO) as the corporation issues new debt ("event risk"), the credit rating agencies were forced during the late 1980s to develop a supplementary rating system for assessing the quality of event risk covenants on new debt issues.

Also, only creditworthy large corporations and sovereign borrowers can efficiently raise funds from the securities markets, where credit ratings predominate. Most borrowers rely on credit from financial intermediaries. However, there is considerable evidence that bank and nonbank financial intermediaries respond to a deterioration in a borrower's creditworthiness in the same way as do the securities markets. Nonetheless, the experience

---

[62]See Bishop and others (1990).

[63]At a minimum, this would require all major financial institutions to limit their exposure to any single borrower (even to the domestic government), and all financial institutions continuously to mark-to-market the value of their holdings of private and public sector debt and deduct losses from their capital bases immediately. Such arrangements would allow institutions gradually to absorb losses arising from the deterioration of a given borrower's creditworthiness without confronting them with the need to absorb a large loss all at once.

with lending to developing countries in the 1970s, with real estate and energy sector loans in the 1980s, and with leveraged buyouts, suggests that the risks inherent in lending operations, especially those arising from systemic or economy-wide shocks, may not always be fully incorporated into lending decisions.

This issue has been examined most extensively in the literature on the behavior of interest rate spreads on bank loans (that is, the loan rate minus the Eurodollar London interbank offer rate) to developing countries in the mid-to-late 1970s.[64] Attention has focused on why the spreads did not widen gradually to reflect the deteriorating relationship between the scale of debt-service payments and capacity, and on why the transition to highly restricted access was so abrupt. One element contributing to the relatively narrow loan spreads during the late 1970s appears to have been the presence of both explicit and perceived guarantees—relating to either debt-servicing support for indebted countries or the safety of the deposit liabilities of large international banks.[65] Such guarantees could produce an underpricing of risk. Lenders also may not always have known the extent and maturity structure of the external debts of some heavily indebted developing countries that lacked centralized debt-management offices. Moreover, some lenders believed that they were holding a diversified portfolio of loans to developing countries that were at different stages of development, in different regions, and with different exports. What was apparently not adequately recognized was that systemic shocks (such as higher real interest rates and depressed commodity prices) might cause a sharp simultaneous downturn in the economic position of all developing countries in certain regions or facing similar economic conditions. The realization that institutions were holding a highly concentrated—rather than diversified—portfolio may have played a major role in the spread of credit rationing to all developing countries in certain regions or facing similar economic conditions.[66]

Concerns about the ability of the market to evaluate creditworthiness properly and to apply discipline smoothly and gradually have led to proposals for fixed rules for fiscal policy. For example, the Delors Committee's *Report on Economic and Monetary Union in the European Community*, published in April 1989, stressed the need to coordinate fiscal and budgetary policies throughout the European Community (EC) to achieve "internal balance." To achieve fiscal prudence, it proposed that binding budgetary rules be set to exclude monetary financing and put limits on external borrowing. Such rules could clearly play a role in establishing fiscal discipline, but they also raise a number of operational questions such as how to take into account the different levels of development of the members of the Community.[67]

The fundamental question is whether the authorities in a country will accept either the market signals about the sustainability of their fiscal position or the constraints imposed on their fiscal actions by existing rules. Experience suggests that governments will from time to time ignore signals and rules until credit becomes unavailable from either private or official sources.[68]

Coordination of Financial and Macroeconomic Policies

The growing integration of major domestic and offshore financial markets has increased the pressure for greater coordination of financial and macroeconomic policies.[69] Since financial institutions are now relatively free to relocate their activities, differences in regulatory or tax policies can induce a shift of activities from one market to another. This has led inter alia to a coordinated and uniform approach to bank capital adequacy requirements across the Group of Ten countries. Efforts are also under way to develop more uniform treatment of capital adequacy for securities houses, disclosure requirements, accounting standards, and the legal codes governing financial transactions. In addition, the authorities in the major industrial countries have faced pressures to

[64]See Folkerts-Landau (1985) for an analysis of these issues.

[65]For example, some lenders appear to have been influenced by the belief that certain large heavily indebted developing countries would be rescued (or bailed out) by large industrial countries with which they had close political and economic ties. In addition, depositors in banks in the large international money centers were generally unconcerned about the riskiness of the banks' loan portfolios (which would affect the deposit rates the banks would have to offer) because of the existence of deposit insurance and the perception that such banks were too large to fail.

[66]In terms of the pricing of risks, the lenders had underestimated the covariances between the returns on loans to different developing countries.

[67]The EC Commission's report, "Economic and Monetary Union: The Economic Rationale and Design of the System" (March 1990) argued for voluntary coordination and surveillance of national budgetary policies rather than for fixed rules.

[68]An example of how constitutional checks on a government's borrowing activities can be evaded was provided during the New York City budgetary crisis in the mid-1970s. Although the city's charter called for a balanced current operations budget, the city government ran up large debts by effectively using the borrowings for capital projects to fund current operating expenses.

[69]Policy coordination can also be important for agreements on the rules for international trade.

eliminate withholding taxes on interest income paid to foreign holders of domestic securities and taxes on transactions in securities.[70]

As noted earlier, the spillover effects from domestic macroeconomic policies have also increased as the linkages between major financial markets have expanded. Monetary policy effects are increasingly transmitted through interest rates and exchange rates, which are at the cutting edge of the short-term linkages between countries. Also, since foreign savers have played an increasingly important role in the financing of fiscal deficits, an economic downturn in one country, which reduces the funds that domestic residents could invest in foreign bonds, could have a major impact on the financing of fiscal imbalances in other countries.

The externalities created by these spillover effects suggest that policies designed in isolation are unlikely to generate an appropriate supply of the international public good of worldwide economic stability. The case for the international coordination of macroeconomic policies rests essentially on internationalizing these externalities.

Major movements in asset prices (especially exchange rates, interest rates, and equity prices) have often played a key role in intensifying efforts to improve policy coordination. News about anticipated policy developments tends to be quickly reflected in asset prices even without immediate changes in output or activity. This link between asset prices and underlying policies underscores the importance of credible and coordinated macroeconomic and financial policies for a stable system of exchange rates, interest rates, and equity prices.

While much of the recent discussion of the coordination of policies has tended to focus on monetary, fiscal, financial, and exchange rate policies, the growing integration of major financial markets has also created a need for coordinated crisis management policies, especially among central banks. Indeed, this may be the area where the need for a coordinated official response has increased most during the 1980s. The equity market crash of October 1987 demonstrated both the speed with which major financial shocks can spread across global markets and the types of liquidity, settlement, and clearance problems that can arise in money and equity markets.[71] Since the global markets for key government securities and foreign exchange operate on a 24-hour basis, emergency liquidity support during a major financial crisis may need to be coordinated to provide both continuing market support and the appropriate amount in different currencies. For example, the transfer of U.S. dollar-denomi-

nated funds occurs continuously throughout the day, with various offshore payments systems operating during the time when U.S. domestic markets and payments systems are closed for business. These systems function smoothly only if the banks, which serve as the "offshore" clearing agencies, are willing to extend the "nighttime" credits that may be needed by some participants to make payments before the U.S. markets open. In a major liquidity crisis, such credits might not be extended if banks were uncertain about what their own liquidity position might be when the U.S. markets opened.

Institutional Structure, Stability, and Contagion

International capital flows will yield an efficient reallocation of savings across countries only if global capital markets generate prices that appropriately reflect the underlying risks of holding financial claims. As discussed in the previous section, both official policies and factors inherent in the operation of private markets (such as asymmetrical information) can work to distort asset prices, to reduce market liquidity, and to prevent the emergence of markets for certain types of financial claims and services. While many industrial countries have undertaken financial liberalizations designed to reduce or eliminate the distortions created by official restrictions, some observers have argued that the process of deregulation, globalization, and innovation in financial markets has been a two-edged sword.[72] On one side, these developments have increased financial market efficiency; on the other, they have increased volatility in financial markets and introduced new and highly complex elements of risk—some of a systemic variety—that make the pricing of financial instruments more difficult and that can contribute to abrupt changes in credit flows once previously unforeseen risks become evident.

Efficiency and Stability in International Financial Markets

Authorities in the major industrial countries have had to confront a number of financial crises during the past two decades that have had an international as well as a domestic dimension. These crises have shared some common features (Table 11). Several were preceded by the introduction of a new financial instrument or by a sharp increase in debt, and lenders accepted a concentration of risks and charged interest rates that, ex post, did not reflect underlying risks. This was particularly evident with the growth of interbank positions prior to

---

[70]The EC has been discussing what uniform Community-wide withholding and transaction taxes should be established.

[71]These problems are discussed further below.

[72]See, for example, Corrigan (1989).

1974, the expansion of developing country debt prior to 1982, the large issuance of floating rate notes in the early 1980s, the accumulation of high-risk real estate loans and noninvestment grade bonds by U.S. thrift institutions during the 1980s, and the highly concentrated lending of Canadian regional banks to the agriculture and energy sectors in the early 1980s. Some crises were also preceded by major, often unanticipated, changes in macroeconomic conditions or policies. To take an example, the emergence of debt-servicing problems for many heavily indebted developing countries was preceded by a collapse of commodity prices, a sharp increase in oil prices, and historically high international real interest rates. Finally, the emergence of a major crisis has typically resulted in sharp increases in the risk premiums charged to certain classes of borrowers and in more restrictive credit rationing. The collapse of Bankhaus Herstatt in June 1974 was such a case, where there was a "tiering" of interest rates charged for interbank borrowing, with some large Italian and Japanese banks paying premiums as high as 200 basis points.[73]

These crises suggest that a disturbance in markets for securities or foreign exchange would be most likely to threaten *systemic* stability if it fundamentally disrupted major national and international payments, settlement, and clearance systems. The global equity markets crash of October 1987 illustrated all too well that the systems for execution of orders, for dissemination of trading information, for clearance and settlement of securities, and for payments of funds can be severely strained during a crisis.[74] If one of these systems collapses, selling pressures are likely to be exacerbated. An insolvency of a major financial institution[75] could also lead to settlement failures that would require clearinghouses either to absorb the losses or to attempt to "unwind" all transactions between the failed institutions and other institutions.[76] Cross-border settlement and payment systems are more exposed to these problems than major domestic systems because the former must operate across mixed legal and fiscal systems that can complicate the transfer of title to securities and the enforcement of settlement arrangements.[77]

Measures to Contain Systemic Risks in International Financial Markets

In addition to efforts to improve the discipline and consistency of macroeconomic policies through surveillance and policy coordination, official measures to limit contagion and to reduce systemic risks in international financial markets have focused on (1) strengthening the structures of major financial institutions and payments, clearance, and settlement systems so that they can better withstand financial crises; and (2) developing improved techniques for crisis management.

Institutional Strengthening. Efforts have been made in both private and official sectors to improve the ability of financial institutions and market structures to withstand the effects of financial shocks. New capital adequacy standards for international banks, which will come into effect fully at the end of 1992, specify the minimum amount of bank capital for such banks in relation to the credit risks that they incur in their on- and off-balance-sheet activities. Capital adequacy standards for securities houses are also being discussed by the International Organization of Securities Commissions (IOSCO). While some progress has been made, there has been a problem in defining equivalent capital standards across systems where banks' participation in security activities and transactions differ markedly (in Japan and the United States versus, say, in the European Community).[78]

Another area of institution strengthening involves efforts by major securities exchanges to increase the computer capacity of their trading systems and to improve their telecommunications

---

[73]During the October 1987 equity market crash, securities houses with large equity exposures reportedly also faced a threat of credit rationing by banks. The access of many heavily indebted developing countries to spontaneous lending was quickly curtailed after the emergence of debt-servicing difficulties for Mexico in 1982.

[74]The private and official reports on the events of October 1987 are reviewed in Section V of International Monetary Fund (1989).

[75]A sharp fall in security prices, for example, can create concerns about the ability of institutions that are large holders of securities to absorb the resulting capital losses. This could lead to a withdrawal of credit lines and an unwillingness by other institutions to trade with the institutions affected. Such institutions could therefore face a sudden funding problem that, if not solved, would lead to insolvency. Major banks may be less vulnerable to this liquidity problem (because of the availability of the central bank's discount window) than large securities houses and other nonbank financial institutions. However, the problems of the Continental Illinois Bank in 1984 illustrated that banks can also be affected by funding shortages.

[76]The problems created by an attempt to unwind transactions in payment systems are discussed in Chapter II, below.

[77]Time zone differences may also contribute to uncertainties during a crisis, since they generally lengthen the period between the sale of the security and the receipt of final payment.

[78]Some industrial countries have already taken steps to increase the minimum capital requirements for brokers and securities houses. In addition, measures have been taken to improve the capital positions of market-makers and clearinghouses. In the United States, for example, the minimum capital requirement for specialists on the New York Stock Exchange was raised from $100,000 to $1 million; and the Chicago Mercantile Exchange increased its pool of security deposits from member firms, which are liquid funds to be used in case of a customer's default, from $4.5 million to $42 million.

Table 11. Characteristics of Selected Financial Crises in Major Industrial Countries and Eurocurrency Markets, 1970–89

	U.S. Commercial Paper Market and the Penn Central Bankruptcy (1970)	U.K. Secondary Banking Crisis (1973)	Interbank Crisis in Eurocurrency Market (1974)	Emergence of External Payments Difficulties for Heavily Indebted Developing Countries (1982)	Continental Illinois Bank Crisis (1984)	Canadian Regional Bank Crisis (1985)	Floating Rate Note Market (1986)	Equity Market Crash (1987)	U.S. Thrifts "Loan Quality" Crises (1985–89)
Prior market development	Rapid growth in commercial paper market.	Expansion of lending to property and financial companies. Rapid growth of wholesale money market.	Foreign currency interbank credits to European banks rose from $9 billion in 1970 to $22 billion in 1974.	Rapid growth of lending to a broad range of developing countries during late 1970s and early 1980s.	Rapid growth of loans to heavily indebted developing countries and energy sector funded by heavy reliance on wholesale (interbank) deposits.	Heavy agricultural and energy-related lending, funded from wholesale money market sources.	Floating rate note (FRN) issuance grew rapidly between 1981 and 1985. Main issuers were government and banks.	Extended global "bull" market for equities with widening yield gap between government bonds and equities in Japan, the United Kingdom, and the United States.	Some thrifts, often those with weak capital positions, undertook high-risk lending in real estate, commercial development, and high-yield bonds.
Triggering event	Bankruptcy of Penn Central Railroad Company.	Failures of some large secondary banks.	Failure of Bankhaus Herstatt in June 1974. Large foreign exchange losses in other major banks.	Suspension of external debt-servicing payments by Mexico in August 1982.	After period when the bank had to pay a higher cost for wholesale deposits, large depositors withdrew funds as concerns about the quality of bank's loan portfolio grew.	Collapse of Northland and Canadian Commercial (CCB) banks.	Concerns about underpricing of risks, liquidity of market, and potential effects of changes in capital adequacy requirements for banks.	Sharp decline in equity prices in the United States spread rapidly to other major markets.	No single event.
Financial innovation	Broadening of instruments used in money markets.	Development of money market and wholesale banking.	—	Development of internationally syndicated bank lending.	—	—	Floating rate note.	Growing cross-border holdings of equity by large institutional investors.	High-yield ("junk") bonds often used to finance corporate takeovers.
Prior changes in financial policy	—	"Competition and Credit Control" of 1971 eliminated some direct credit controls and excluded clearing banks' interest rate cartel.	Movement to system of generalized floating exchange rates.	—	—	—	Proposals for establishing uniform bank capital adequacy standards in Group of Ten countries.	—	Deregulation of thrifts' lending powers, relaxation of capital standards, and interest rate deregulation.

Monetary policy and macroeconomic developments	Tightening of monetary policy in 1969 continuing into spring 1970.	Series of base rate increases and call for special deposits by banks at Bank of England.	Some tightening of U.S. monetary policy in early 1974.	General rise of interest rates to post-World War II peaks. Slower world economic growth.	—	Collapse of primary producer prices.	—	Large fiscal and current account imbalances in major industrial countries. Rise in global interest rates.	Collapse of real estate prices and primary product prices (especially for oil).
Aspects of crises									
1. Credit rationing in affected markets	Issuance of commercial paper declined sharply as corporates turned to banks to obtain credit.	Wholesale funding to secondary banks cut sharply.	Significant tiering of interbank interest rates, with premiums as high as 2 percent for even large Japanese and Italian banks. Many smaller banks excluded from market.	"Spontaneous" syndicated lending to borrowers from Latin America and Eastern Europe in particular virtually disappeared.	Withdrawals reached $8 billion a day.	Banks with characteristics similar to CCB threatened with cutoff of funds.	Market for perpetual (no maturity) FRNs affected in December 1986. The market for dated (finite maturity) FRNs affected a month later. After crises, market makers withdrew, and liquidity in market remained low.	Sales of international equity came virtually to a halt.	No runs on thrifts with federal deposit insurance, but state-insured systems experienced runs.
2. Contagion to other markets	Nonfinancial companies found borrowing in all markets more expensive.	Official support operations motivated by concerns about contagion to other institutions.	Depositors moved funds from Eurocurrency market to national markets.	Loans to borrowers in industrial countries not significantly affected. Average interest rate spreads and final maturities for these borrowers relatively stable.	None, primarily owing to large-scale intervention by authorities and other private banks.	None.	None.	Concerns that commercial banks in some countries would cut credit lines to securities houses. Trading in futures and options markets for equity instruments disrupted. Issues of equity-related Eurobonds dropped sharply. "Flight to quality" reflected in shift from equities to government bonds.	Market for high-yield bonds adversely affected.
3. International transmission	None.	None.	Yes.	Yes—across broad range of markets for loans and bonds of developing countries.	None.	None.	Yes—across the FRN market.	Yes.	None.

Table 11 (concluded). Characteristics of Selected Financial Crises in Major Industrial Countries and Eurocurrency Markets, 1970–89

	U.S. Commercial Paper Market and the Penn Central Bankruptcy (1970)	U.K. Secondary Banking Crisis (1973)	Interbank Crisis in Eurocurrency Market (1974)	Emergence of External Payments Difficulties for Heavily Indebted Developing Countries (1982)	Continental Illinois Bank Crisis (1984)	Canadian Regional Bank Crisis (1985)	Floating Rate Note Market (1986)	Equity Market Crash (1987)	U.S. Thrifts "Loan Quality" Crises (1985–89)
4. Official actions	Suspension of ceiling interest rate on short-term certificates of deposit. Indication that discount window available to banks needing reserves to extend loans to corporations.	Support loans ("Lifeboat") given to a large number of secondary banks.	In September 1974, the central bank governors of the Group of Ten and Switzerland expressed their commitment to the continued stability of the markets.	Authorities intervened to prevent an immediate crisis in the interbank market and to persuade creditor banks to roll over their claims on Mexican banks.	Major rescue program that included a $5.5 billion line of credit arranged by 28 banks led by Morgan Guaranty Trust. The Federal Deposit Insurance Corporation and a group of commercial banks infused $2 billion of new capital, and the Federal Reserve used discount window to provide funds ($4.5 billion of discounts were done in the week ended May 16, 1984).	Funds provided to CCB but were insufficient to prevent insolvency. Federal government guaranteed those deposits not covered by federal deposit insurance.	—	Some central banks indicated commitment to help maintain market liquidity.	Major rescue program enacted, with changes in supervisory structure and policies.
5. Other features	—	Sharp fall in asset prices followed (and aggravated) crisis.	The collapse of the Bankhaus Herstatt created serious difficulties in the Clearing House Interbank Payments System (CHIPS).	—	Government placed representative on Continental Illinois Executive Board.	—	Market remains weak.	Abrupt equity price changes occurred subsequently (e.g., in October 1989).	—

Source: Davis (1989).

systems. Delays experienced by investors in October 1987 in either accessing their brokers or getting their orders executed acted as an incentive for these efforts. Fewer problems were reported with processing orders or with contacting brokers in October 1989 than in October 1987.

Limits on daily price movements have also been employed to give investors time to evaluate the fundamentals and therefore to avoid contagion effects.[79] However, uncoordinated trading halts, whether within a country or across borders, may generate cross-market selling pressures as portfolio managers excluded from using one market shift their selling to other markets that remain open.

Since October 1989, pressure has been renewed to limit certain types of program trading.[80] In the United States, it has been argued that computer-driven program trading contributed to the fall in equity prices in October 1987 and October 1989 either directly, by generating sales of stock-index futures contracts in a declining market, or indirectly, by creating a negative market psychology.[81] One response to these criticisms in the United States has been the imposition of circuit breakers (which stop trading for some period after prices decline by a prespecified amount) in both the stock and stock-index futures markets, as well as limitations on the use of New York Stock Exchange (NYSE) facilities by program traders.

While higher capital adequacy standards, circuit breakers, and other structural reforms can improve a financial system's ability to cope with abrupt changes in asset prices, they can raise the costs of financial intermediation and create incentives for large portfolio managers and corporate treasurers to transact directly with each other rather than through financial intermediaries or exchanges. Computer and telecommunications technologies now make such direct trading between large traders both feasible and (in a growing number of activities) efficient.[82] This may lead to an increasing share of securities transactions taking place off the principal exchanges and without the use of financial intermediaries—just as the late 1960s and early 1970s witnessed a shift from national to offshore markets.[83] If that happens, it would be even more difficult to obtain an accurate view of the scale and direction of international capital flows.

Strengthening Clearance, Settlement, and Payment Systems. A principal reason why the major international financial crises of the 1970s and 1980s had only a modest short-run impact on real economic activity[84] is that they did not extensively disrupt major national and international clearance, settlement, and payment systems. During the past two decades, however, the growing integration of major financial markets has sharply increased the volume of transactions both within and across these systems.[85] As a result, there is a legitimate concern whether existing institutional arrangements can cope efficiently with the new volume of transactions and manage effectively the risks created by counterparty failure and liquidity crises.

In response, the authorities and private institutions in the clearinghouses have taken steps to limit the risks they face by requiring higher-quality and larger amounts of collateral from members, by shortening the settlement period,[86] by moving

---

[79]The stock markets in some countries (such as France and Japan) have employed limits on daily price movements for some time, but the United States implemented "circuit breakers" (see below) on the basis of the recommendation of the Brady Commission report (*Report of the Presidential Task Force on Market Mechanisms* (Washington: Government Printing Office, January 1988).

[80]Such trading typically involves purchases or sales of securities triggered by some predetermined rule built into a computer software program.

[81]While portfolio insurance (or dynamic hedging) activities were cited by some as an important source of price variability in 1987, recent attention has focused on the role of stock-index arbitrage. Portfolio insurance is designed to allow institutional investors to participate in a rising market, yet protect their portfolio if the market falls. Using computer-based models derived from stock options analysis, portfolio insurers would calculate and aim to achieve optimal stock-to-cash ratios at various stock market price levels. While such optimal ratios could be achieved by buying and selling stocks, most portfolio insurers found it less costly to trade stock-index futures. In stock-index arbitrage, an arbitrageur attempts to profit from disparities between the price of the stock-index future (or option) and the price of the basket of stocks underlying the index. When the futures price is at a discount, for example, the arbitrageur will sell the basket of stocks underlying the index, and buy the stock-index futures contract.

[82]Between October 1987 and October 1989, for example, such off-exchange trading was evident whenever the NYSE suspended the processing of program trading orders after the Dow Jones Industrial Average had moved by 50 points. Program traders responded by transacting directly with each other and only later reporting these transactions to the exchanges (to satisfy regulatory requirements).

[83]In the United States, the Securities and Exchange Commission recently modified its regulations (Rule 144A) so that large domestic and foreign institutional investors will be able to operate more easily in U.S. private placement markets.

[84]The emergence of the external payments problems of heavily indebted developing countries clearly had adverse medium-term effects on income and trade flows in both developing and industrial countries.

[85]The domestic and international U.S. dollar wholesale payments systems alone experienced an average *daily* payments flow of $1.4 trillion in 1988.

[86]The Group of Thirty, *Clearance and Settlements Systems in the World's Securities Markets* (1989) includes recommendations that (1) each country should have a central securities depository in place by 1992; (2) a trade netting system should be implemented by 1992 if it would help reduce risk and promote efficiency; and (3) a "rolling settlement" system would be adopted with final settlement occurring on $T+3$ (where T is the trade date) by 1992.

toward delivery versus payments (DVP) methods,[87] by placing limits on "daylight" overdrafts in payments systems, and by making more intensive use of netting arrangements to reduce the volume of transactions.[88] The members of clearinghouses have also clarified the legal arrangements governing the sharing of losses arising from a payments or settlement failure.

Crisis Management. During a financial crisis, uncertainty about the evolution of asset prices and about the solvency of financial institutions can result in a "shortage" of liquidity, as intermediaries become reluctant to extend credit and as depositors (or creditors) withdraw funds from institutions experiencing difficulties. Authorities have sought to contain the spread of major financial crises through a "safety net" encompassing the provision of emergency liquidity assistance by central banks, intervention to assist particular institutions, and the establishment of official or private deposit insurance arrangements. Emergency liquidity assistance is designed to prevent a sharp rise in interest rates and to allow creditors to make lending decisions on the basis of normal creditworthiness rather than on concerns about short-term liquidity shortages. At times, large financial institutions have also been assisted through the central bank's discount window, through infusions of new capital, and through support from other private (and public) sector entities.

Deposit insurance has traditionally been viewed as a means of eliminating the need for depositors to flee into currency during a crisis and thereby helping to reduce contagion among banks or other institutions. Since deposit insurance has been limited in scope, it has been more relevant for retail deposits than for the placement of funds through the wholesale international interbank markets.[89] Indeed, experience with the events surrounding the bankruptcies of Bankhaus Herstatt, the Continental Illinois Bank, and Drexel Burnham Lambert indicate that concerns about the solvency of a major financial institution can lead to a rapid withdrawal of wholesale deposits.[90]

As with other types of insurance, however, an official safety net must confront the problem that the insured may behave differently simply because insurance exists. A potentially serious "moral hazard" arises if the official safety net induces the managers of some financial institutions, especially those close to insolvency, to undertake an unduly large share of potentially high-return but also high-risk activities; this can occur if managers perceive that, with good outcomes, they will earn high profits for shareholders, but, with bad outcomes, the losses will be absorbed by the taxpayer. Also, if some institutions are viewed as being too large to fail, creditors and depositors might not be concerned with the risks being assumed by these institutions. In the end, insufficient "market discipline" (in the form of a higher cost of funds when the firm undertakes more risky activity) may be imposed on the institutions. Such a risk-taking bias could eventually lead to significant future public sector liabilities, as the recent savings and loan institutions crisis in the United States so vividly illustrated.

Deposit insurance systems have therefore taken steps appropriately to limit their risk exposure by restricting the extent of their coverage of deposits, by enhancing supervision of the activities of insured institutions, by developing procedures for more rapid closing of insolvent institutions, and by relating insurance premiums more closely to the riskiness of the institutions' portfolios. In a number of countries, including the United States, the authorities are reassessing the future role of deposit insurance in their systems.

---

[87]DVP requires that the transfer of a security be matched by delivery of payment. In most systems, payments occur more quickly than the transfer of securities.

[88]The Bank for International Settlements has published a "Report on Netting Schemes" examining how netting arrangements could help reduce the scale of transactions and risks in clearance and payments systems for foreign exchange and securities. Such arrangements could involve systems based on (1) position netting—which nets the amount to be delivered but leaves the underlying original contracts intact; (2) netting by novation—which extinguishes the original contracts and replaces them with a new net contract; and (3) close-out netting—which, when liquidation occurs, brings forward all outstanding contracts for settlement as a single netted amount. The differences between the legal and fiscal systems employed in the major countries create a variety of obstacles to implementing these arrangements.

[89]Even in systems without explicit official deposit insurance, a system with a majority of state-owned banks or a history of central bank or regulatory intervention to shore up or merge failing institutions, to avoid depositor losses, could create the perception of implicit deposit insurance.

---

[90]The effects of a depositor (or creditor) run on the stability of a financial system depend on the financial condition of the institutions affected and the reactions of the monetary and regulatory authorities. A run on a financial institution, for example, could result in a shift of deposits (or credits) to other institutions, a flight to quality in which deposits are used to purchase "safe" securities, or (especially in the case of a bank) a transfer into currency. The first two types of runs principally redistribute deposits or credits within the financial system and implicitly reflect the belief that the financial system as a whole is sound. Nonetheless, such a run could still adversely affect economic activity by creating uncertainty and breaking traditional financial connections between borrowers and lenders. A run into currency or foreign exchange could indicate a lack of confidence in the financial or banking systems. In the absence of offsetting central bank actions, such a run could lead to a sharp contraction of the money supply, a sharp rise in short-term interest rates, and either an abrupt depreciation of the exchange rate under a flexible exchange rate system or a balance of payments deficit with a fixed exchange rate.

In an environment in which financial institutions are now relatively free to relocate their activities, efforts by any country on its own to impose stiffer regulatory standards faces the problem of regulatory arbitrage. Again, here, a coordinated approach can accomplish what a competitive, uncoordinated approach cannot.

Role of Official Capital Flows

As noted above, official capital flows have at times been a major component of total capital flows—both to indebted developing countries and between industrial countries during periods of foreign exchange market instability. While some official flows (such as military assistance) have been motivated by noneconomic considerations, others have reflected attempts either to alter the redistribution of global savings and investment produced by private capital flows or to influence the asset prices (especially exchange rates) produced by financial markets.

Leaving aside military assistance, the dominant official flows among industrial countries have reflected exchange market intervention.[91] Such intervention often took place when there were concerns that exchange rates were either excessively volatile or were moving in a direction inconsistent with fundamentals. While the ultimate objectives of macroeconomic policies are price stability and economic growth rather than exchange market stability, stable exchange market conditions and sustainable current account positions are widely regarded as having favorable feedback effects on economic performance. There may, therefore, be scope to use exchange market intervention both to offset bandwagon effects and to signal the authorities' policy intentions. The effects of such intervention are likely to be larger and more lasting if backed by other policy changes that help to make the signal credible. Also, "concerted" intervention by a number of countries seems to have a greater and more sustained effect on exchange rates than intervention by a country alone. Nevertheless, exchange market intervention cannot by itself be counted upon to achieve an appropriate pattern of exchange rates.

With increasingly integrated financial markets, the question arises of how to select the set of asset prices to be stabilized. Exchange rates, important as they are, are only one element in the set of asset prices that influence private sector portfolio and trade decisions. Asset price volatility in a major segment of international financial markets (such as

for bonds or equities) could create just as much private sector uncertainty as exchange rate instability. However, intervention in a broad range of markets would raise the issue of how private risk-taking activities would be affected by the knowledge that the authorities would regularly intervene to stabilize asset prices during periods of financial disturbance.

Proposals for throwing "sand in the wheels" of the world capital market (for example, by imposing transaction taxes on trades in short-term securities) reflect the view that short-run trading in foreign exchange and securities markets can be dominated by "noise" traders who ignore fundamentals and thereby contribute to excess asset price volatility. Transaction taxes create two problems. One is that they may also discourage trades based on fundamentals, as well as those based on noise. The second is that, to be effective, they need to be imposed on a global basis. If implemented in only a few markets, activity would quickly shift to other markets.

Official transfers and credits from industrial to developing countries encompass a broad range of economic, humanitarian, and military assistance. Official lending has encompassed both direct bilateral credits and lending through multilateral institutions. The terms and conditions under which these official credits are made available vary considerably. Some development credits are supplied on concessionary terms for long periods; other official flows represent short- and medium-term credits that are subject to conditionality and carry market-related interest rates. Despite the heterogeneous nature of the terms and conditions of these loans, their availability helped cushion the sharply reduced access to private international financial markets experienced by many indebted developing countries in 1982. Since the experience of the 1980s suggests that re-establishing creditworthiness can be a lengthy process—even for countries undertaking strong adjustment measures—official credits are likely to play an important role during the 1990s as well.

International Capital Markets and Developing Countries

Developing countries should be major beneficiaries of an international system that efficiently transfers resources from relatively capital-abundant to relatively capital-scarce regions. The 1970s and 1980s have, however, provided only mixed evidence of a smooth transfer of resources. Some developing countries that have consistently implemented sound policies have maintained or achieved good access to international financial markets, and still others have even been net creditors to these markets. At the same time, eight years

---

[91]In 1987, for example, reserve accumulation by Germany and Japan represented 37 percent of the financing of their current account surpluses.

after the emergence of the debt crisis, many indebted developing countries still have very limited access to spontaneous credits from international financial markets. As a result, official transfers and long-term credits, rather than private financial flows, have become the primary source of financing for this latter group's current account deficit.

Current Linkages

Experience since 1982 has demonstrated that creditworthiness considerations play a dominant role in determining both the cost and availability of credit from international markets. While there is considerable debate about how well the markets evaluate the willingness and ability of borrowers to service their debt obligations, it is clear that the perception that a borrower's creditworthiness has deteriorated, or is about to deteriorate, can lead to an abrupt curtailment of funding that may be difficult to reverse even in the medium term (see above).

One key issue is whether perceptions of creditworthiness are subject to "contagion effects" in the sense that an otherwise creditworthy country's access to international credits is curtailed because other countries at a similar stage of development or with a similar external debt position are experiencing external payments difficulties. Even in the industrial countries, it is evident that debt-servicing difficulties for a particular institution lead to a close scrutiny of similar institutions. The experience with financial crises (see above) suggests that contagion can occur both when information about a borrower's current financial position is lacking and when the adverse economic news is such that all similar borrowers are viewed as equally likely to be affected. Both of these factors were evident during the early stages of the debt crisis in 1982. For example, some heavily indebted developing countries lacked comprehensive reporting systems for keeping track of the level and composition of the external debts of not only the central authorities but also local governments and public sector enterprises. In addition, the downturn in economic activity in the industrial countries in 1981–82, the rise in international real interest rates, and the decline in commodity prices may have contributed to the view that *every* heavily indebted developing country might face serious external debt-servicing difficulties.[92,93] While contagion may be difficult to

avoid in the uncertain environment created by a major financial or macroeconomic shock, it may be easier to contain when there is updated information on a borrower's debt and debt-servicing capacity and when debt-servicing obligations are perceived to be low relative to debt-servicing capacity.

Access to international markets by public and private sector entities in developing countries has also been influenced by capital controls. In general, private residents of developing countries face much more significant restrictions on their ability to move capital in and out of their economies than do residents of the industrial countries. While many considerations have influenced the severity of these restrictions, they are typically motivated by a desire to prevent capital flight, to limit foreign ownership of domestic enterprises, or to conserve scarce foreign exchange. There is nonetheless some evidence that the restrictiveness of capital controls is being relaxed in some developing countries with good access to international markets, particularly in Asia.[94]

While capital controls could break the linkages between external and domestic financial markets, experiences with capital flight during periods of political and economic instability suggest that these restrictions are far from effective. As discussed in the study by Rojas-Suarez, below, capital flight has been influenced by such factors as the difference between the real yields on domestic and external financial assets, the presence (or absence) of high and variable domestic inflation, differential tax treatment of interest income at home and abroad, the credibility of domestic macroeconomic policies, and political uncertainty. Whatever the specific factors that have motivated such capital movements, residents of many developing countries are now more aware of how to place and manage funds in international financial markets and are becoming increasingly sensitive to differences between financial conditions in domestic and external markets. For this reason, there is a growing consensus that capital flight needs to be addressed by dealing with the underlying distortions or policy inadequacies at the source, rather than by attempting to restrict the symptom or manifestation of these inadequacies (that is, the capital flow itself).

Prospects

Any net capital flows to (or from) developing countries during the 1990s will naturally reflect saving and investment balances in both the developing and industrial countries. As discussed by Aghevli

---

[92]Even as the debt crisis emerged, some indebted developing countries, especially those that had pursued sound macroeconomic and debt-management policies, avoided contagion and maintained access to private flows.

[93]Some shocks, such as a sharp rise in energy prices, could benefit some developing countries while adversely affecting others.

[94]Mathieson (1988) found that this had occurred most often in those Asian countries undertaking trade and domestic financial liberalizations.

and others (1990), savings rates in both the industrial and developing countries have declined since the mid-1970s.[95] Medium-term World Economic Outlook projections suggest little change in these saving patterns in the early 1990s. At the same time, demands for the use of world savings are likely to be increasing. The successful implementation of growth-oriented adjustment programs in countries in Africa and Latin America would create opportunities for new and profitable investments. Similarly, the restructuring of the Eastern European economies will require major new investments, and the industrial countries also face the need to rebuild infrastructure capital and to undertake investments to cope with a variety of environmental investments. This suggests that without measures to stimulate either private or public sector saving in both industrial and developing countries high real interest rates (especially on long-term instruments) could be a characteristic of the 1990s.

Although World Economic Outlook projections imply that total financial flows to the net debtor countries in 1990–95 are expected to be roughly the same as in 1983–89,[96] the access of individual net debtor developing countries to international capital markets during the early 1990s is likely to vary widely. Those developing countries that either maintain or develop good access to international capital markets will be able to use a wide array of financial instruments and markets to fund domestic investments and to manage external debt positions and foreign exchange reserves. Other developing countries will also have access to financial markets and instruments as suppliers of funds, or where institutional arrangements (including collateralization requirements) minimize the barriers associated with creditworthiness considerations.

Developing Countries' Use of Markets and Instruments. Although private capital flows to developing countries in the 1970s were dominated by commercial bank lending, flows of securities (including the use of market-based hedging instruments) and direct foreign investment appear likely to play a relatively more important role in the 1990s. While short-term trade credits from commercial banks have remained a regular feature of

capital flows between developing and industrial countries, the use of medium-term general purpose syndicated bank loans declined dramatically in the 1980s. This instrument is unlikely to be a major vehicle for transferring resources to indebted developing countries in 1990–95; such loans are not an attractive vehicle for financing long-term domestic investment. They create an "open exposure" to variations in nominal and real interest rates, since they typically carry a floating interest rate tied to the London interbank offer rate (LIBOR), and their availability cannot be guaranteed for the life of the investment project.

During the late 1800s and 1920s, long-term bond financing was the principal financial vehicle for resource transfers between industrial and developing countries. Such bonds matched the maturity of a long-term investment with its financing and provided certainty about the time profile of nominal (though not necessarily real) debt-servicing obligations. Long-term bond financing is currently available only to borrowers that are perceived to be among the best credit risks. As a result, only a limited number of developing countries have been able to issue regularly on international bond markets. Long-term bond markets are therefore unlikely to be a major source of direct funding for developing countries during the *early* 1990s.[97]

As developing countries' creditworthiness is restored, however, bond markets could become a much more prominent source of external finance. Although the international bonds issued by indebted developing countries during the 1970s constituted only a small fraction of their accumulation of external debts, the recent debt exchanges undertaken by Mexico have created a sizable stock of new bonds.[98] In addition, developing countries have generally had a good record of servicing their external bond holding throughout the 1980s.[99] In part, this reflects the fact that bond payments constituted a relatively small fraction of developing countries' total external debt-service obligations.[100] Nonetheless, there is some evidence that

---

[95]For example, gross saving in industrial countries declined from 26 percent of GNP in 1973 to 20.5 percent in 1988, whereas net saving fell from 17 percent of GNP in 1973 to about 10 percent in 1988. For developing countries, the gross saving rate fell from an average of 27 percent in 1976–81 to 22½ percent in 1982–88.

[96]Since a major resumption of spontaneous commercial bank lending to developing countries with recent debt-servicing difficulties appears unlikely, official creditors are expected to provide nearly all of the total net external credit extended during 1990–95 to this group of countries.

[97]These markets have been a major indirect source of funding as a result of bond issuance by multilateral development institutions.

[98]About $44 billion of 30-year bonds were issued by Mexico in exchange for its debt.

[99]It is estimated that the four largest indebted developing countries in Latin America have repaid about $24 billion of principal and interest on their external bonds issued over the past 15 years.

[100]In 1989, for example, it is estimated that debt service on the bonds of the four largest Latin American countries amounted to only 5½ percent of total debt-service payments. The large debt exchanges by countries such as Mexico will increase the relative importance of bond-related debt-servicing payments.

this record of repayment has facilitated a limited return to the bond market, especially for the borrowers that are residents of those indebted developing countries that have participated in debt-reduction programs.[101]

One problem associated with the use of fixed interest rate bond financing is that debt-service payments would be fixed even if a country's debt-servicing capacity changed abruptly owing to an economic shock. This problem has led to proposals that developing countries consider issuing index or commodity-linked bonds that would tie interest and/or amortization payments to movements of a specified price index (such as an exchange rate) or commodity price. But such bonds could be more costly than conventional (nonindexed) bonds, since investors would require a higher interest rate to compensate for the more variable income stream. Although proposals for the use of commodity-linked bonds have been made throughout the 1970s and 1980s,[102] there has been limited use of these instruments.

One new instrument that combines the elements of collateralized loans and of commodity-linked bonds is the commodity swap. The commodity swap undertaken by Mexican de Cobre (Mexcobre),[103] which was one of the first spontaneous foreign currency borrowings by a private sector Mexican company since 1982, illustrates the structure of such transactions. Mexcobre obtained a $210 million loan from a consortium of ten commercial banks. The loan was secured by the dollar proceeds of one third of Mexcobre's copper production over the next three years, sold to Sogem, a subsidiary of Société Générale de Belgique. The transaction fixed the copper price at about $2,000 a ton, and fixed the loan rate at 12 percent a year using a floating-to-fixed interest rate swap. The swap effectively allowed Mexcobre to lock in both fixed-term funding and a known price for a portion of its copper exports. The copper user in turn achieved a fixed input cost and the banks obtained a collateralized loan secured by copper output that represents a relatively low portion of the producer's output.

It is estimated that to date there have been about $2.5 billion of commodity swaps, with the vast majority of the transactions being oil swaps. While the market appears to be growing rapidly, implementing long-term commodity swaps can be very time consuming without organized markets in which to hedge long-term commodity price risks.[104] As a result, the intermediary must search for commodity producers and users that have complementary needs.

Equity-related capital flows could potentially provide an important source of external resources through both foreign direct investment and portfolio investments in equities. Foreign direct investment can be motivated by a variety of factors, including a desire to utilize abundant local raw material, to take advantage of differences in factor costs, and to penetrate local markets.[105] As a source of external finance, foreign direct investment is attractive in the sense that foreign exchange remittances are tied to the local producer's capacity to pay. Since foreign direct investors are exposed to a variety of commercial and transfer risks, however, they will expect to earn a higher rate of return than other investors providing funds through loans or bonds.

While there has been growing interest in equity portfolio investment in certain developing countries, the ability of foreign investors to make such investments varies considerably across developing countries. According to the International Finance Corporation (IFC), only Argentina, Indonesia, Jordan,[106] Malaysia, Portugal, and Turkey offered foreign investors generally free and unrestricted repatriation of capital and income from shares at the end of 1989. Some markets (in Chile, Costa Rica, Venezuela, Mexico, and Thailand) were classified by the IFC as "relatively open," with some registration requirements and restrictions on repatriation of capital and income. About 40 percent of the emerging markets were classified as "relatively closed." Some of these economies (Brazil, India, Taiwan Province of China, and Korea) permit foreign portfolio investment through country-specific funds that are listed on major stock exchanges in industrial countries. These funds have expanded

---

[101]For example, Banco Nacional de Comercio Exterior of Mexico privately placed $100 million of bonds with investors in Europe, the Far East, Central America, and South America in June 1989. The bonds reportedly carried a five-year maturity with a coupon of 10.25 percent and an issue price of 88.5. Euromarket issues were also made in early 1990 by two Mexican borrowers (Petróleos Mexicanos (DM 100 million) and Tamtradu ($30 million)) and a Venezuelan borrower (Swensa Steel Investment ($40 million)).

[102]The different proposals are reviewed in Lessard and Williamson (1985).

[103]Mexcobre is the copper-exporting subsidiary of Group Mexico, a large Mexican mining group.

[104]The Mexcobre transaction apparently took three months to complete.

[105]Debt-equity swaps have also provided a source of funding for foreign direct investment in some developing countries. The determinants of foreign direct investment are discussed in the study by Lizondo, below.

Stable macroeconomic policies, labor market conditions, and exchange rate policies are also likely to play key roles in attracting foreign direct investment.

[106]Some limitations exist on how quickly capital can be repatriated.

sharply, with the total market capitalization of a group of 40 funds reaching nearly $7 billion at the end of 1989. Although many of these markets are thin and volatile, they have provided attractive total returns in comparison with many major markets in the industrial countries.[107]

Foreign portfolio investment inflows can have a beneficial effect on the cost of capital in a developing country; if they are from venture capital funds, they could increase the availability of funds to new enterprises. Despite these potential benefits, many developing countries maintain restrictions on foreign portfolio equity purchases because of concerns about the effects of foreign control of domestic enterprises and the potential loss of foreign exchange reserves through repatriation of capital and dividends. While views differ on the benefits and costs associated with foreign ownership of domestic institutions, foreign control could potentially be addressed by limiting the percentage of total equity in a company that could be held by foreign investors or by creating specific classes of stocks without voting rights. The right to repatriate dividends and capital is more fundamental and is likely to be crucial in attracting significant amounts of foreign equity investment.

International capital markets can also be used in developing countries to manage existing foreign asset and liability positions. Periods of high variability in international interest rates, in primary commodity prices, and in exchange rates of major currencies present a particular problem for developing countries because this variability is essentially "beyond their control." For example, countries with large floating rate obligations have faced complicated debt-management problems because they have effectively taken on a relatively "open" (unhedged) position regarding interest rate variability. While developing countries have attempted to limit or offset the impact of external shocks through self insurance and official multilateral agreements or assistance (for example, through the IMF's compensatory and contingency financing facility), market-based hedging instruments are also available.[108]

Creditworthiness considerations directly limit access to some hedging instruments. For example, creditworthy borrowers in industrial countries often use the interest rate swap market to convert their floating interest rate debt into the equivalent of fixed interest rate debt. However, since an interest rate swap involves an exchange of debt-servicing obligations (the fixed interest rate borrower agrees to service the obligations of the floating interest rate borrower and vice versa), a swap is an effective hedging instrument only if each counterparty fulfills its debt-servicing obligations. Most borrowers will therefore engage in a swap only when credit risk is perceived to be low; indebted developing countries with debt-servicing difficulties have thus not had access to this market.

Certain other hedging instruments are not as directly restricted by creditworthiness considerations. The futures exchanges, for example, have sought to minimize credit risks by adopting margin calls, which involve both the posting of an initial performance bond (margin requirements) when a futures contract is either purchased or sold and the allocation to the margin account of the capital gains or losses on outstanding future contracts at the end of each business day. This requirement limits credit risks by reducing the scale of potential losses and by shortening the performance period to a single day.[109] Similarly, when a developing country enters into an interest rate cap agreement provided by a large international bank or manufacturing firm, the creditworthiness of the bank or manufacturing firm is the factor that will influence the effectiveness of the hedge.

Although the use of financial and commodity hedging markets does not directly increase the scale of financing available to developing countries, it restores some access to international capital markets for debt-management purposes and provides greater certainty about external receipts and payments. Short-term hedging operations can potentially be carried out using financial and commodity futures and options. Medium-term hedges can be constructed with interest rate caps and forward agreements for major exchange rates and commodity prices. Moreover, as noted earlier, hedging operations can be combined with other lending arrangements (for example, in a commodity swap) to secure both access to additional funds and greater certainty about external interest rates and commodity prices.

While market-based hedging instruments can benefit stability, a number of factors limit the use of such instruments. The cost of hedging can include the payment of up-front premiums (such as with interest rate caps), which countries that are short of reserves and experiencing external payments difficulties may find excessively costly. As already noted, creditworthiness considerations also

---

[107]From the end of 1984 to the end of 1989, the total return index for the IFC's emerging market rose from 100 to 306, while the United States Standard and Poor's 500 stock index rose to 224.

[108]These hedging instruments were examined in detail in Mathieson and others (1989).

---

[109]Should the hedger be unable to meet any daily margin calls, this position is immediately closed out by the exchange.

restrict access to some hedging instruments (such as interest rate swaps). In addition, the management of hedging operations requires skilled personnel capable of dealing in wholesale hedging markets, as well as implementing internal control mechanisms that effectively limit the activities of risk managers to legitimate hedging operations.

Despite these barriers, the use of market-based hedging instruments by developing countries has continued to expand in recent years (Table 12). While much of this growth has involved the use of currency options and swaps, there has been increasing use of interest rate swaps, interest rate caps, and commodity-linked facilities. Moreover, the data in Table 12 do not reflect the growing use of financial and commodity futures contracts.[110]

Policies to Increase the Availability of Savings to Developing Countries. One means of increasing the external resources that could potentially be made available to developing countries would be to increase the level of public sector saving (or to reduce dissaving) in the *industrial countries.* While the export credit policies and official capital flows of these countries have played an important role in sustaining the availability of external resources to developing countries in the 1980s, the financing of large fiscal deficits in some major industrial countries has naturally drawn heavily on existing global savings. However, the extent to which a reduction in these fiscal deficits would increase the resources available to developing countries would depend on the developing countries' access to international financial markets. If all developing countries had good access to international capital markets, a reduction in fiscal deficits in the industrial countries could stimulate capital flows to developing countries. But if their access remained limited, a reduction of fiscal deficits in the industrial countries would affect developing countries only indirectly through the effects of income and interest rate movements on trade flows rather than through a surge of new capital inflows.

Without any other policy changes, previous World Economic Outlook analyses have indicated that a reduction in fiscal deficits in the industrial countries would result in lower international interest rates and, initially, a decline in industrial country GNP, which would be reversed in the medium term. While lower interest rates would reduce developing countries' debt-service payments, the offsetting short- and medium-term movements in industrial country GNP would also imply correspondingly modest changes in the exports and

---

[110]For example, Chile has made extensive use of the Eurodollar futures markets to hedge against the effects of interest rate movements on its debt-service payments.

Table 12. External Risk Management in Developing Countries[1]
(In millions of U.S. dollars)

Type of Instrument	1988	1989
Currency options/swaps	1,231	2,186
Of which:		
Algeria	100	—
Bulgaria	25	—
China	30	290
Hungary	156	50
India	324	50
Indonesia	318	—
Korea	—	49
Nauru	—	150
Oman	100	100
Portugal	50	—
Thailand	8	16
Trinidad and Tobago	20	—
Turkey	100	—
Interest swaps	262	391
Of which:		
China	60	100
India	—	68
Korea	—	68
Portugal	132	—
Thailand	70	155
Interest caps	51	140
Of which:		
China	51	—
Malaysia	—	140
Commodity-linked facility	—	310
Of which:		
Algeria (oil-linked)	—	100
Mexico (copper swap)	—	210
Other[2]	280	725
Of which:		
China	—	50
India	—	50
Indonesia	—	225
Korea	30	—
Thailand	250	—
Turkey	—	400
Total	1,824	3,752

Source: World Bank, *Financial Flows to Developing Countries.*

[1]This table does not necessarily provide a complete list of all risk management activities undertaken by developing countries.

[2]Includes such instruments as floating rate certificates of deposit, floating rate notes, and note issuance facilities with put and call options.

income levels of developing countries. Thus, with relatively limited access to international financial markets, the developing countries would be likely to share only modestly in the benefits associated with reducing fiscal deficits in the industrial countries.[111]

Previous staff studies of capital flight and saving[112] have identified a number of measures that over time could promote domestic savings in developing countries, a return of flight capital, and renewed access to international capital markets. At a minimum, domestic fiscal, monetary, exchange rate, and financial policies must be designed to create stable domestic economic and financial market conditions, to provide domestic residents with clear incentives to hold their savings in domestic financial claims, and to ensure that available domestic and foreign savings are used to support productive investments.[113] Moreover, since it is difficult for any financial system to insulate domestic savings from the adverse effects of high and variable rates of inflation, a reasonable degree of price stability will be a key factor in providing an attractive return on domestic financial instruments. Such price stability will not be possible unless fiscal deficits can be financed in a noninflationary manner.

Fiscal policy also impinges directly on post-tax rates of return on assets. Income taxes on interest, profits, and dividends, and property taxes on private wealth can drive a wedge between the post-tax returns on domestic assets and external assets, especially when returns on external assets escape taxation. Large fiscal imbalances can also create the expectation of higher future taxes either directly through higher tax rates or indirectly through an inflation tax.

Exchange rate policies that are perceived as inconsistent with monetary and fiscal policies can also create strong incentives for residents to acquire foreign assets, especially when the exchange rate appears likely to depreciate strongly in the near term. Although countries have often experienced a reverse capital inflow after a large exchange rate depreciation, repeated episodes of rapid inflation followed by sharp adjustments in exchange rates can create a strong incentive for domestic residents to hold assets abroad.

Excessive domestic money creation and inflexible interest rate policies often combined to create negative real rates of return on domestic assets in many developing countries. Residents in indebted developing countries were therefore faced with the choice of accepting negative real rates of return on domestic financial claims—amounting to an average 5 percent per annum during 1979–82—or positive real rates of return on foreign assets—equivalent to about 17 percent per annum, after taking exchange rate movements into account. Even with exchange controls, such large real interest rate differentials can create a significant incentive for an outflow of funds. The demonstrated ability and willingness of developing country residents to place their wealth in external markets suggests that to limit capital flight, it will generally be necessary to offer yields on domestic financial claims that are comparable to those available on external assets.[114]

Even if restoration of normal market access is delayed,[115] the sustained implementation of credible macroeconomic and financial policies may result in a return of flight capital. Nonetheless, since the residents of developing countries probably want to hold internationally diversified portfolios, it is unlikely that all previous flight capital would return even with "good" policies. However, the return of even a limited proportion of past outflows could have a significant impact on economic performance. Moreover, the combination of a return of flight capital and reduced fiscal deficits in the industrial countries could have mutually reinforcing positive medium-term effects on investment and growth in developing countries.

---

[111]If spontaneous capital flows to developing countries are affected by expected tax payments associated with the servicing of their external debts, industrial countries' support of debt reduction and enlarged access into their markets for developing country products could also indirectly influence developing countries' access to external markets.

[112]See Deppler and Williamson (1987) and Aghevli and others (1990), respectively.

[113]Stable economic conditions are also important for encouraging foreign direct investment.

---

[114]The degree of competition and stability of the domestic financial system will affect the willingness of residents to accumulate domestic financial claims and the ability of that system to identify and fund productive investments. Improving financial market efficiency and stability requires the implementation of policies to encourage increased competition, improvements in the management of financial institutions, the establishment of uniform accounting and legal arrangements (especially regarding bankruptcy), and strengthened supervision.

[115]Experience in both the industrial and the developing countries suggests that a return to normal market access may not occur quickly, in part reflecting the need to establish the perception that the borrower's debt-service capacity is adequate to service both existing and any additional obligations. For example, serious budget difficulties led credit rating agencies to suspend New York City's credit rating in April 1975, which essentially made it impossible for the city and its agencies to refinance their short-term debts. The State of New York created the Emergency Control Board to oversee the city's financial recovery and to authorize the Municipal Assistance Corporation to issue bonds (which were guaranteed by the "moral obligation" of the state) to raise funds for the refinancing of the city's debts. Despite this extensive assistance, the city's credit rating was not restored to the minimum investment grade (Standard and Poor's BBB) until 1981.

References

Adler, Michael, and Bruce Lehmann, "Deviations from Purchasing Power Parity in the Long Run," *Journal of Finance*, Vol. 38 (December 1983).

Aghevli, Bijan, and others, *The Role of National Savings in the World Economy*, IMF Occasional Paper, No. 67 (Washington: International Monetary Fund, March 1990).

Bank for International Settlements, *Report on Netting Schemes* (Basle, February 1989).

Barro, Robert, "Are Government Bonds Net Wealth?" *Journal of Monetary Economics* (November/December 1974).

Batten, Dallas S., Michael Blackwell, In-Su Kim, Simon E. Nocera, and Yuzuru Ozeki, *The Conduct of Monetary Policy in the Major Industrial Countries: Instruments and Operating Procedures*, IMF Occasional Paper, No. 70 (Washington: International Monetary Fund, July 1990).

Bayoumi, Tamim, "Saving-Investment Correlations: Immobile Capital, Government Policy or Endogenous Behavior?" *Staff Papers*, International Monetary Fund, Vol. 37 (July 1990).

Bishop, Graham, and others, *Market Discipline Can Work in the EC Monetary Union* (New York: Salomon Brothers, 1989).

————, *Creating an EC Monetary Union With Binding Market Rules* (New York: Salomon Brothers, February 1990).

Black, Fischer, and Myron Scholes, "The Pricing of Options and Corporate Liabilities," *Journal of Political Economy*, Vol. 81 (May–June 1973).

Boughton, James M., *The Monetary Approach to Exchange Rates: What Now Remains?* Essays in International Finance, No. 171 (Princeton, New Jersey: Princeton University, Department of Economics, 1988).

Branson, William H., *Financial Capital Flows in the U.S. Balance of Payments* (Amsterdam: North-Holland, 1968).

————, "Financial Market Integration, Macroeconomic Policy and the EMS," Centre for Economic Policy Research, Discussion Paper Series, No. 385, March 1990.

Brimmer, Andrew F., "International Finance and the Management of Bank Failures: Herstatt vs. Franklin National," paper presented at a joint session of the American Economic Association and the American Finance Association, Atlantic City, New Jersey, September 16, 1976.

Bryant, Ralph, David Currie, Jacob A. Frenkel, Paul Masson, and Richard Portes, eds., *Macroeconomic Policies in an Interdependent World* (Washington: International Monetary Fund, 1989).

Corrigan, E. Gerald, "Reflections on the 1980s," *Federal Reserve Bank of New York Seventy-Fifth Annual Report for the Year Ended December 31, 1989*, pp. 5–22.

Davis, E.P., "Instability in the Euromarkets and the Economic Theory of Financial Crisis," Bank of England Discussion Paper No. 43 (October 1989).

de Vries, Margaret Garrison, *The International Monetary Fund 1972–1978: Cooperation on Trial, Volume I: Narrative and Analysis* (Washington: International Monetary Fund, 1985).

Deppler, Michael, and Martin Williamson, "Capital Flight: Concepts, Measurement, and Issues," *Staff Studies for the World Economic Outlook* (Washington: International Monetary Fund, August 1987), pp. 39–58.

Dooley, Michael, "Country-Specific Risk Premiums, Capital Flight and Net Investment Income Payments in Selected Developing Countries" (Washington: International Monetary Fund; unpublished, March 1986).

————, Jeffrey Frankel, and Donald J. Mathieson, "International Capital Mobility: What Do Saving-Investment Correlations Tell Us?" *Staff Papers*, International Monetary Fund, Vol. 34 (September 1987).

Feldstein, Martin, "Time to Bid Farewell to the Louvre Accord," *Financial Times*, March 29, 1990.

————, and Phillipe Bacchetta, "National Saving and International Investment," in *National Saving and Economic Performance,* ed. by Douglas Bernheim and John B. Shoven (Chicago: University of Chicago Press, forthcoming June 1991).

Feldstein, M., and C. Horioka, "Domestic Saving and International Capital Flows," *Economic Journal*, Vol. 90 (June 1980).

Folkerts-Landau, David, "The Changing Role of International Bank Lending in Development Finance," *Staff Papers,* International Monetary Fund, Vol. 32 (June 1985).

————, and Donald J. Mathieson, "Innovation, Institutional Changes, and Regulatory Response in International Financial Markets," in *Restructuring Banking and Financial Services in America,* ed. by William S. Haraf and Rose Marie Kushmeider (Washington: American Enterprise Institute, 1988).

Frankel, Jeffrey A., "Quantifying International Capital Mobility in the 1980s," in *National Saving and Economic Performance*, ed. by Douglas Bernheim and John B. Shoven (Chicago: University of Chicago Press, forthcoming June 1991).

————, and Alan T. MacArthur, "Political vs. Currency Premia in International Real Interest Differentials: A Study of Forward Rates for 24 Countries," *European Economic Review*, Vol. 32 (June 1988).

Frenkel, Jacob A., and Richard M. Levich, "Transaction Costs and Interest Arbitrage: Tranquil versus Turbulent Periods," *Journal of Political Economy*, Vol. 85 (December 1977).

Friedman, B., "Capital, Credit and Money Markets," in *The New Palgrave: Money*, ed. by John Eatwell, Murray Milgate, and Peter Newman (New York: W.W. Norton, 1989).

Greenspan, Alan, Testimony before the Task Force on the International Competitiveness of U.S. Financial Institutions, Committee on Banking, Finance and Urban Affairs, U.S. House of Representatives (April 4, 1990).

Hacche, Graham, "The Demand for Money in the United Kingdom: Experience Since 1971," *Bank of England Quarterly Bulletin*, Vol. 14 (September 1974).

International Monetary Fund, *International Capital Markets: Developments and Prospects, April 1989*, By a Staff Team from the Exchange and Trade Relations and Research Departments (Washington: International Monetary Fund, 1989).

————, *International Capital Markets: Developments and Prospects, April 1990*, By a Staff Team from the Exchange and Trade Relations and Research Departments (Washington: International Monetary Fund, 1990).

Isard, Peter, and Liliana Rojas-Suarez, "Velocity of Money and the Practice of Monetary Targeting: Experience, Theory, and the Policy Debate" in *Staff Studies for the World Economic Outlook* (Washington: International Monetary Fund, July 1986), pp. 73–114.

Johnson, Manuel H., "Monetary Policy in an Integrated World Economy," address delivered at the Cato Conference on Global Monetary Order (February 22, 1990).

Kouri, J.K. Pentti, and Michael G. Porter, "International Capital Flows and Portfolio Equilibrium," *Journal of Political Economy*, Vol. 82 (May/June 1974).

Lessard, Donald R., and John Williamson, *Financial Intermediation Beyond the Debt Crisis* (Washington: Institute for International Economics, 1985).

Lintner, John, "The Valuation of Risk Assets and the Selection of Risky Investments in Stock Portfolios and Capital Budgets," *Review of Economics and Statistics*, Vol. 47 (February 1965).

Makin, John H., *Capital Flows and Exchange-Rate Flexibility in the Post-Bretton Woods Era*, Essays in International Finance, No. 103 (Princeton, New Jersey: Princeton University, February 1974).

Markowitz, Harold M., *Portfolio Selection: Efficient Diversification of Instruments* (New York: John Wiley and Sons, 1959).

Mathieson, Donald J., "Exchange Rate Arrangements and Monetary Policy," in *Monetary Policy in Pacific Basin Countries*, ed. by Hang-sheng Cheng (Norwell, Massachusetts: Kluwer Academic Publishers, 1988).

————, David Folkerts-Landau, Timothy Lane, and Iqbal Zaidi, *Managing Financial Risks in Indebted Developing Countries*, IMF Occasional Paper, No. 65 (Washington: International Monetary Fund, June 1989).

Morawetz, David, *Twenty-Five Years of Economic Development, 1950 to 1975* (Washington: World Bank, 1977).

Portes, Richard, and Alexander Swoboda, eds., *Threats to International Financial Stability* (Cambridge, England; New York: Cambridge University Press, 1987).

Reid, Margaret, *The Secondary Banking Crisis, 1973–75: Its Causes and Course* (London: Macmillan, 1982).

Salomon Brothers, *How Big Is the World Bond Market?—1989 Update* (New York, 1989).

Sharpe, William F., "Capital Asset Prices: A Theory of Market Equilibrium Under Conditions of Risk," *Journal of Finance*, Vol. 19 (September 1964).

Spero, Joan Edelman, *The Failure of the Franklin National Bank: Challenge to the International Banking System* (New York: Columbia University Press, 1980).

Stekler, Lois, "Adequacy of International Transactions and Position Data for Policy Coordination," Board of Governors of the Federal Reserve System, International Finance Discussion Paper No. 337 (Washington, November 1988).

Stevens, Guy V.G., and others, *The U.S. Economy in an Interdependent World: A Multicountry Model* (Washington: Board of Governors of the Federal Reserve System, 1984).

Tobin, James, "Liquidity Preference as Behavior Towards Risk," *Review of Economic Studies*, Vol. 25 (February 1958).

————, *Asset Accumulation and Economic Activity: Reflections on Contemporary Macroeconomic Theory* (Oxford, England: Basil Blackwell, 1980).

van der Werff, A.A., and Th.J. Sluijter, "Informal Restriction of Banks' Money Creation (1986 and 1987)," De Nederlandsche Bank, Reprint Series No. 235 (1989).

Watson, Maxwell, and others, *International Capital Markets: Developments and Prospects, January 1988* (Washington: International Monetary Fund, 1988).

Wellink, A.H.E.M., "Dutch Monetary Policy in an Integrating Europe," De Nederlandsche Bank, Reprint Series No. 238 (1989).

Yeager, Leland B., *International Monetary Relations: Theory, History, and Policy* (New York: Harper & Row, 2nd ed., 1976).

II

Systemic Financial Risk in Payment Systems

David Folkerts-Landau

At the core of current international monetary arrangements lies an interlocking network of national and international payment systems that facilitate the exchange of funds associated with almost all international trade and financial transactions. These payment systems have been an almost invisible component of the international monetary system because, to a large degree, they have functioned smoothly and efficiently. However, during the past two decades, the growing size and integration of major financial markets has sharply increased the volume of transactions both within and across national payment systems. As a result, private and official sector observers have expressed concerns about whether existing institutional arrangements in the major payment systems can both efficiently cope with the new volume of transactions and effectively manage the risks created by such factors as counterparty failure and liquidity crises. An extended disruption in the largest payment systems would clearly have a highly adverse effect on international trade and financial flows.

This study examines both the nature of systemic risks in payment systems and the policies being implemented by the authorities in major countries to manage or curb them. The first section of this study briefly reviews the role, evolution, and public policy issues associated with modern payment systems. The next two sections identify the main characteristics of systems for clearing and settling payments and examine the financial risks in payment systems. Then policy initiatives aimed at containing payment system risks are discussed, and finally the issues are summarized.

Payment Systems: Role, Evolution, and Public Policy Issues

Role of Payment Systems

Most economic transactions in market economies involve an exchange of goods, services, or securities for money. In modern economies, money largely consists of bank liabilities; hence, the role of a payment system is to effect the transfer of bank liabilities among transactors.[1] Although the payment systems in the major industrial countries share a common objective, their institutional arrangements differ as a result of differing patterns on the use of checks versus electronic fund transfers, the use of post office accounts versus bank accounts, and the relative importance of large wholesale payments.[2] Retail payments tend to be large in volume of transactions but small in size, while wholesale payments are by their very nature large in size and are executed electronically in all major payment systems.[3] Moreover, retail payments made by checks tend to be free of systemic risk since the liability for payment falls on the payor only and the failure of a single payor or a group of payors to make payments is unlikely to affect the depository intermediary.

In contrast, most wholesale payments involve exchanges between large institutions that arise from transactions by their customers in securities markets. Banks are typically the main participants in wholesale payments systems.[4] Banks play an im-

---

[1] The evolution of modern banking systems received strong impetus from the demand for an efficient mechanism to facilitate the payments flows needed to sustain a growing economy. The transfer of securities among buyers and sellers in spot and futures markets has also received increased attention recently (see Group of Thirty (1989) and Kessler (1988)).

[2] Tables 4–9 of Appendix I summarize the main characteristics of major payment systems in the industrial countries.

[3] For example, in the United States, paper checks account for about 95 percent of noncurrency payments but for only 14 percent of dollar volume, whereas electronic payments account for 0.1 percent of the number of transactions, but for 80 percent of the dollar volume.

[4] The importance of the wholesale payments system in the United States to the international economy is a reflection of the growth of the liquid and deep money and securities markets where trading activity gives rise to large transfers of funds. Furthermore, the U.S. dollar system is also the major system for transfers of international funds because of the dollar's role as a vehicle currency and the importance of Eurodollar markets; see also the following section of this study.

portant role both because of their ability to establish efficient payments arrangements and because of their direct access to "good funds" (reserves at the central bank) for payments. Such good funds constitute the core of any payment system because they are available for the use of the owner to make payments under all market conditions (especially during market crises).

At first glance, the payments side of a transaction appears to be straightforward—the payor instructs his bank to transfer an amount of funds agreed upon to the bank of the payee. But closer inspection reveals a number of difficulties that could prevent a successful transfer from taking place. First, there is the problem of how best to achieve a simultaneous exchange of goods or securities for money so as to minimize the risk that one party to the transaction could renege on his payment or his delivery obligation, while the other party is fulfilling his side of the transaction. This risk can be minimized by closely tying the delivery of securities or goods to the receipt of good funds by the seller. The payments system is therefore closely linked to the system of transferring securities and legal arrangements for securing title to goods.

Second, there is the problem of how to transfer funds from one bank to another. In most systems, this problem is ultimately solved by having the central bank transfer central bank liabilities (that is, high-powered money) from the reserve account of the sending bank to the reserve account of the receiving bank. However, this transfer of funds is often achieved indirectly by using correspondent bank relationships or clearinghouse arrangements. A clearing or money center bank may clear payments among a number of smaller correspondent banks that have accounts with the clearing bank. Under this arrangement, each correspondent bank would only have to transfer (or receive) the net amount of his payment to and receipt from the other correspondent banks. In addition, groups of banks in some countries have created clearinghouses that net payments among the banks before achieving final settlements on the books of the central bank, for example, CHIPS in the United States and giro clearinghouses in Germany.

Third, the issue arises of how to deal with a payments failure. It is common practice in most countries for banks to send and receive payments instructions from a clearinghouse or central bank throughout the day and to achieve final settlement only at the end of the day or at the beginning of the next day by transferring the net amounts owed/due on the books of the clearinghouse or the central bank. If an insolvent bank fails to have sufficient good funds at settlement time, the issue of which

parties bear the losses is typically resolved by either (1) unwinding all the payment instructions sent out by this bank during the day (thereby imposing the losses on the counterparties to the bank's transactions); (2) letting the settlement stand and imposing a cooperative assessment of losses on the members of the clearinghouse or payments system; or (3) providing temporary public sector credits and resolving the sharing of loss through legal channels.

Evolution of Payment Systems

Structural changes in major payment systems have reflected the evolving transaction requirements of modern banking systems. To an important degree, the growth of modern fractional reserve banking systems was initially stimulated by reductions in the transaction and payment costs that could be obtained by substituting promises to pay of banks for commodity money or currency.[5] To obtain these cost savings, however, the depositor had to relinquish good funds (such as currency) and become a general creditor of the bank. Further gains in payment efficiencies were made by banks through the holding of interbank credit and debit balances on each other overnight or for longer periods, which allowed banks more time to adjust to payments shortages.

However, the bilateral clearing and settling of checks between large banks meant that messengers went with bundles of checks from bank to bank on which they were drawn. Such bilateral methods resulted in long periods between settlement during which large amounts of "float" (free credit to the bank on which the check was drawn) would accumulate. The next stage in the evolution of banking and payments systems, therefore, was the displacement of bilateral bank payment relationships by multilateral clearinghouses. In the United States, for example, such clearinghouses first emerged during the middle of the nineteenth century in the form of private cooperative arrangements to economize on check collection.[6] The clearinghouse member banks brought checks to the clearinghouse at a fixed settlement time, and after the checks were netted, each member's net credit or debit position against the clearinghouse was computed and banks with debit positions were required to deliver government currency or coins, which were then passed on to the net creditor banks. The later practice of keeping reserves at clearinghouses facilitated an overnight interbank market that produced a more efficient distribution of reserves

---

[5]See Goodfriend (1988).

[6]Timberlake (1984). The New York Clearing House was founded in 1853 by about 50 member banks.

among banks and allowed banks to reduce their reserve holdings. The period of float was also reduced to a period of hours.[7]

The clearinghouse traditionally provided another benefit, namely, some payment finality. Clearinghouse members usually agreed to cover the net debit positions of a failed member bank out of an assessment on their transactions. The clearinghouse then became a general creditor of the failed bank. Thus payment finality meant that the depositor of the check was at least partially insured against the failure of the paying bank from the time of deposit to the time when his account was credited. Such clearinghouse corporations thus allowed member banks to delegate the monitoring of each bank's solvency to the clearinghouse. In return, the clearinghouse restricted membership, imposed capital requirements on members, and held periodic inspections. Nonmember banks cleared their checks through correspondent banks.

The clearance of payments required clearing banks to offer lines of credit to their correspondent banks, which meant that clearing banks had to acquire expertise in monitoring and managing interbank credit, which frequently arose in the clearing process on short notice and without the safety of collateral. Since clearing banks usually were best able to evaluate the creditworthiness of correspondent banks, they became the main supplier of short-term liquidity for the payments system.

Public Policy Issues

The growing involvement of central banks was the final step in the development of modern banking and payment systems. For payment systems in a fractional reserve system to be stable and to work efficiently, checkable deposits must remain convertible into currency. If a clearinghouse restricted conversion of deposits into currency, deposits would sell at a discount in terms of currency. Thus the prospect of restricted convertibility could cause forward-looking depositors to convert deposits immediately into currency, thereby precipitating a liquidity crisis.

The ability to create currency through the open market purchase of securities or direct lending against eligible collateral has allowed central banks to offset these liquidity shortages and thereby helped maintain the exchange rate between bank deposits and currency.[8] In addition, central banks have also served as clearinghouses where banks can hold their clearing balances. In providing short-term liquidity to banks, however, central banks have taken on a certain amount of credit risk as the cost of providing a more efficient payments system. In effect, the public as a whole has assumed some of the credit risk inherent in bank assets that serve as collateral for central bank lending in return for having an efficient payments system.

The role of the central bank in maintaining the stability of payment systems has raised important policy issues. The real economic costs of a breakdown in the wholesale payments system provide a key rationale for central bank intervention. Nevertheless, such intervention implies a policy of supporting clearing or money center banks that are the main participants in the payments system— creating the perception in some countries that some banks are "too large to fail." As a result, depositors and other creditors of these institutions may tend to underplay the riskiness of the institution's assets. Moreover, central banks have during crises sometimes not only provided general liquidity but have also indicated support for certain large institutions. The problem then is that such an extension of the official safety net can encourage the very kinds of excessive risk-taking that ultimately transpose the safety net into a large contingent liability of the official sector.

This problem has been magnified because large clearing or money center banks have supplied liquidity to facilitate not only payments transactions but also to finance short-term positions.[9] Liquidity is supplied to the nonbank financial sector through revolving lines of credit that are designated to "back" the issue of securities, such as commercial paper. These revolving lines of credit assure the lender that he has access to good funds if the borrower is unable to roll over the security at maturity. Moreover, banks finance the inventory of securities dealers and other market makers through repurchase agreements. As a result central bank liquidity support for large banks implicitly extends official support to other institutions that rely on the liquidity provided by banks.

In recent years, there has also been a growing concern that developments in the major financial

---

[7]See Cannon (1911) and Timberlake (1984).

[8]Schwartz (1988) has argued that in the United States there were at least 17 banking crises during the period from 1793 to 1933, but none have occurred since 1933, the beginning of active Federal Reserve intervention.

[9]For example, Corrigan (1987) argued that "the efficient working of a large modern economy clearly requires the presence of a stock of financial assets which are highly liquid *and* readily transferable, thereby facilitating the broad range of transactions needed to sustain the real and financial sectors of the economy. To be highly liquid, such assets must be available to the owner at very short notice (a day or less) at par. To be readily transferable, ownership rights in such assets must be capable of being readily shifted to other economic agents, also at par and in a form in which they are acceptable by that other party" (pp. 12–13).

markets—increased international integration, higher volatility of asset prices, growth of derivative markets, and, above all, substantially larger trading volumes in all markets—are severely testing the adequacy of the existing infrastructure for clearing and settling large-value payments among major international financial institutions. The settling of payments, by the delivery of good funds at periodic, usually daily, intervals is a key test of the solvency of financial institutions in the international financial system. An international financial crisis, if it occurred, would most likely first manifest itself through the inability of a financial institution, or a group of institutions, to settle its obligations in one of the major payment systems. The fear is that such an event would cause an inadequately prepared payments system to "freeze"—become unable to effect payments among institutions. Such an inability to settle payments could then be expected to lead to a severe liquidity shortage, as healthy institutions—not having received payments expected at settlement time—might be unable to settle their own payments obligations.

Without central bank intervention, such a liquidity crisis could easily lead to a loss of confidence in depository institutions, which in turn could precipitate multiple failures of otherwise healthy financial institutions.[10] As a result, major central banks have reassured financial markets of their liquidity support during times of stress. However, the sheer size of average *daily* payments flows—$1.4 trillion in 1988—through the domestic and international U.S. dollar wholesale payments system and the difficulties experienced in settling trades and payments following a computer breakdown at a single clearing bank in New York in 1985[11] and during the October 1987 equity price downturn have contributed to a sense of unease. In fact, some observers believe "that the greatest threat to the stability of the financial system as a whole during the October stock market crash was the danger of a major default in one of the clearing and settlement systems."[12]

In addition, the growth of private, frequently offshore, payment netting arrangements has raised questions not only about systemic risk, but also about monetary control. If a central bank accommodates an abrupt increase in the demand for central bank money during a financial crisis, it could make it more difficult to control the expansion of the monetary base over the medium term. But failure to increase the supply of central bank money during times of liquidity shortages may result in a systemic liquidity crisis. Central banks have sought to improve the trade-off between control of the monetary base and the stability of the payments system by regulating and supervising private payments clearing arrangements. However, when private settlement systems operate outside the jurisdiction of the central bank, such supervision is more difficult to implement. Nonetheless, problems in an offshore clearinghouse might adversely affect the stability of a national payments system. For example, if private financial institutions set up a clearinghouse for dollar-denominated payments outside the United States, final settlement of payments would still ultimately involve clearing payments through the U.S. wholesale payments system. In this situation, problems in this offshore clearinghouse might adversely affect the stability of the U.S. payments system.

Such growing interdependence between national and offshore payment systems has led financial authorities in the major countries to undertake an extensive program to strengthen wholesale payment systems. First, steps have been taken to enhance the ability of payment systems to withstand operational and liquidity shocks and to allow for an orderly completion of the settlement process in the event of insolvency of a single institution or group of institutions. Second, a strengthening of the capital positions of international money center banks, as agreed in the recently implemented Basle Agreement, was aimed at improving confidence in the ability of these key players to withstand adverse credit or liquidity shocks and thereby enabling them better to fulfill their settlement obligations. Before considering these policy measures in detail, it is useful first to examine some examples of major payments systems to identify more specifically what characteristics generate liquidity and credit risks.

Main Features and Examples of Payment Systems

Main Features

Most wholesale payment systems consist of (1) a central bank that settles payments among a group of clearing banks via their reserve accounts (such as the Fedwire system in the United States); and

---

[10]Some of these concerns have been discussed in recent conferences and symposia: the Group of Thirty Symposium on Clearance and Settlement Issues in the Global Securities Markets in London in March 1988; the International Symposium on Banking and Payment Services sponsored by the Board of Governors of the U.S. Federal Reserve System in June 1989; and the Williamsburg Payments System Symposium of the Federal Reserve Bank of Richmond in May 1988.

[11]The Bank of New York, a major clearing bank in the U.S. payments system, experienced a computer breakdown on November 21, 1985, which led the U.S. Federal Reserve to make an overnight loan of $22.6 billion from the discount window, collateralized by $36 billion in securities.

[12]Greenspan (1989).

(2) various private clearinghouse arrangements among subgroups of banks (such as the CHIPS for international dollar payments or regional or giro clearing systems in Germany). The main characteristics of these payment systems that are relevant for a discussion of systemic risk and public sector credit risk are gross or continuous settlement systems and net periodic settlement systems (Tables 4–9 of Appendix I summarize the key characteristics of major national payment systems).

In gross or continuous settlement systems, each payment instruction to the clearinghouse (central bank or private clearing corporation) results in an immediate debit for the sender and credit for the receiver in the settlement accounts that the sending and receiving banks hold with the clearinghouse. If gross or continuous settlement systems do not allow overdrafts against the clearinghouse, as is the case in Switzerland, payment instructions can be executed only if the payor has a sufficiently large credit in his account. If the clearinghouse allows overdrafts, as in the Fedwire system in the United States, it is necessary to determine the length of the period at the end of which the overdraft has to be eliminated. In this case, the clearinghouse is exposed to the intrasettlement period credit risk arising from these overdrafts.

In net periodic settlement systems, payment instructions are accumulated by the clearinghouse over a period of time, and only net debits and credits are entered into the settlement accounts of the members at the end of the settlement period. An important determinant of systemic risk in these systems is the presence or absence of settlement finality. Under a regime of settlement finality, any payment instruction received by the clearinghouse is irrevocably executed even if the bank sending the message defaults.[13] Settlement finality precludes the clearinghouse from unwinding payment instructions if one or several members are unable to supply good funds at the end of the clearing day to settle their debit balances. Moreover, the non-defaulting participants of the settlement system are obliged to cover the shortfall at settlement. Liquidity crises are therefore avoided, while the claim against the defaulting institutions is resolved through legal recourse.

The risk-sharing rules adopted by the clearinghouse have to be explicitly formulated and must define the position of the defaulting institution vis-à-vis the remaining participants. The longer the settlement period, the greater the credit risk to which

the clearinghouse is exposed. Most payment settlement periods are therefore one day or shorter. On the other hand, the shorter the settlement period, the greater is the need for institutions to hold costly reserves to be able to settle payment balances.

Gross settlement systems automatically achieve settlement finality, since each individual payment instruction is executed without netting, and thus unsettled balances do not accumulate. Furthermore, most gross settlement systems also have payments finality, that is, the payment instruction is irrevocably executed and cannot be revoked.

Examples of Major Payment Systems

The most prominent example of a gross payments system with payment finality and intrasettlement period overdraft facilities is Fedwire, the world's largest wholesale payment settlement mechanism. Fedwire is the U.S. Federal Reserve's nationwide wire system for transferring funds and U.S. Government securities among foreign and domestic depository institutions operating in the United States. The depository institutions participating in Fedwire operate through the Federal Reserve Banks in their districts. As of January 1989, Fedwire had 11,398 active participants, of which 6,163 participated on-line. During the first quarter of 1989, the average daily transaction volume was 231,000, while the average daily value was almost $700 billion (excluding CHIPS net settlement). Direct access to Fedwire is restricted to depository institutions, while other financial and non-financial firms, securities firms, and insurance companies can gain access to the system only on terms and conditions set by their depository institutions.

Fedwire payments are made by debiting and crediting reserve accounts maintained by the respective depository institutions at their Federal Reserve Banks. The Fedwire payment is finally and irrevocably paid when a reserve bank sends the payment message to the receiving bank. Funds are immediately made available to the receiving customer (Federal Reserve Regulation J). Thus payment and settlement are final. The Federal Reserve Bank will execute a payment instruction even if it leads to a debit balance, and the execution of the payment does not depend on the account of the sender. If the sending bank failed while in overdraft, the risk would be borne by the Federal Reserve Bank, which would then become a general creditor of the failing bank. Such an overdraft must, however, be settled by the end of the day; hence, the term "daylight overdraft" indicates recourse to the federal funds market if necessary.

Fedwire intraday overdrafts occur when a depository institution's outgoing Fedwire payments

---

[13]It is possible to refine the concept of finality further into payments, settlement, and receiver finality, depending on the stage of the funds transfer transaction (see United States, Board of Governors of the Federal Reserve System (1989)).

exceed the sum of its opening balance and its incoming Fedwire credits. The precise measurement of daylight overdrafts requires rules to determine when, during the day, debits and credits to a depository institution's account at a reserve bank occurred. For Fedwire transactions the timing is clear, since they are considered to be final payments when the receiver of funds is advised of the credit. Since intraday reserve balances do not count toward meeting reserve requirements, banks are then primarily concerned about their reserve balances as of the end of the day—as daylight overdrafts do not carry a charge. A bank generally brings its reserve position up to that required by the end of the day through borrowing in the federal funds market or reduces its reserves to required levels by lending in this market. These funds are then returned the following morning.

U.S. Government securities are also transferred among banks over Fedwire. Each Federal Reserve Bank maintains ownership records of the securities in its computer system. Depository institutions can transfer securities held in their name to other institutions through a system of book entries. Such a transfer can be arranged either in conjunction with a transfer of reserves of equal value or as a separate transaction. Such security transactions also contribute to daylight overdrafts. Since reserve accounts are typically debited when book entry securities accounts are credited, a few clearing banks that specialize in transactions with dealers in government securities generate a large share of total daylight overdrafts of bank reserve accounts. For example, in the second quarter of 1988, four clearing banks accounted for about 70 percent of the daylight overdrafts attributable to transactions in book entry securities. Dealers in government securities maintain book entry securities accounts and demand deposit accounts with clearing banks but have no direct access to the Fedwire book entry system. They generally hold large inventories of securities during the day to meet the anticipated demands of their customers, but sell most of their securities by the end of the day through repurchase agreements ("repos") to minimize the cost of holding the inventories. Investors who enter into these repurchase agreements own the securities overnight and resell them to dealers early the next day.[14]

Fedwire daylight overdrafts averaged between $60–65 billion a day in 1989, with book-entry-related overdrafts accounting for about 60 percent of all Fedwire peak intraday overdrafts. The six largest clearing banks account for about two thirds of all book-entry-related daylight overdrafts, while the ten largest clearing banks account for approximately 80 percent of all such overdrafts. Transfers of book entry securities over Fedwire averaged $312 billion a day in 1987.

The largest net settlements system without receiver finality is CHIPS (the Clearing House Interbank Payments System), the international dollar payments system. CHIPS is a private payments network owned by the New York Clearing House Association, with about 140 participating domestic and foreign banks, of which 22 are settling banks (banks that settle daily transactions on a net basis for their own account and as correspondents for nonsettling participants). Settlements among the 22 settling banks are made at the end of the day through the Fedwire system. CHIPS was the first private clearinghouse arrangement that permitted a real-time exchange of electronic payment information with net balances being at first settled the next morning. In October 1981, CHIPS began same-day settlement through a special account at the New York Reserve Bank. Hence, overnight and weekend float disappeared from the CHIPS system, leaving only daylight float. Most payments on CHIPS are associated with foreign exchange and Eurodollar transfers. The payments volume is about $700 billion a day, about the same as on Fedwire during the fourth quarter of 1988. Peak volume was reached on November 14, 1988, at $1.2 trillion. The peak intraday net debit position on CHIPS of about $45 billion a day has been smaller than the Fedwire daylight overdrafts of about $60–65 billion a day.

In 1986, the Federal Reserve Bank of New York undertook a special survey that focused on CHIPS and Fedwire to ascertain the nature, timing, and composition of payments on a single day (June 4, 1986) by sampling individual transactions (see Table 1). On that day, there were 120,000 CHIPS transactions with an aggregate value of $432 billion, and there were 56,000 Fedwire payments with a dollar value of $265 billion (these were payments

[14]Dealers generally make commitments to deliver specific securities by the end of the day. While the customer receives interest on the promised securities for the day, he pays the dealer only when the securities are delivered. Failure to deliver would expose the dealer to losses, and, to minimize the probability of such losses, the dealer waits until early afternoon before directing his clearing bank to send the securities sold to the book entry accounts of the banks of the purchasers. When the

investor in a repurchase agreement returns the securities to the dealer, the dealer's securities account at the clearing bank increases and his demand deposit account decreases, while at the Federal Reserve Bank the book entry account of the clearing bank increases and its reserve account decreases. The dealer will also finance his inventory of securities by overdrawing his account with the clearing bank. The overdraft on the reserve and deposit accounts is reversed later in the day as dealers enter into repurchase agreements.

Table 1. Estimated Aggregate Transactions by Survey Category by Wire System[1]

Transactions Category	CHIPS				Fedwire			
	Number of transactions	Percent	Amount[2]	Percent	Number of transactions	Percent	Amount[2]	Percent
Securities purchases/ redemption/financing	274	1.0	2,842	1.4	4,458	37.7	54,856	27.8
Bank loans	399	1.4	3,476	1.7	272	2.3	3,956	2.0
Federal funds	107	0.4	788	0.4	2,361	19.9	66,269	33.5
Commercial and miscellaneous	1,295	4.5	12,793	6.2	2,690	22.7	33,593	17.0
Settlement	945	3.3	16,198	7.9	915	7.7	18,664	9.5
Eurodollar placements	4,800	16.8	56,255	27.5	966	8.2	18,848	9.6
Foreign exchange	20,674	72.6	112,505	54.9	173	1.5	858	0.4
Total	28,494	100.0	204,857	100.0	11,836	100.0	197,043	100.0

Source: Federal Reserve Bank of New York, *Quarterly Review* (Winter 1987–88).
[1]The sample consisted of 13 banks accounting for 48 percent of all CHIPS payments on June 4, 1986 and of 9 banks accounting for 76 percent of all Fedwire payments on that day.
[2]In millions of dollars.

originating in the New York Federal Reserve district only).[15] The sample showed that Fedwire accounted for virtually all payments related to transactions for securities purchases/redemption/financing and for purchases and sales of federal funds, while CHIPS handled payments for almost all foreign exchange transactions. Overlap between the two systems occurred in the categories of payment-related bank loans, commercial and miscellaneous transactions, settlement, and Eurodollar placements. Foreign exchange and Eurodollar placements made up more than 80 percent of CHIPS dollar volume, while accounting only for 10 percent of Fedwire transactions.

Of the 265 foreign-based depository institutions that have a banking presence in the United States, 91 are CHIPS participants (two thirds of all CHIPS participants). Virtually all major depository institutions based in the United States are Fedwire participants, but fewer than 50 of these are represented on CHIPS. On the sample day, $270 billion of payments of Fedwire were related to securities

transactions, while only $1 billion of CHIPS transactions were related to securities business. Bank loan transactions were generally low in frequency and value, indicating that much of this business is done on the bank's own books. Almost all federal fund transactions occur over Fedwire. CHIPS usage is largely confined to foreign bank customers without direct access to Fedwire. The adjustment of correspondent balances constituted the dominant purpose for settlement transactions on both CHIPS (67 percent of transactions, 84 percent of dollar volume) and Fedwire (81 percent of transactions, 61 percent of dollar volume). CHIPS settlement transactions over Fedwire represent 5 percent of the settlement transactions on Fedwire, but more than 30 percent of the dollar volume. CHIPS transacted $23 billion related to foreign transactions, while Fedwire transacted $250 billion of foreign exchange transactions.

A net settlement system that nets payments on a continuous basis avoids, or at least reduces, the systemic risk associated with the possibility of a participant failing to settle at settlement time. An example of such a system is the FXNET, a U.K.

---

[15]See Federal Reserve Bank of New York (1987).

limited partnership owned by subsidiaries of 12 banks, which was developed largely to deal with foreign exchange transactions. For any given value date and currency, the successive trades between two FXNET participants are continuously netted throughout the day. Such netting is bilateral, that is, it occurs between any two participants in FXNET. Thus, the decisions regarding creditworthiness exposure and risk management are under the control of each counterparty. Such netting is done by novation, that is, each trade is folded into the previous obligations and creates a new net position. This new obligation represents the only remaining binding bilateral currency payment obligation for all of the previous trades. Each counterparty either makes or receives one payment for each currency dealt on each settlement date. The exchange of two payments is no longer required for each pair of currencies dealt.

Netting by novation transforms a FXNET obligation into a stream of net payments over all forward dates dealt. Such netting reduces settlement risk, since the average amounts to settle are reduced and the volatility around the average is reduced. Without an effective netting agreement, a liquidator could choose not to honor the solvent party's profitable contracts but could honor all the contracts that were profitable for the liquidating firm. Under the netting scheme, the liquidator has a claim only to net credits due to a liquidating firm and can default only on net debits. This feature greatly reduces systemic risk since it reduces the exposure of the overall system to the defaulting participant.

An example of a gross settlement system with payment finality that does not extend intraday overdraft to the senders of payments is the Swiss Interbank Clearing System (SIC).[16] The SIC is a gross settlement system with payments being settled individually on reserve accounts. It uses queuing to prevent daylight overdrafts on these accounts, operates 24 hours on bank working days, and has a capacity of approximately 600,000 payments a day. Payments are irrevocable and final. Payment orders that would lead to an overdraft are automatically queued until sufficient funds have accumulated from incoming payments and are then automatically released for settlement on a first-in/first-out basis. This centralized facility relieves participants of having to synchronize incoming and outgoing payments to prevent overdrafts on reserve accounts. The queued orders may be canceled by the sending bank at any time. This rule was designed to minimize incentives for participants to make use of payments held in the queue.

A value day starts at around 6:00 p.m. and ends at around 4:15 p.m. of the following bank working day. The 24-hour operations feature allows the coordination of settlement of foreign exchange transactions, in which currencies of countries located in different time zones are involved. Further globalization of financial markets might lead to increased use of this feature in other settlement and payment systems. The SIC participant has real-time access to all data entered into this system relating to his account, that is, he can monitor settled incoming and outgoing payments as well as payment orders stored in the waiting queue and pre-value data file, as well as the actual balance of the reserve account. The value of payments reached Sw F 140 billion on an average day in April 1989—about 50 percent of annual GNP. The value of payments drops to approximately 10 percent of the average on U.S. bank holidays, indicating that foreign exchange transactions are the major source of large payments. Payments of about Sw F 1 million or more comprise 97.9 percent of total value.

Since a change of liquidity regulations in January 1988 in Switzerland made reserve account balances voluntary, all reserves became excess reserves. As a result, the balances held by SIC participants decreased from Sw F 7.5 billion to Sw F 2.6 billion in April 1988, or to about one third of their original level. The daily turnover ratio—the relation between daily payment value and reserves—has increased from 12 to 54 on an average day. Almost one third of payments are made and settled within ten minutes of being validated, while nearly two thirds are made within two hours, and only 2.5 percent of payments are in the queue for more than five hours. While the Swiss SIC system has eliminated daylight overdrafts, it is nevertheless subject to the risk of having a payments grid lock, a situation in which no payments move over the system because the accumulated credit balances are too small.

There are indications that, if the composition of the payment stream is not changed by subdividing very large payments (those in excess of Sw F 0.5 billion), further reductions in the reserve account balances may increase the frequency of payment grid locks. Grid locks are currently resolved at the end of the day with funds raised in the market or through collateralized lines of credit with the Swiss National Bank at a penalty rate. Alternatively, payments pending in the queue may remain unexecuted. Moreover, it is unclear whether sufficient incentives exist to prevent participants from reducing their holdings of reserve account balances to a level where major grid locks become likely.

---

[16]See Mengle, Humphrey, and Summers (1987) and Vital and Mengle (1988).

Risk in Payment Systems

There are four basic parties to each transaction in a payments system: the payor originating the transfer, the sending bank that transmits the payments message of the payor, the receiving bank that acts on behalf of the payee, and the payee. Credit risk arises from the possibility that one of the parties in the chain of transactions defaults on its obligations. For example, the sender could initiate a transfer with his sending bank without having sufficient funds in his account to cover the transfer. The sending bank incurs credit risk if it transmits the payments message before the sender supplies the covering funds. Second, the sending bank may fail to provide funds to the receiving bank at settlement. Finally, the payee runs the risk that the receiving bank will not make the funds available. These three risks—sender risk, receiver risk, and settlement risk—are to be found in most payment systems. If the clearinghouse operates under settlement finality, the credit risk of the sending bank is distributed over the receiving banks according to the loss-sharing formula adopted by the clearinghouse.[17]

There is also systemic risk, which occurs as an outgrowth of settlement risk (see Appendix II). The failure of one participant to settle deprives other institutions of expected funds and in turn prevents these institutions from settling. Thus, although a participant does no business directly with a failed institution, chains of obligation may make it suffer because of the impact that the failed institution has on an intermediate participant's ability to settle, that is, the cost of settlement failure reaches beyond the exposure of the credited bank to the failing bank. While it is generally not difficult to identify credit risk in a payments system, it is difficult to identify systemic risk properly.

While a private or public payments system with settlement finality, such as the Fedwire system in the United States, is not subject to systemic risk, its participants are subject to credit risk, especially risk generated by intraday credit exposure. Moreover, liquidity crises are avoided by sharing the debit balance of the failed institutions among the solvent members of the system or by the central bank funding the debit balance. Concerns about intraday credit exposure led the U.S. Federal Reserve to introduce caps on debit positions with Fedwire and CHIPS (Table 2), and to propose interest charges on such debit positions. The presence of a cap on the debit position that an individual bank is allowed to run with Fedwire effectively limits the loss that could be incurred by the Federal Reserve

as a result of payment instructions sent out over the Fedwire by a failing bank. However, in a situation where investors have lost confidence in a large money center bank and fail to renew short-term funds (such as maturing certificates of deposit and repurchase agreements), the bank would quickly reach its net debit limit and might then be unable to repay its short-term creditors. As a result, the central bank could be faced with the need to provide funds to the bank through the discount window and hence be once again subject to the credit risk inherent in bank assets being used as collateral.[18] Thus, if some banks are regarded as too large to fail, it may be difficult for the central bank to avoid credit risk completely in a liberalized financial system.

In contrast, the main international payments system—CHIPS—has only recently adopted payment finality and its members were therefore significantly exposed to the credit risk of lending banks. The 150 member banks of CHIPS are international banks with varying credit ratings. Credit risk arises when banks send out payments for a customer during the day before receiving good funds in the customer's account. For example, a bank might receive a message from the clearinghouse that an account will be credited with a given amount of dollars at the end of the day. The bank might then be asked by the account holder to make payments to other banks from the account through CHIPS even though the bank has not received good funds. Competition has generally forced banks to be prepared to make such payments. All such payment messages are netted at the end of the day by CHIPS, and net balances are cleared through Fedwire transfers among the settlement banks.[19] Thus a central element of the international payments system is the extension of credit among the banks that are members of CHIPS.[20]

If a disturbance occurs in the financial markets, such as the bankruptcy of a major nonfinancial company, some CHIPS members might be unable to settle their debit balances by borrowing in the interbank market for federal funds. In this case, payments to and from that participant would be unwound, and new net positions would be calcu-

---

[17]See New York Clearing House Association (1989), for the proposed loss-sharing formula for CHIPS.

[18]A large proportion of the assets of a money center or a clearing bank are financed by short-term funds—certificates of deposit, repurchase agreements, interbank loans—and a loss of such funding might make it necessary for the bank to discount assets other than the eligible government securities. In this case the central bank would be exposed to the private credit risk inherent in such assets.

[19]Foreign banks clear through a CHIPS settlement bank.

[20]CHIPS operates under the legal environment of the U.S. Uniform Commercial Code and wire transfers therefore represent noncontingent commitments among banks.

Table 2. Caps on Daylight Overdrafts Across Payment Systems
(Multiples of adjusted primary capital)

Self-Assessment Category	Cap Applied to	Period Caps in Effect		
		March 27, 1986–January 13, 1988	January 14, 1988–May 18, 1988	May 19, 1988–present
High	Two-week average	2.000	1.700	1.500
	Single day	3.000	2.550	2.250
Above average	Two-week average	1.500	1.275	1.125
	Single day	2.500	2.125	1.875
Average	Two-week average	1.000	0.850	0.750
	Single day	1.500	1.275	1.125
Limited	Two-week average	0.500	0.425	0.375
	Single day	0.500	0.425	0.375

Note: Adjusted primary capital for U.S.-chartered banks is the sum of primary capital less all intangible assets and deferred net losses on loans and other assets sold.

Source: *Federal Reserve Bulletin* (November 1987), p. 843.

lated for the remaining participants. If one of these remaining participants was unable to settle them, this process of calculating new net positions would continue until settlement was achieved. Participants in CHIPS permit most of their customers to use credits for CHIPS payments during the day prior to settlement while reserving the right to charge back such credits if the transferring bank does not settle its CHIPS position. Simulations of the unwinding of transactions under the assumption that one large CHIPS participant would be unable to meet its payments obligations suggest that such failures could drastically change the net positions of other participants, thus inducing a series of failures to settle by the remaining participants.[21] Current CHIPS rules and the practice of unwinding could thus potentially contribute to systemic risks in the banking system and put pressure on the Federal Reserve to provide liquidity assistance while losses and solvency problems are determined.

Since the Federal Reserve does not regulate and supervise the foreign members of CHIPS, it could only guarantee the domestic transactors on CHIPS

(as is done on Fedwire). Moreover, attempts by CHIPS itself to impose regulations on its foreign member banks would require the approval of bank regulators in those countries. Under current arrangements, the failure of a major international banking institution could nonetheless cause a systemic crisis if it were to spread illiquidity across the CHIPS system.

Policy Initiatives to Reduce Risk in Payment Systems

This section reviews the major policy initiatives undertaken to reduce credit risk arising from daylight overdrafts in gross payment systems and to reduce systemic risk in net payment systems. The thrust of these initiatives has been to reduce the credit exposure of the clearinghouse, such as Fedwire, and to introduce payments finality in net settlement systems, such as CHIPS, as well as to strengthen the operational, financial, and liquidity characteristics of the private net settlement systems.

In 1986, the U.S. Federal Reserve Board introduced a risk reduction program for the payments system that focused on controlling the direct

---

[21] Humphrey (1986).

Federal Reserve credit risk exposure arising with the extension of intraday credit on Fedwire (see Tables 2 and 3). The policy was later extended to CHIPS, in that it established a maximum amount of intraday overdraft that depository institutions are permitted to incur over Fedwire and private large dollar payment systems such as CHIPS. Such caps are defined as a multiple of the depository institution's adjusted primary capital and are based on the institution's self-evaluation of its credit-worthiness, credit policies, and operational controls. This policy was further strengthened in July 1987 when the Board adopted a two-step 25 percent reduction in cross-system net debit caps. In addition to the cross-system caps, which apply to the daylight overdraft position on Fedwire and CHIPS, caps apply to the sum of a bank's overdraft on its reserve account and its net debit position on CHIPS at each moment during the day. Each bank places itself in one of four self-assessment categories to determine its caps for both a one-day and a two-week average maximum daylight overdraft as a percentage of primary adjusted capital (see Table 2).

In addition, the Federal Reserve requires each participant on CHIPS to set a limit on its net credit position vis-à-vis each of the other participants in the system. Finally, CHIPS is required to establish limits on the net debit positions of each participant with all other participants in the system. This limit is set at 5 percent of the sum of all bilateral credit limits for a given participant extended by all other CHIPS participants.[22]

In June 1988, the Board of Governors Large-Dollar Payments System Advisory Group made recommendations on how to achieve further reductions in payment system risks. It concluded that (1) some level of public and private intraday credit was desirable to absorb the inevitable lack of synchronization of payments flows; (2) the unconstrained access to Federal Reserve overdrafts induces private institutions to use more intraday credit than is optimal; (3) either caps or pricing can in principle be used to discourage the use of daylight over-

drafts; and (4) binding caps will produce a more volatile intraday rate than pricing. With regard to the pricing of daylight overdrafts, it has been proposed that the Board charge 25 basis points on daily average overdrafts, less a deductible equal to 10 percent of capital. This fee would be phased in over a three-year period beginning in 1991. The Large-Dollar Payments System Advisory Group judged that this price should be set so as to "induce the creation of a private-sector market to replace much of Federal Reserve funding of intraday credit."[23] It is expected that the assessment of a fee for daylight overdrafts will create incentives for depository institutions to reduce their demand for intraday extensions of credit for transfers of funds by reserve banks, thus reducing the reserve banks' direct credit exposure.[24] Such a reduction in daylight overdrafts could be achieved by delaying less critical payments, shifts of payments to CHIPS, greater use of netting, and the development of an intraday federal funds market.

In view of the anticipated shift of settlement from Fedwire to CHIPS, the Federal Reserve has also been concerned with reducing the systemic risks associated with private sector large dollar payment and clearing systems. It has therefore encouraged the New York Clearing House to adopt settlement finality for CHIPS. If fully adopted, settlement finality assures that CHIPS net debits and credits will be settled each day even if some participants are unable to settle. This procedure therefore separates liquidity from credit risk, since the allocation of losses can be resolved later. In consultation with the Board of Governors of the Federal Reserve System, the New York Clearing House recommended that all CHIPS participants sign a loss-sharing agreement to provide funds necessary to complete CHIPS settlements if one or a limited number of participants are unable to meet their respective debit balances. In addition, if any participant fails, or is otherwise unable to meet his balance, the remaining participants would make up the shortfall. They will contribute amounts computed by a formula under which each bank makes up a portion of the failed participant's balance in relation to its own credit judgment regarding the failed banks, that is, the bilateral limit, which enables the participants to incur the obligation on the system. This procedure is also expected to improve the assessment of bilateral credit limits.

---

[22]An important category of transactions not yet subject to the daylight overdraft caps are book entry transfers of U.S. Government and federal agency securities. It is proposed that book-entry-related overdrafts also be included within the existing caps on depository institutions' daylight overdrafts. Since the majority of book entry overdrafts appear to be concentrated in a few clearing banks that act on behalf of major dealers and brokers in government securities, it has been feared that a restriction on the overdrafts of such institutions could impair the smooth functioning of the Government's securities markets. It is therefore proposed to permit such institutions to pledge book entry securities in transit as collateral for the amount of the total funds and book entry overdrafts.

---

[23]United States, Board of Governors of the Federal Reserve System (1989), p. 23.

[24]Faulhaber, Phillips, and Santomero (1990) suggested that efficient pricing of overdrafts would involve a per unit price per transaction, a charge on daylight overdraft, and a premium covering possible default on daylight overdraft.

Table 3. Summary of U.S. Federal Reserve Board Proposals for Risk Reduction in Payments System

Issue	Current Policy	Proposed Policy	Proposed Effective Date
Private book entry delivery against payment systems.	No policy.	If settlement on books of Federal Reserve Bank, must adopt certain liquidity and credit safeguards, prohibit unwinds, and provide open settlement information to participants.	On publication of policy statement.
Offshore dollar clearing networks.	No policy.	Interim policy applicable to systems that settle directly or indirectly through Fedwire or CHIPS: (1) must be subject to oversight as a system by some authority; (2) participants responsible for risks and prudent management; (3) system must assure settlement finality; and (4) must be assured that satisfactory settlement can be ascertained.	On publication of policy statement.
Rollovers and continuing contracts.	No policy.	Board supports efforts to reduce daylight overdrafts through conversion of overnight borrowing to term and continuing contracts, as well as rollovers of net amount of overnight amounts not repaid; lenders must be aware of additional risk.	On publication of policy statement.
Book entry overdrafts.	Exempt.	Include under cap; require collateral for total Fedwire overdrafts (funds and book entry) if they exceed cap because of book entry overdrafts.	1990.
U.S. agencies and branches of foreign banks.	Collateralized that part of Fedwire overdrafts that *exceed* cap multiple times U.S. capital equivalency.	Collateralized *total* Fedwire overdraft exceeds cap multiples times U.S. capital equivalency.	1990.
Defining overdrafts through nonwire posting sequence.	All automatic clearinghouses (ACH) posted at opening; other nonwire posted net at opening if net is a credit and posted net at close if net is a debit; wire transactions as they occur.	U.S. Treasury book entry interest, redemption, and net issue entries, and U.S. Treasury ACH credits at opening; U.S. Treasury direct and special direct investment at 2:00 p.m.; all nonwire and commercial ACH at close; wire transactions as they occur.	Late 1990 or early 1991.
Sender net debit cap:	Applies to intraday peak each day and two-week average of daily peak values:	Same.	
(1) small overdrafters;	(1) included under cap;	(1) exempt from caps if overdrafts are less than $10 million and 20 percent of capital;	(1) when net posting rule is implemented;
(2) CHIPS;	(2) included under cap;	(2) excluded from cap when settlement finality is implemented;	(2) when NYCH implements settlement finality on CHIPS;
(3) book entry overdrafts;	(3) excluded; and	(3) included; and	(3) 1990;
(4) *de minimis* cap.	(4) applicable only to infrequent overdrafters with overdrafts.	(4) no frequency test or dollar limit but retain 20 percent of capital.	(4) when new posting rule is implemented.
Capital (used with cap multiple to define sender net debit cap).	No price.	Applies price of 25 basis points (annual rate): (1) to total Fedwire overdraft (funds and book entry); (2) to intraday average amount in excess of 10 percent of capital; (3) regardless of cap status.	Phased in over three years beginning mid-1991 (10 basis points first year; 10 basis points second year; and 5 basis points third year).

Source: United States, Board of Governors of the Federal Reserve System (1989).

An important element involved in instituting payment finality is that the multilateral netting rules on CHIPS be upheld legally. CHIPS and its individual participants cannot take the risk that the general creditors of a failed participant bank will demand immediate payment of the *gross* amount of payment sent to the failed bank, while treating payments made by the failed bank as unsecured (and possibly depositor-subordinated) claims against the receivership.

Finality of payment rules, such as those proposed for CHIPS, internalize the costs of a settlement failure and thus provide incentives for market participants to control payment risks. Such finality rules are of particular interest now because the U.S. National Conference of Commissioners on Uniform State Laws is currently drafting provisions of the uniform commercial code that codify a law of electronic funds transfer (EFT). This effort will largely determine the future statutory environment that guides the rights, obligations, and risk assignments of network participants. Finality rules need to specify with certainty who pays the cost of a settlement failure.

In the absence of established law and precedent, the New York Clearing House is seeking rulings concerning the proposed arrangements from the Federal Reserve and other regulatory agencies, and has proposed an amendment to the Federal Reserve Act. It is envisioned that settlement finality will become fully operative in 1991. While settlement finality on CHIPS will reduce private credit risk, it does not entirely eliminate it. It is possible, for example, that the debit balance of a group of failed banks is larger than that covered by the contributions of the remaining CHIPS participants.

One further possibility for eliminating the direct credit exposure of the central bank is to establish payment queues with payment transfers being held in the queue until covering funds have arrived, rather than allowing overdrafts. Hence, a payment without temporary cover is not rejected but is instead placed in a queue and then processed on a first-in first-out basis after covering funds are received. However, as noted above, the problem with adopting such a centralized payment queuing system is that, without reserve requirements or some price incentive, there is no guarantee that the level of reserves held voluntarily will remain above that required to avoid grid lock of the system.

An important public policy issue in reducing payments risk relates to the growth of offshore clearance and settlement systems. This issue has led to the preparation of a report on such systems by a group of experts on payment systems of the central banks of the Group of Ten countries.[25] The incentive to develop offshore payment networks or netting systems derives from a less stringent regulatory environment and from significant time zone differences between North America, Asia, and Europe. Offshore dollar arrangements must ultimately settle in the United States through either CHIPS or Fedwire since good funds can only be transferred in accounts held with the U.S. Federal Reserve Banks. Significant disruptions in offshore clearance and settlements systems for foreign exchange and securities owing to the failure of a participating institution could well result in systemic problems in the United States and other major countries. Offshore clearing of U.S. dollar payments for subsequent net settlement in the United States has been viewed as obscuring and possibly increasing the level of systemic risk in the U.S. large dollar payments system and in the international settlements process.

Finally, offshore multilateral netting arrangements complicate the allocation of supervisory responsibilities. Formalized netting arrangements and offshore payments systems (that is, groupings of individual banks with interrelated credit and liquidity risks) have shifted risks among participants, and it is at times unclear at which level a supervisor should examine the credit, liquidity, and operational risks facing these institutions. Both the host country authorities of an offshore system and the home country of the multinational participants in that system have an interest in supervising it if it affects the solvency and liquidity of their institutions. In addition, the central bank for the currency that is being cleared in the offshore system could have a supervisory interest in the system for monetary policy reasons.

Another concern is that a shift away from the use of the central payments system toward the offshore netting system might amount to the decentralization of the major monetary mechanisms and thus undermine the relationship between key monetary aggregates and domestic activity. In particular, netting arrangements can serve as a close substitute for money in terms of economizing on transaction costs.[26]

---

[25]Bank for International Settlements (1989a).

[26]The development of multilateral clearinghouses could also significantly alter the structure of interbank credit relationships. For example, several large over-the-counter markets such as the interbank foreign exchange markets and the interbank swap market could evolve into an organized exchange, as has happened with Eurodollar futures markets. If this occurred, net claims on the clearing organization would replace gross interbank credit exposure in the deposit markets. Under the Basle capital adequacy standards, bank claims on organized financial exchanges subject to daily margining have a zero-risk weight in determining a bank's required regulatory capital.

In response to these concerns, the U.S. Federal Reserve Board published a draft interim policy statement on offshore dollar clearing and netting systems.[27] This statememt indicated that (1) any subsystem that settled directly or indirectly through CHIPS or Fedwire should be subject to oversight as a system by a relevant central bank or supervisory authority; (2) participants should clearly identify the operational, liquidity, and credit risks created within the system; (3) the system should provide for the finality of settlement obligations; and (4) the direct or indirect settlement of the system's obligations through CHIPS or Fedwire should be done by a U.S. settlement bank.

The increasing globalization of securities markets and foreign exchange markets and the shift toward 24-hour trading in certain types of securities have also led to proposals for extending settlement hours, preferably toward a 24-hour settlement period. Such an option is currently under review by the Federal Reserve System. For example, in foreign exchange transactions, the delivery of each currency is made at a bank in the country that issues the currency. If the banking hours of the respective central banks do not overlap, a time lag will appear between final settlements in the home currencies. Currently settlement of spot transactions in foreign exchange markets occurs on the second day after the contract has been entered into.[28]

The counterparty risks in the settlement process for foreign exchange transactions could be minimized by moving toward a system based on delivery against payment. However, if a yen-U.S. dollar foreign exchange transaction took place in New York, such a simultaneous matching of the yen settlement to the dollar settlement would require the Bank of Japan to effect the interbank settlement during New York daytime or during nighttime in Japan. Some major U.S. correspondent clearing bank would then have to make transfers into a dollar account during the night.

Without 24-hour settlement, offshore settlement systems have developed, with the attendant liquidity and credit risks. The inability to make a Fedwire transfer outside the 9:00 a.m. to 6:30 p.m. eastern time slot has led banks to use other networks to make dollar payments.[29]

Summary and Conclusions

Efficient and stable payment systems are of fundamental importance in maintaining an orderly international monetary system. Major disruptions of national and international payment systems would have highly adverse effects on international trade, capital flows, and real activity. A key issue now being addressed by the authorities in a number of major countries is whether existing institutional arrangements need to be modified to manage better the sharp increases in the volume of payments transactions and the liquidity and credit risks that have arisen from the expansion of international trade and capital flows and the growing integration of major financial markets. For example, the direct credit exposure in the form of daylight overdrafts on the world's largest payments system, the Fedwire, has grown significantly during the last decade, as daily average overdrafts have risen to about $65 billion.

The internationalization of financial markets and of clearing arrangements has further contributed to systemic risk. Clearinghouses directly link the financial solvency of members through credit and debit positions in the clearinghouse. Periodic settlements are major points in time where the liquidity and solvency of banks are tested by the market. Many major international banks play the role of settlement banks for international transactions undertaken by smaller regional or local national banks. Thus, disturbances in one payments system would tend to spread rapidly to other systems.

---

[27]United States, Board of Governors of the Federal Reserve System (1989), Appendix B.

[28]If a yen purchase occurs in New York and if the buyer would like to have the yen delivered during that day, for example, the Bank of Japan would have to make a transfer settlement at night. Under the current system, final dollar settlement in a yen-dollar transaction in the New York foreign exchange market is made through Fedwire during New York daytime, while the yen settlement is done through the GAITAME-YEN Settlement System during Japanese daytime, that is, early in the morning of the next day in New York. Hence, a time lag occurs between the two operations.

[29]For example, Chase Tokyo operates a dollar settlement system in Tokyo. Transfers among the correspondent's dollar deposit accounts with Chase are made in Tokyo. Balances are then transferred from Chase Tokyo to Chase New York after business hours in Tokyo. The final settlement occurs after the opening of the New York market. A net debit dollar position with Chase is financed by an overdraft extended by Chase Tokyo until the net debit bank is in a position to raise dollar funds in New York through CHIPS and finally deliver them through Fedwire. If the net debit bank in Tokyo exceeds its credit line with Chase, it will then have to raise dollar funds, which may be difficult when the Federal Reserve's funds market is closed. If Fedwire operated on a 24-hour basis, it would become necessary to define when and how reserve positions are measured. Currently reserve balances are measured at the end of the day and counted as reserve balances for that day. In a 24-hour payment system, banks might be tempted to deposit funds for the measurement of reserve balances at a particular time and withdraw the funds immediately afterward. Another difficulty might occur in monitoring institutions. If, for example, a U.S. bank branch in Tokyo runs a negative balance on its accounts for the Federal Reserve, the latter may be unable to ascertain whether there is a problem, since the bank is located in Tokyo.

One source of concern has been the growth of international or offshore netting arrangements, in particular in foreign exchange markets. Netting arrangements that are located outside the country whose currency is being netted have the potential to alter significantly the structure of the international interbank clearing and settlement process. Multilateral netting schemes without settlement finality in which participants retain some responsibility for the gross transactions are particularly exposed to credit risks. The unwinding necessary if a participant is unable to settle is a significant source of systemic risk. Hence, netting by novation is emphasized, which reduces the overall credit exposure of participants to their net position vis-à-vis the clearinghouse. Furthermore, novation with settlement finality is the solution desired by regulatory authorities.

Since many of the credit and liquidity risks cannot be directly controlled by individual participants, it is unlikely that market forces alone would produce international payment arrangements that would adequately manage the systemic risks. Private cooperative arrangements without central bank involvement are unlikely to reduce systemic risk to acceptable levels, because the power of private clearinghouses to impose restrictions on members, as well as to provide the liquidity occasionally required by members at closing time, is limited. Furthermore, the ability of private financial institutions to undertake regulatory arbitrage (to relocate activities to a less regulated environment) suggests that cooperation between major central banks will have to be an important element in the management of payments system risks. Central bank cooperation in strengthening international payments would complement the cooperation already achieved in the area of bank supervision and monetary policy.[30] Nonetheless, the allocation of supervisory responsibility among the various national supervisory authorities remains unresolved. In part, this reflects the fact that while the efficiencies of netting arrangements may be enjoyed by banks located in one country, the credit and liquidity risks associated with the settlement of payments resulting from that netting system may be experienced in the banking system of another country. This issue is of particular concern to U.S. authorities, as most of the offshore netting arrangements are subsequently settled through CHIPS and Fedwire.

These developments have led monetary authorities, particularly the U.S. Federal Reserve Board, to design policy initiatives to reduce risks in payment systems. The Federal Reserve's program of risk reduction in the payments system began in 1986 and has focused on controlling levels of intraday credit extension on both U.S. large dollar payment systems, Fedwire and CHIPS, by limiting the total net debit position of participants in the systems. In addition, the Federal Reserve proposed that intraday credit on Fedwire be subject to a 25-basis points interest charge, and CHIPS began to introduce settlement finality in late 1990.

Since the proposed constraints on Fedwire and private payment systems in the United States are likely to stimulate the use of other private netting systems and offshore networks, the Central Bank Committee of the Group of Ten produced a series of proposals to strengthen such netting schemes, with emphasis on the finality of payments. Furthermore, the globalization of financial markets and the development of continuous 24-hour trading in some spot and futures contracts may necessitate operating the major clearing systems such as Fedwire on a 24-hour basis to avoid the systemic risk associated with current and proposed offshore large dollar payment networks.

A key element containing and reducing systemic risk in payment systems is the *finality* of payments—reducing the period during which balances remain unsettled. In addition, improvements in the operational efficiency and financial resources of clearing and settlement systems are important in containing credit and liquidity risks. Efficient operational features allow participants to keep track of exposures, including intraday positions. A clearing entity should have in place the financial resources and commitments (in the form of reserves, collateral, committed bank loans, guarantees, etc.) to ensure that if a participant defaults, settlement will still take place—that is, no unwinding of the transaction will occur. The financial resources of payment systems are reflected in the capital structure of member firms, the level of margins, and access to liquidity and collateral. A strengthening of these features is deemed to increase the ability of the institutions to withstand disturbances and thereby reduce payments system risk.

---

[30]Padoa-Schioppa (1989).

Appendix I

Table 4. United States: Payments System, 1987

Instruments	Volume of Transactions (in millions)	Volume per Capita	Percentage of Total Volume	Value of Transactions (in billions of U.S. dollars)	Value per Capita (in U.S. dollars)	Percentage of Total Value
Checks issued[1]	49,200	201.0	82.9	55,917.0	228,140	16.40
Credit card transactions[2]	9,100	37.0	15.3	375.0	1,530	0.10
Payments by debit card on EFT	55	0.2	0.1	0.8	3	0.01
Large-value paperless credit transfers[3,4]	84	0.3	0.1	281,000.0	1,146,471	82.60
Other credit transfers by ACH and ATM[5]	613	2.5	1.0	805.0	3	0.20
Direct debits	269	1.1	0.5	2,235.0	9	0.70
Total	59,321	242.1	100.0	340,332.8	1,388,069	100.00

Note: EFT = electronic funds transfers; ACH = automatic clearinghouses; ATM = automated teller machines.

Source: Bank for International Settlements (1989b).

[1] Includes traveler's checks (1.4 billion with a value of $47 billion) and money orders (0.8 billion valued at $70 billion).

[2] The Nilson Report, May 1988 (Los Angeles, California). Includes all types of credit card transactions; bank card volume: 2.5 billion valued at $165.3 billion. Credit card payment volume and value included in check data.

[3] Includes Fedwire volume of 53 million valued at $142 trillion and CHIPS volume of 31 million valued at $139 trillion.

[4] Approximately 40 percent of the dollar value of Fedwire transfers are for interbank loan transactions, 10 percent for Eurodollar transactions, and 10 percent for commercial transactions, whereas 55 percent of the dollar value of CHIPS transactions are for foreign exchange transactions and 28 percent for Eurodollar transactions.

[5] ACH credit payments: 584 million transactions with a value of $803 billion; ATM payments: 29 million transactions with a value of $2 billion.

Table 5. Japan: Payments System, 1987[1]

Instruments	Volume of Transactions (in millions)	Volume per Capita	Percentage of Total Volume	Value of Transactions (in billions of yen)	Value per Capita (in yen)	Percentage of Total Value
Checks issued	269.4	2.2	7.4	4,129,848.9	33,768,184.0	67.4
Payments by credit card	211.9	1.7	5.8	4,672.2	38,202.8	0.1
Paper-based credit transfers	446.1	3.6	12.2	55,126.5	450,748.2	0.9
Paperless credit transfers	869.1	7.1	23.8	1,917,181.8	15,676,057.2	31.3
Direct debits	1,855.9	15.2	50.8	17,453.0	142,706.5	0.3
Total	3,652.4	29.9	100.0	6,124,282.4	50,758,898.6	100.0

Source: Bank for International Settlements (1989b).

[1] Estimated figures.

Table 6. Germany: Payments System, 1987

Instruments	Volume of Transactions (*in millions*)	Volume per Capita	Percentage of Total Volume	Value of Transactions (*in billions of deutsche mark*)[1]	Value per Capita (*in deutsche mark*)	Percentage of Total Value
Checks issued	545.0	9	8.6	3,355.0	54,910.0	18.8
Checks paperless collect[2]	(300.0)	(5)	(4.7)	(85.0)	(1,391.0)	(0.5)
Payments by credit card[3]	38.0	1	0.6	8.0	131.0	0.1
Payments by debit card on EFT	0.4	—	—	0.1	0.9	—
Paper-based credit transfers[4]	1,805.0	30	28.5	10,420.0	170,540.0	58.4
Paperless credit transfers[5]	1,665.0	27	26.3	2,560.0	41,899.0	14.3
Direct debits[6]	2,285.0	38	36.0	1,505.0	24,632.0	8.4
Total	6,338.4	105	100.0	17,848.1	292,112.0	100.0

Note: EFT = electronic funds transfers; ATM = automated teller machines.
Source: Bank for International Settlements (1989b).
[1]Partly estimated.
[2]Not included in direct debits to avoid double counting.
[3]Charge cards and bank cards, excluding retail cards; the card companies' settlements with the retailers (normally credit transfers) and payment of the monthly totals by cardholders to card issuers by credit transfers, direct debit, or check are contained in the corresponding items.
[4]Excluding interbank transfers. Interbank transfers via Bundesbank, partly estimated:

	Volume of Transactions (*millions*)	Value of Transactions (*billions of deutsche mark*)
Local credit transfers	1.0	6,099.0
Local clearinghouse credit transfers	213.8	64,571.0
Intercity wire transfers	0.8	4,942.0

[5]Including customers' paper-based credit transfers that were routed into the paperless procedure by the bank to which they were first submitted.
[6]Including cash dispenser/ATM withdrawals made with EC-cards at banks other than the one issuing the card.

Table 7. United Kingdom: Payments System, Year-End 1987

Instruments	Volume of Transactions (in millions)	Volume per Capita	Percentage of Total Volume	Value of Transactions (in billions of pounds sterling)	Value per Capita (in pounds sterling)	Percentage of Total Value
Checks issued[1]						
Town[2]	5	less than 1	less than 1	10,612	186,830	53.0
Other	2,963	52.0	57	1,253	22,059	6.0
Payments by credit card[3]	592	10.0	11	36	334	less than 1
Paper-based credit transfers[4]	483	8.5	9	527	9,278	2.5
Paperless credit transfers						
Of which						
Large-value transfers[5]	4	less than 1	less than 1	7,332	129,084	36.5
Others	678	12.0	13	231	4,067	1.0
Direct debits	486	8.5	9	127	2,236	less than 1
Total[6]	5,211	91.0	100	20,101	353,888	100.0

Source: Bank for International Settlements (1989b).
[1]Excluding an estimated 300 million cashed checks, valued at $25 billion (some £13 billion).
[2]Including interbranch checks.
[3]Excluding transactions by holders of an estimated 9 million charge and budget cards issued by retailers, but including transactions by holders of over 1.5 million travel and entertainment cards.
[4]Including standing orders.
[5]Via Clearing House Automated Payment System (CHAPS).
[6]Excluding government payments in cash from post offices against state benefit vouchers.

Table 8. France: Payments System, 1987[1]

Instruments	Volume of Transactions (in millions)	Volume per Capita	Percentage of Total Volume	Value of Transactions (in billions of French francs)	Value per Capita (in French francs)	Percentage of Total Value
Checks issued[2]	4,406.4	80.6	65.4	15,225.5	278,345.5	29.9
Payments by debit card on EFT[3]	530.0	9.7	7.9	163.0	2,979.9	0.3
Paper-based credit transfers[4]	128.7	2.4	1.9	30,719.4	561,597.8	60.3
Paperless credit transfers[5]	1,039.5	19.0	15.4	3,893.3	71,175.5	7.7
Direct debits[6]	637.3	11.6	9.4	921.0	16,837.3	1.8
Total	6,741.9	123.3	100.0	50,922.2	930,936.0	100.0

Note: EFT = electronic funds transfers.
Source: Bank for International Settlements (1989b).
[1]The figures in this table combine the data relating to all payments instruments, whether they are routed via "official" circuits or not.
[2]Including postal checks.
[3]Of which 45 percent (by volume) did not give rise to electronic payment.
[4]These figures include credit transfers of a purely interbank nature that could not be isolated.
[5]A breakdown is not available.
[6]Including the universal payment order.

Table 9. Switzerland: Payments System, 1987

Instruments	Volume of Transactions (in millions)	Volume per Capita	Percentage of Total Volume	Value of Transactions (in billions of Swiss francs)[1]	Value per Capita (Swiss francs)
Checks issued[1]	42.1	6.40	13.8	127.7	19,436.0
Payments by credit card[2]	9.2	1.40	3.0	2.7	410.0
Payments by debit card on EFT	1.0	0.15	0.3	0.04	5.0
Paper-based credit transfers	123.7	18.80	40.6	. . .	. . .
Paperless credit transfers	119.4	18.20	39.3	. . .	. . .
Direct debits[3]	9.1	1.40	3.0	. . .	. . .
Total	304.5	46.35	100.0	36.101[4]	5.50[5]

Note: EFT = electronic funds transfers.
Source: Bank for International Settlements (1989b).
[1] Euro, bank, Swiss Bankers Traveller, and postal checks.
[2] Rough estimates.
[3] Without payments by debit cards.
[4] Total giro transfers including interbank payments.
[5] In millions of Swiss francs.

Appendix II
Example of Systemic Risk

Consider three participating banks (A, B, and C) on the CHIPS system. These banks receive and send payments during the day as follows:

A		B		C	
Receipts	Payments	Receipts	Payments	Receipts	Payments
$10 from C	$5 to B	$5 from A	$10 to C	$10 from B	$10 to A
$15 from C	$10 to B	$10 from A			$15 to A

Assume that A issues an order to pay $5 to B; B makes a $10 payment to C; and C makes a payment of $10 to A. Then C makes an additional payment of $15 to A. Finally, A makes a payment of $10 to B; all these payments are made during the course of one settlement day. After CHIPS clears these payments: A is a net creditor for $10, B is a net creditor for $5, and C has a net debt balance of $15. Thus C would have to send $15 over Fedwire into the CHIPS clearing account at the Federal Reserve either directly or through its clearing bank. CHIPS would then pay out $10 to A's account and $5 to B's account. However, if C was unable to pay its settlement obligation, CHIPS would unwind the day's transactions and delete B's receipts and pay-

ments from the relevant net payments. The new transaction structure would become:

A		B		C	
Receipts	Payments	Receipts	Payments	Receipts	Payments
	$5 to B	$5 from A		—	—
	$10 to B	$10 from A		—	—

Thus A would be left with a $15 net debit position as opposed to a $10 net credit position. If A does not have $15 in its Federal Reserve account, it has to borrow from the federal funds market. However, the bankruptcy of a major bank might make it difficult for a net debit bank to borrow, particularly if its net debit is large relative to its capital. Simulation exercises[31] have shown that the unwinding of transactions of one large CHIPS participant would make a high percentage of other participants unable to meet their commitments on CHIPS without acquiring additional reserves in the federal funds market. In such a situation, the Federal Reserve could lend reserves to bank A against collateral, or, at an earlier stage, to bank C so that the initial settlement could go through.

[31] Humphrey (1986).

References

Anvari, Mohsen, "The Canadian Payment System: An Evolving Structure," in *The U.S. Payment System: Efficiency, Risk and the Role of the Federal Reserve*, ed. by David B. Humphrey (Boston: Kluwer, 1990).

Association of Reserve City Bankers (ARCB), *Finality in Private Payments Systems: Issues and Alternatives* (Washington: ARCB, December 1985).

————, *Report of the Working Group of the Association of Reserve City Bankers on Book-Entry Daylight Overdrafts* (Washington: ARCB, June 1986).

Banca d'Italia, *White Paper on the Payment System in Italy* (Rome: Banca d'Italia, April 1988).

Bank for International Settlements (1989a), *Report on Netting Schemes*, Prepared by the Group of Experts on Payment Systems of the central banks of the Group of Ten countries (Basle, February 1989).

———— (1989b), *Payment Systems in Eleven Developed Countries* (Basle, 3rd ed., May 1989).

Bank of Canada, "Matters Arising from Transactions of the Northland Bank with its *Clearing Agent* The Royal Bank of Canada, and with the Bank of Canada on August 30th, 1985" (Press Statement, September 18, 1985).

Bank of Japan, "Japanese Transfer Systems in the Era of Financial Deregulation and Globalization" (July 1989).

Baxter, William F., "Bank Interchange of Transactional Paper: Legal and Economic Perspectives," *Journal of Law and Economics*, Vol. 26 (October 1983).

Belton, Terrence M., and others, "Daylight Overdrafts and Payments System Risk," *Federal Reserve Bulletin*, Vol. 73 (November 1987).

Benston, George J., and George G. Kaufman, "Regulating Bank Safety and Performance," in *Restructuring Banking and Financial Services in America*, ed. by William S. Haraf and Rose Marie Kushmeider (Washington: American Enterprise Institute, 1988).

————, Robert Eisenbeis, Paul Horvitz, Edward Kane, and George Kaufman, *Perspectives on Safe and Sound Banking: Past, Present, and Future* (Cambridge, Massachusetts: MIT Press, 1986).

Brickley, James A., and Christopher M. James, "Access to Deposit Insurance, Insolvency Rules and the Stock Returns of Financial Institutions," *Journal of Financial Economics*, Vol. 16 (July 1986).

Brown, John Prather, "Toward an Economic Theory of Liability," *Journal of Legal Studies*, Vol. 2 (June 1973).

Cannon, James G., *Clearing Houses: Their History, Models, and Administration* (London: Smith, Elder, and Company, 1901), reprinted in *National Monetary Commission*, Vol. 6 (Washington, 1911).

Clarke, John J., "An Item is an Item is an Item: Article 4 of the U.C.C. and the Electronic Age," *Business Lawyer*, Vol. 25 (November 1969).

Cooter, Robert D., and Edward L. Rubin, "A Theory of Loss Allocation for Consumer Payments," *Texas Law Review*, Vol. 66 (November 1987).

Corrigan, E. Gerald, "Financial Market Structure: A Longer View," Federal Reserve Bank of New York, *Seventy-Second Annual Report For the Year Ended December 31, 1986* (1987).

de Roover, Raymond, *The Dawn of Modern Banking* (New Haven, Connecticut: Yale University Press, 1979).

Dudley, William C., "Controlling Risk on Large-Dollar Wire Transfer Systems," in *Technology and the Regulation of Financial Markets: Securities, Futures, and Banking*, ed. by Anthony Saunders and Lawrence J. White (Lexington, Massachusetts: Lexington Books, 1986).

Edwards, Franklin R., "The Future Financial Structure: Fears and Policies," in *Restructuring Banking and Financial Services in America*, ed. by William S. Haraf and Rose Marie Kushmeider (Washington: American Enterprise Institute, 1988).

Eisenbeis, Robert A., "Eroding Market Imperfections: Implications for Financial Intermediaries, the Payments System, and Regulatory Reform," in *Restructuring the Financial System* (Federal Reserve Bank of Kansas City, 1987).

Fama, Eugene, "Banking in a Theory of Finance," *Journal of Monetary Economics*, Vol. 6 (January 1980).

————, "What's Different About Banks?" *Journal of Monetary Economics*, Vol. 15 (January 1985).

Faulhaber, Gerald R., Almarin Phillips, and Anthony M. Santomero, "Payment Risk, Network Risk, and the Role of the Fed," in *The U.S. Payment System: Efficiency, Risk and the Role of the Federal Reserve*, ed. by David B. Humphrey (Boston: Kluwer, 1990).

Federal Reserve Bank of New York, "Large-Dollar Payment Flows from New York," Federal Reserve Bank of New York, *Quarterly Review*, Vol. 12 (Winter 1987–88).

————, *Clearing and Settling the Euro-Securities Market: Euro-Clear and Cedel* (New York, March 1989).

————, *An Overview of the Operation of the Options Clearing Corporation* (New York, April 1989).

Fédération Internationale des Bourses de Valeurs, *Improving International Settlement*, Report of the Task Force appointed by the FIBV (1989).

Flannery, Mark J., "Payments System Risk and Public Policy," in *Restructuring Banking and Financial Services in America*, ed. by William S. Haraf and Rose Marie Kushmeider (Washington: American Enterprise Institute, 1988).

Folkerts-Landau, D., "Coordination of Financial Policy," in *International Policy Coordination and Exchange Rate Fluctuations*, ed. by W. Branson, J.A. Frenkel, and M. Goldstein (Chicago: University of Chicago Press, 1990).

Friedman, Milton, *A Program for Monetary Stability* (New York: Fordham University Press, 1959).

————, and Anna J. Schwartz, *A Monetary History of the United States, 1867–1960* (Princeton, New Jersey: Princeton University Press, 1963).

Garbade, Kenneth D., and William L. Silber, "The Payment System and Domestic Exchange Rates: Technological Versus Institutional Change," *Journal of Monetary Economics*, Vol. 5 (January 1979).

Gelfand, Mathew D., and David E. Lindsey, "The Simple Microanalytics of Payments System Risk," Finance and Economics Discussion Series, No. 61 (Washington: Federal Reserve Board, March 1989).

Goodfriend, Marvin S., "Central Banking Under the Gold Standard," in *Money Cycles, and Exchange Rates: Essays in Honor of Allan H. Meltzer*, ed. by Karl Brunner and Bennett McCallum, Carnegie-Rochester Conference Series on Public Policy, Vol. 29 (1988).

————, "Money, Credit, Banking, and Payment System Policy," in *The U.S. Payment System: Efficiency, Risk and the Role of the Federal Reserve*, ed. by David B. Humphrey (Boston: Kluwer, 1990).

————, and Robert G. King, "Financial Deregulation, Monetary Policy, and Central Banking," in *Restructuring Banking and Financial Services in America*, ed. by William S. Haraf and Rose Marie Kushmeider (Washington: American Enterprise Institute, 1988).

Goodhart, C.A.E., "Why Do Banks Need a Central Bank?" *Oxford Economic Papers*, Vol. 39 (March 1987).

————, *The Evolution of Central Banks*, (Cambridge, Massachusetts: MIT Press, 1988).

Gorton, Gary, and Donald J. Mullineaux, "The Joint Production of Confidence: Endogenous Regulation and Nineteenth Century Commercial-Bank Clearinghouses," *Journal of Money, Credit, and Banking*, Vol. 19 (November 1987).

Greenspan, Alan, "International Payment Systems Developments," speech at the International Symposium on Banking and Payment Services (Washington, June 9, 1989).

Group of Thirty, *Clearance and Settlement Systems in the World's Securities Markets* (New York: Group of Thirty, 1989).

Guttentag, Jack M., and Richard J. Herring, *Disaster Myopia in International Banking*, Brookings Discussion Papers in International Economics, No. 31 (Washington: Brookings Institution, 1985).

Heurtas, Thomas F., "Risk in the Payments System," in U.S. Congress, House, Committee on Government Operations, *Structure and Regulation of Financial Firms and Holding Companies* (*Part 3*), 99th Congress, 2nd Session (Washington: Government Printing Office, 1987), pp. 361–89.

Humphrey, David B., *The U.S. Payments System: Costs, Pricing, Competition, and Risk*, Monograph Series in Finance and Economics (New York: New York University, 1984).

————, "Payments Finality and Risk of Settlement Failure," in *Technology and the Regulation of Financial Markets: Securities, Futures, and Banking*, ed. by Anthony Saunders and Lawrence J. White (Lexington, Massachusetts: Lexington Books, 1986).

Ireland, Oliver I., "Payment System Risk," in U.S. Congress, House, Committee on Government Operations, *Structure and Regulation of Financial Firms and Holding Companies* (*Part 1*), 99th Congress, 2nd Session (Washington: Government Printing Office, 1987), pp. 500–508.

James, Christopher, "Some Evidence on the Uniqueness of Bank Loans," *Journal of Financial Economics*, Vol. 19 (December 1987).

Jensen, Michael C., and William H. Meckling, "Theory of the Firm: Managerial Behavior, Agency Costs and Ownership Structure," *Journal of Financial Economics*, Vol. 3 (October 1976).

Jevons, William S., *Money and the Mechanism of Exchange* (New York: Appleton, 1898).

Johnson, Manuel H., "Challenge to the Federal Reserve in the Payments Mechanism," *Issues in Bank Regulation* (Summer 1988).

Kantrow, Yvette D., "Big NY Banks May Spin Off Chips Network," *American Banker*, Vol. 23 (June 27, 1988).

Kareken, John H., "Ensuring Financial Stability," in *The Search for Financial Stability: The Past Fifty Years* (San Francisco: Federal Reserve Bank of San Francisco, 1985).

Kessler, J., *Study on Improvements in the Settlement of Cross-Border Securities Transactions in the EEC* (Commission of the European Communities, July 1988).

King, Robert G., and Charles I. Plosser, "Money as the Mechanism of Exchange," *Journal of Monetary Economics*, Vol. 17 (January 1986).

Lindow, Wesley, "Bank Capital and Risk Assets," *National Banking Review*, Comptroller of the Currency, U.S. Treasury Department (September 1963).

Litan, Robert E., "Taking the Dangers Out of Bank Deregulation," *Brookings Review*, Vol. 4 (Fall 1986).

Lumpkin, Stephen A., "Repurchase and Reverse Repurchase Agreements," in *Instruments of the Money Market*, ed. by Timothy Q. Cook and Timothy D. Rowe (Richmond, Virginia: Federal Reserve Bank of Richmond, 6th ed., 1986).

McCallum, Bennett, "Bank Deregulation, Accounting Systems and Exchange, and the Unit of Account: A Critical Review," in *The New Monetary Economics, Fiscal Issues and Unemployment*, ed. by Karl Brunner and Allan H. Meltzer, Carnegie-Rochester Conference Series on Public Policy, Vol. 23 (1985).

Mengle, David L., "Legal and Regulatory Reform in Electronic Payments: An Evaluation of Payment Finality Rules," in *The U.S. Payment System: Efficiency, Risk and the Role of the Federal Reserve*, ed. by David B. Humphrey (Boston: Kluwer, 1990).

————, David B. Humphrey, and Bruce J. Summers, "Intraday Credit: Risk, Value, and Pricing," *Federal Reserve Bank of Richmond Economic Review*, Vol. 73 (January/February 1987).

Mullineaux, Donald J., "Competitive Monies and the Suffolk Bank System: A Contractual Perspective," *Southern Economic Journal*, Vol. 53 (April 1987).

New York Clearing House Association, *Constitution of the New York Clearing House Association* (May 1903).

————, Memorandum on "Increased Assurances of Settlement Formality or CHIPS" (April 1989).

Padoa-Schioppa, T., "Payment System: A New Ground for Central Bank Cooperation," unpublished (June 1989).

"Proposals for International Convergence of Capital Measurement and Capital Standards," *Issues in Bank Regulation* (Winter 1988).

Rothschild, Michael, and Joseph E. Stiglitz, "Increasing Risk: I. A Definition," *Journal of Economic Theory*, Vol. 2 (September 1970).

Schwartz, Anna J., "Financial Stability and the Federal Safety Net," in *Restructuring Banking and Financial Services in America*, ed. by William S. Haraf and Rose Marie Kushmeider (Washington: American Enterprise Institute, 1988).

Timberlake, Richard H., Jr., "The Central Banking Role of Clearinghouse Associations," *Journal of Money, Credit and Banking*, Vol. 16 (February 1984).

United States, Board of Governors of the Federal Reserve System, "Policy Statement Regarding Risks on Large-Dollar Wire Transfer Systems," *Federal Register*, Vol. 50, No. 99 (May 22, 1985).

————, "Interim Policy Statement Regarding Risks on Large-Dollar Wire Transfer Systems," *Federal Register*, Vol. 52, No. 151 (August 6, 1987).

———— (1988a), Large-Dollar Payments System Advisory Group, *A Strategic Plan for Managing Risk in the Payments System*, Report of the Large-Dollar Payments System Advisory Group to the Payments System Policy Committee of the Federal Reserve System (Washington, August 1988).

———— (1988b), *Controlling Risk in the Payments System*, Report of the Task Force on Controlling Payments System Risk to the Payments System Policy Committee of the Federal Reserve System (Washington, August 1988).

————, *Proposals for Modifying the Payments System Risk Reduction Policy of the Federal Reserve System*, Prepared by the Staff of the Federal Reserve System (Washington, May 1989).

————, Congress, House, Committee on Government Operations and Committee on Banking, Finance, and Urban Affairs, *The Role of the Federal Reserve in Check Clearing and the Nation's Payments System*, Joint Hearings before Subcommittees of the Government Operations and Banking, Finance and Urban Affairs Committees, 98th Congress, 1st Session, June 15, 1983 (Washington: Government Printing Office, 1983).

Van Hoose, David, "The Angell Proposal: An Overview" (Board of Governors of the Federal Reserve System, June 6, 1988).

Vital, Christian, and David L. Mengle, "SIC: Switzerland's New Electronic Interbank Payment System," *Federal Reserve Bank of Richmond Economic Review* (November/December 1988).

Westerfield, Ray B., *Banking Principles and Practice*, Vol. 3 (New York: Ronald Press Company, 1921).

Whitney, D.R., *The Suffolk Bank* (Cambridge, Massachusetts: Riverside Press, 1878).

Williamson, Stephen D., "Bank Failures, Financial Restrictions, and Aggregate Fluctuations: Canada and the United States, 1870–1913," *Federal Reserve Bank of Minneapolis Quarterly Review* (Summer 1989).

Young, John E., "The Rise and Fall of Federal Reserve Float," *Federal Reserve Bank of Kansas City Economic Review*, Vol. 71 (February 1986).

III

Foreign Direct Investment

J. Saúl Lizondo

J. Saúl Lizondo

oreign direct investment has long been a subject of interest. This interest has been renewed in recent years for a number of reasons. One of them is the rapid growth in global foreign direct investment flows, which increased from $47 billion in 1985 to $139 billion in 1988.[1] Another reason is the recent sharp increase in foreign direct investment inflows into the United States, which caused some concern about the causes and consequences of such an expansion in foreign ownership. A third reason is the possibility offered by foreign direct investment for channeling resources to developing countries. Although foreign direct investment has not been a significant component of total capital inflows into developing countries, its relative importance may increase now that many of them have quite limited access to other sources of financing.[2]

As a result of the continuous interest in foreign direct investment, a large number of studies have analyzed both the determinants and the effects of such investment. This study reviews the conclusions reached in some of these studies about the determinants of foreign direct investment, and it includes hypotheses that emphasize a variety of factors. Some of these hypotheses use arguments that could also be applied, and in some cases were typically applied, to analyzing portfolio investment. In contrast, other hypotheses stress that to understand foreign direct investment it is essential to take into account the fundamental difference between portfolio investment and direct investment in terms of the control exercised over the operations of the firm.[3]

The structure of this study is based on that employed in the comprehensive survey by Agarwal (1980).[4] It first examines the determinants of foreign direct investment identified in theories that assume perfect markets, which focus on differential rates of return, portfolio diversification, and market size. Then it considers the factors viewed as important in theories that assume imperfect markets and emphasizes the role of industrial organizations, internalization, the product cycle, and oligopolistic reaction. The next sections discuss the theories based on liquidity, currency areas, diversification with barriers to international capital flows, and the Kojima hypothesis and examine some factors that are considered to have an important effect on foreign direct investment, but that sometimes are not included explicitly in the theories mentioned above. Finally, it presents the overall conclusions.

Theories Assuming Perfect Markets

Differential Rates of Return

This approach argues that foreign direct investment is the result of capital flowing from countries with low rates of return to countries with high rates of return. This proposition follows from the idea that, in evaluating their investment decisions, firms equate expected marginal returns with the

---

[1]International Monetary Fund, *Balance of Payments Statistics*. Recent studies describing the evolution of foreign direct investment include Thomsen (1989), DeAnne and Thomsen (1989a and b), and Lipsey (1989).

[2]Foreign direct investment inflows into net debtor developing countries increased gradually from $2 billion in 1970 to $15 billion in 1981. These inflows then declined, remaining at about $10 billion for a few years, before increasing again to $17 billion in 1988.

[3]It is not obvious what constitutes control of a firm. In general, countries classify as direct investment enterprises those in

which the percentage of foreign ownership is above a certain limit, usually between 10 and 25 percent. Although there are no uniform criteria among countries, moderate differences in the percentage used for the classification do not alter significantly the measurement of foreign direct investment, since the share of foreign ownership in firms considered to be foreign affiliates is usually much larger. For discussion of some of these issues, and other methodological and data problems, see Thomsen (1989).

[4]There are also alternative ways of organizing the discussion. For example, Boddewyn (1985) groups the theories according to whether they refer to conditions, motivations, or precipitating circumstances for foreign direct investment. Kojima and Ozawa (1984) distinguish between macro- and micromodels of foreign direct investment.

marginal cost of capital. If expected marginal returns are higher abroad than at home, and assuming that the marginal cost of capital is the same for both types of investment, there is an incentive to invest abroad rather than at home.

This theory gained wide acceptance in the late 1950s when U.S. foreign direct investment in manufacturing in Europe increased sharply. At that time, after-tax rates of return of U.S. subsidiaries in manufacturing were consistently above the rate of return on U.S. domestic manufacturing. However, this relationship proved to be unstable. During the 1960s U.S. foreign direct investment in Europe continued to rise, although rates of return for U.S. subsidiaries in Europe were below rates of return on domestic manufacturing.[5]

Empirical tests of this hypothesis proceeded along several lines. Some authors tried to find a positive relationship between the ratio of a firm's foreign direct investment to its domestic investment and the ratio of its foreign profits to its domestic profits. Others tried to relate foreign direct investment and the rate of foreign profits, usually allowing for a certain time lag. Another approach was to examine the relationship between relative rates of returns in several countries and the allocation of foreign direct investment among those countries.

As reported by Agarwal (1980), these empirical studies failed to provide strong supporting evidence, maybe partly owing to the difficulties of measuring expected profits. In the various tests, reported profits were used to represent expected profits. However, reported profits are likely to differ from actual profits, which in turn may differ from expected profits. The main reason for a divergence of reported profits from actual profits is intra-firm pricing for transactions between a subsidiary and the parent firm, and among subsidiaries. Multinational firms may establish intra-firm prices that are different from market prices, for example, to reduce their overall tax burden, or to avoid exchange controls. In turn, actual profits may differ from expected profits owing to unexpected events and the difficulties of using observations for a few years to represent the expected results from an investment with a longer time horizon.

In addition to these inconclusive empirical results, there are certain aspects of foreign direct investment that this theory cannot explain. Since this theory postulates that capital flows from countries with low rates of return to countries with high rates of return, it assumes implicitly that there is a single rate of return across activities within a country. Therefore, this theory is not consistent with some

countries experiencing simultaneously inflows and outflows of foreign direct investment. Similarly, it cannot account for the uneven distribution of foreign direct investment among different types of industries. These considerations, as well as the weak empirical results, suggest that the differential rates of return theory does not satisfactorily explain the determinants of foreign direct investment flows.

Portfolio Diversification

Since expected returns did not appear to provide an adequate explanation of foreign direct investment, attention was next focused on the role of risk. In choosing among the various available projects, a firm would presumably be guided by both expected returns and the possibility of reducing risk. Since the returns on activities in different countries are likely to have less than perfect correlation, a firm could reduce its overall risk by undertaking projects in more than one country. Foreign direct investment can therefore be viewed as international portfolio diversification at the corporate level.

Various attempts to test this theory have been made. One approach was to try to explain the share of foreign direct investment going to a group of countries by relating it to the average return on those investments, and to the risk associated with those investments, as measured by the variance of the average returns. A variant of this procedure was to estimate first the optimal geographical distribution of assets of multinational firms based on portfolio considerations, and then to assume that firms gradually adjust their flow of foreign direct investment to obtain that optimal distribution. Another line of inquiry was to ascertain whether large firms with more extensive foreign activities showed smaller fluctuations in global profits and sales.

The results from these tests offered only weak support for the portfolio diversification theory, as documented in Hufbauer (1975) and in Agarwal (1980). In some cases, results that were favorable for a group of countries failed to hold for individual countries. In others, the results were not significant or were more consistent with alternative theories. Although the lack of strong empirical support may be due partly to the difficulties associated with measuring expected profits and risk, there are more basic, theoretical, problems with this approach.

The portfolio diversification theory is an improvement over the differential rates of return theory in the sense that, by including the risk factor, it can account for countries experiencing simultaneously inflows and outflows of foreign direct investment. However, it cannot account for the observed differences in the propensities of different industries to invest abroad. In other words, it does

---

[5]See Hufbauer (1975).

not explain why foreign direct investment is more concentrated in some industries than in others.

A more fundamental criticism of this theory has been the argument that in a perfect capital market there is no reason to have firms diversifying activities just to reduce risk for their stockholders. If individual investors want reduced risk, they can obtain it directly by diversifying their individual portfolios. This criticism implies that for the diversification motive to have any explanatory power for foreign direct investment, the assumption of perfect capital markets must be dropped.[6]

Output and Market Size

Two other approaches worth reporting relate foreign direct investment to some measure of output of the multinational firm in the host country. The output approach considers the relevant variable to be output (sales), while the market size approach uses the host country's GNP or GDP, which can be considered as a proxy for potential sales. The relevance of output for foreign direct investment can be derived from models of neoclassical domestic investment theory, whereas the relevance of the host country's market size has generally been postulated rather than derived from a theoretical model. Despite this lack of explicit theoretical backing, the market size model has been very popular, and a variable representing the size of the host country appears in a large number of empirical papers.

These hypotheses have been tested in a variety of ways.[7] One approach was to take models of domestic investment and estimate them using foreign direct investment data to see whether the output of multinational firms in host countries is a significant explanatory variable. Another technique was to see whether the share of foreign direct investment of a given country going to a group of countries was correlated with the income level of the individual host countries. Sometimes, the rate of growth of income in the host country, or the difference between the rate of growth of income in the host and the investing country, were also used as explanatory variables. Some authors distinguished between external and internal determinants of foreign direct investment with market size being an external factor and sales of foreign subsidiaries an internal factor.

These empirical studies support the notion that higher levels of sales by the foreign subsidiary and of the host country's income, or income growth,

have been associated with higher foreign direct investment. The broad support for these hypotheses is generally valid across a variety of countries, periods, estimation techniques, and specification of the variables.

This support, however, has to be carefully interpreted (Agarwal, 1980). As mentioned above, proponents of the market size hypothesis have seldom presented an explicit theoretical model from which the estimated relationships are derived. Therefore, the correlation between foreign direct investment and market size may be consistent with various structural models. Also, the size and growth of the host country's market should affect foreign direct investment that is used to produce for the domestic market, not for exports. In most of the empirical studies, however, no distinction is made between the two types of investment. Finally, some evidence suggests that the decisions of firms regarding foreign direct investment may be guided by different considerations depending on whether it is the firm's initial investment in the country. In this case, it would be incorrect to use the same variables to explain all types of foreign direct investment.

Theories Based on Imperfect Markets

The theories outlined in the previous section did not make any specific assumption about market imperfections or market failures. Hymer (1976) was perhaps the first analyst to point out that the structure of the markets and the specific characteristics of firms should play a key role in explaining foreign direct investment.[8] The role of these factors has been analyzed in both a static context, which focuses on issues associated with industrial organization and the internalization of decisions, and in a dynamic framework, which highlights oligopolistic rivalry and product cycle considerations.

Industrial Organization

Hymer (1976) argued that the very existence of multinational firms rests on market imperfections. Two types of market imperfection are of particular importance: structural imperfections and transaction-cost imperfections.[9] Structural imperfections, which help the multinational firm to increase its market power, arise from economies of scale, advantages of knowledge, distribution networks, product diversification, and credit advantages. Transaction costs, on the other hand, make it profitable for the multinational firm to substitute

---

[6]The discussion of this point is continued in the section on diversification with barriers to international capital flows.
    [7]See Agarwal (1980).

[8]Although Hymer's dissertation was completed in 1960, it was not published until 1976.
    [9]See Dunning (1981).

an internal "market" for external transactions. The literature focusing on structural imperfections gave rise to the industrial organization theory of foreign direct investment, whereas that focusing on transaction costs led to the internalization theory of foreign direct investment.[10]

The industrial organization approach argues that when a foreign firm establishes a subsidiary in another country, it faces a number of disadvantages when competing with domestic firms. These include the difficulties of managing operations spread out in distant places, and dealing with different languages, cultures, legal systems, technical standards, and customer preferences. If, in spite of those disadvantages, a foreign firm does engage in foreign direct investment, it must have some firm-specific advantages with respect to domestic firms. The advantages of the multinational firm are those associated with brand name, patent-protected superior technology, marketing and managerial skills, cheaper sources of financing, preferential access to markets, and economies of scale.

The industrial organization approach has been used recently by Graham and Krugman (1989) to explain the growth of foreign direct investment in the United States. They argue that 20 years ago U.S. firms had significant advantages over firms from other countries in terms of technology and management skills. U.S. firms were also superior to foreign rivals in producing abroad, as well as at home. As a result, there was not much foreign direct investment in the United States. Since then, U.S. technological and managerial superiority has declined, and foreign firms can therefore compete with U.S. firms in the U.S. market. Thus, the authors interpret the growing inflow of foreign direct investment into the United States as evidence supporting their hypothesis.

The industrial organization theory, in the restrictive sense employed in this paper, is not a complete theory of foreign direct investment. While the existence of some firm-specific advantages explains why a foreign firm can compete successfully in the domestic market, such advantages do not explain why this competition must take the form of foreign direct investment. The foreign firm could just as well export to the domestic market, or license or sell its special skills to domestic firms. The internalization theory and the eclectic approach, discussed below, offer explanations of why firms choose foreign direct investment over the other alternatives.

Internalization

This hypothesis explains the existence of foreign direct investment as the result of firms replacing market transactions with internal transactions. This in turn is seen as a way of avoiding imperfections in the markets for intermediate inputs (see Buckley and Casson, 1976). Modern businesses conduct many activities in addition to the routine production of goods and services. All these activities, including marketing, research and development, and training of labor, are interdependent and are related through flows of intermediate products, mostly in the form of knowledge and expertise. However, market imperfections make it difficult to price some types of intermediate products. For example, it is often hard to design and enforce contractual arrangements that prevent someone who has purchased or leased a technology (such as a computer software program) from passing it on to others without the knowledge of the original producer. This problem provides an incentive to bypass the market and keep the use of the technology within the firm. This produces an incentive for the creation of intrafirm markets.

The internalization theory of foreign direct investment is intimately related to the theory of the firm. The question of why firms exist was first raised by Coase (1937) and later examined by Williamson (1975). They argued that, with certain transaction costs, the firm's internal procedures are better suited than the market to organize transactions. These transaction costs arise when strategic or opportunistic behavior is present among agents to an exchange, the commodities or services traded are ambiguously defined, and contractual obligations extend in time. When these three conditions are present, enforcement and monitoring costs may become prohibitive. Under those circumstances, the firm opts to internalize those transactions. The main feature of this approach therefore is treating markets on the one hand, and firms on the other, as alternative modes of organizing production.[11]

It is the internalization of markets across national boundaries that gives rise to the international enterprise, and thus, to foreign direct investment. This process continues until the benefits from further internalization are outweighed by the costs. As indicated in Agarwal (1980), the benefits include avoidance of time lags, bargaining and buyer uncertainty, minimization of the impact of government intervention through transfer pricing,

---

[10]The concept of "industrial organization theory of foreign direct investment" is not uniformly used in the literature. Sometimes it is used to encompass all the theories derived from Hymer's work, that is, all the theories included in this section. In this study, the concept is used in its more restrictive sense, to refer to the literature focusing on structural imperfections.

[11]This approach also implies that the motivation behind multinational production, and therefore foreign direct investment, may well be the search for efficiency rather than the attempt to profit from monopoly power. This change in focus has important welfare implications. See Dunning and Rugman (1985) and Teece (1985).

and the ability to use discriminatory pricing. The costs of internalization include administrative and communication expenses.

The internalization hypothesis is a rather general theory of foreign direct investment. In fact, Rugman (1980) has argued that most, if not all, of the other hypotheses for foreign direct investment are particular cases of this general theory. As a result of this generality, this approach has been accused of being almost tautological, and of having no empirical content. Rugman (1986), however, argues that with a precise specification of additional conditions and restrictions, this approach can be used to generate powerful implications.

The difficulties in formulating appropriate tests for the internalization theory were examined further by Buckley (1988). He agreed that the general theory cannot be tested directly, but argued that it may be sharpened to obtain relevant testable implications. Since much of the argument rests on the incidence of costs in external and internal markets, the specification and measurement of those costs is crucial for any test. Empirical evidence suggests that transaction costs are particularly high in vertically integrated process industries, knowledge-intensive industries, quality-assurance-dependent products, and communication-intensive industries. Therefore, the internalization theory predicts that those will be the industries dominated by multinational firms. Buckley also cited evidence showing that the pattern of foreign direct investment across industries, and nationalities, is broadly consistent with the theory's predictions, but he emphasized that tests need to be more precise and rigorous to increase our confidence in the theory.

An Eclectic Approach

Dunning (1977, 1979, 1988) developed an eclectic approach by integrating three strands of the literature on foreign direct investment: the industrial organization theory, the internalization theory, and the location theory. He argued that three conditions must be satisfied if a firm is to engage in foreign direct investment. First, the firm must have some ownership advantages with respect to other firms; these advantages usually arise from the possession of firm-specific intangible assets. Second, it must be more beneficial for the firm to use these advantages rather than to sell or lease them to other independent firms. Finally, it must be more profitable to use these advantages in combination with at least some factor inputs located abroad, otherwise foreign markets would be served exclusively by exports. Thus, for foreign direct investment to take place, the firm must have ownership and internationalization advantages, and a foreign country must have locational advantages over the firm's home country.[12]

The eclectic approach postulates that all foreign direct investment can be explained by reference to the above conditions. It also postulates that the advantages mentioned above are not likely to be uniformly spread among countries, industries, and enterprises and are likely to change over time. The flows of foreign direct investment of a particular country at a particular point in time depend on the ownership and internationalization advantages of the country's firms, and on the locational advantages of the country, at that point in time. Dunning (1979, 1980) used this approach to suggest reasons for differences in the industrial pattern of the outward direct investment of five developed countries, and to evaluate the significance of ownership and location variables in explaining the industrial pattern and geographical distribution of the sales of U.S. affiliates in 14 manufacturing industries in seven countries.

Product Cycle

This hypothesis postulates that most products follow a life cycle, in which they first appear as innovations and ultimately become completely standardized. Foreign direct investment results when firms react to the threat of losing markets as the product matures, by expanding overseas and capturing the remaining rents from development of the product. This hypothesis, developed by Vernon (1966), was mainly intended to explain the expansion of U.S. multinational firms after World War II.

Innovation can be stimulated by the need to respond to more intense competition or to the perception of a new profit opportunity. The new product is developed and produced locally (in the United States) both because it will be designed to satisfy local demand and because it will facilitate the efficient coordination between research, development, and production units. Once the first production unit is established in the home market, any demand that may develop in a foreign market (Europe) would ordinarily be satisfied by exports. However, rival producers will eventually emerge in foreign markets, since they can produce more cheaply (owing to lower distribution costs) than the original innovator. At this stage, the innovator is compelled to examine the possibility of setting up a production unit in the foreign location. If the conditions are considered favorable, the innovator engages in foreign direct investment. Finally, when the product is standardized and its production technique is no longer an exclusive possession of the

---

[12]Dunning (1979) lists the advantages of each of the categories mentioned above.

innovator, he may decide to invest in developing countries to obtain some cost advantages, such as cheaper labor.

Agarwal (1980) describes a number of studies offering support for the product-cycle hypothesis. Those studies generally refer to U.S. foreign direct investment, although they also cover some German and U.K. foreign direct investment.

Despite those favorable results, the explanatory power of the product-cycle hypothesis has declined considerably as a result of changes in the international environment. Vernon (1979) has noted that, since U.S. multilateral firms now have better knowledge of market demands all around the world, they no longer follow the typical geographical sequence of first setting up subsidiaries in the markets with which they are most familiar, such as in Canada and the United Kingdom, and then in less familiar areas, such as Asia and Africa. Therefore, the assumption that U.S. firms receive stimulus for the development of new products only from their home market is no longer tenable. Furthermore, since the income and technological gap between the United States and other industrial countries has declined, it is less defensible to assume that U.S. firms are exposed to a very different home environment from that faced by firms from other countries. Vernon (1979) speculated that the hypothesis is likely to remain important in explaining foreign direct investment carried out by small firms and in developing countries.

Oligopolistic Reaction

Knickerbocker (1973) suggested that, in an oligopolistic environment, foreign direct investment by one firm will trigger similar investments by other leading firms in the industry to maintain their market shares.[13] Using data from a large number of U.S. multinational firms, he calculated an entry concentration index for each industry, which showed the extent to which subsidiaries' entry dates were bunched in time. As indicated in Hufbauer (1975), the entry concentration index was positively correlated with the U.S. industry concentration index, implying that increased industrial concentration caused increased reaction by competitors to reduce the possibility of one rival gaining a significant cost or marketing advantage over the others. The entry concentration index was also positively correlated with market size, implying that the reaction was stronger, the larger the market at stake. The entry concentration index was

negatively correlated with the product diversity of the multinational firms and with their expenditure on research and development. This suggested that the reaction of firms was less intense if they had a variety of investment opportunities, or if their relative positions depended on technological considerations. Flowers (1976) also tested this hypothesis with data on foreign direct investment by Canadian and European firms in the United States. He found a significant positive correlation between the concentration of foreign direct investment in the United States and the industrial concentration in the source countries.

An implication of this hypothesis is that the process of foreign direct investment by multinational firms is self limiting, since the invasion of each other's home market will increase competition and thus reduce the intensity of oligopolistic reaction (Agarwal, 1980). However, while foreign direct investment has increased competition in many industries, this has not resulted in a corresponding reduction in foreign direct investment. This hypothesis has also been criticized for not recognizing that foreign direct investment is only one of several methods of servicing foreign markets. In addition, there is no explanation of the reason for the initial investment that starts the foreign investment process.

To examine the factors motivating the initial investment of multinational firms, Yu and Ito (1988) studied one oligopolistic and one competitive industry. Their results suggest that in an oligopolistic industry, foreign direct investment is motivated by the behavior of rivals, as well as host country-related and firm-related factors; in contrast, in more competitive industries, firms do not generally match their competitors' foreign direct investments. As a result, the authors argued that firms in oligopolistic industries, besides considering their competitors' activities, make their foreign direct investment decisions on the basis of the same economic factors as firms in competitive industries.

Other Theories of Foreign Direct Investment

Liquidity

U.S. multinational firms have traditionally committed only modest amounts of resources to their initial foreign direct investment, and subsequent expansions of their activities were carried out by reinvesting local profits. As a result, it has been postulated that there is a positive relationship between internal cash flows and the investment outlays of subsidiaries of multinational firms. This relationship is said to arise because the cost of

---

[13]A variant of this "follow the leader" hypothesis is the "exchange of threat" hypothesis, in which intra-industry foreign direct investment results from firms invading each other's home markets owing to oligopolistic rivalry (see Graham, 1978).

internal funds is lower than the cost of external funds.

Agarwal (1980) presented the results of empirical studies, which provided mixed support for this hypothesis. Some studies concluded that there was no evidence that the expansion of subsidiaries was financed only by their retained earnings. Internally generated funds seemed to be allocated between the parent and the subsidiaries to maximize the overall profits of the firm. However, other studies found that the most important sources of funds for the expansion of subsidiaries were undistributed profits and depreciation allowances, although the share of new investment thus financed varied from country to country. In other studies, liquidity-related variables had a higher explanatory power for foreign direct investment than variables based on the accelerator theory of investment.

Some other studies, based on interview data, suggested that small and large international firms may behave differently, with subsidiaries of smaller firms being more dependent on internally generated funds to finance their expansion and therefore behaving more in agreement with the liquidity hypothesis. These studies also suggested that it is important to distinguish between the overall cash flow of the firm and the cash flow of the subsidiary, particularly when examining foreign direct investment in developing countries. Since new investment in developing countries is likely to be only one component of a variety of reinvestment opportunities open to the firm, the overall cash flow of the firm may not be an important determinant in a particular country. Cash flows of the subsidiary, on the other hand, may be important, particularly in countries that place restrictions on repatriation of profits and capital.

Based on the results mentioned above, Agarwal (1980) concludes that the liquidity hypothesis has some empirical support. An expansion of foreign direct investment seems to be partly determined by the subsidiaries' internally generated funds. This factor may be particularly valid for investment in developing countries owing to their restrictions on movements of funds of foreign firms and the lower degree of development of their financial and capital markets.

Currency Area

Aliber (1970, 1971) postulated that the pattern of foreign direct investment can be best explained in terms of the relative strength of the various currencies. The stronger the currency of a certain country, the more likely it is that firms from that country will engage in foreign investment, and the less likely it is that foreign firms will invest in the domestic country. The argument is based on capital

market relationships, exchange rate risks, and the market's preference for holding assets in selected currencies.

The crucial assumption of this theory is the existence of a certain bias in the capital market. This bias is assumed to arise because an income stream located in a country with a weak currency has associated with it a certain exchange risk. Investors, however, are less concerned with this exchange risk when the income stream is owned by a firm from a strong currency country than when owned by a firm from a weak currency country. According to Aliber (1971), this could reflect the view that the strong currency firm might be more efficient in hedging the exchange risk or that the strong currency firm can provide the investors with a diversified portfolio at a lower cost than the investor can acquire on his own. Alternatively, investors may take into account exchange risk for a strong currency firm only if a substantial portion of its earnings are from foreign sources.

For any of these reasons, an income stream is capitalized at a higher rate by the market (has a higher price) when it is owned by a strong currency firm than when owned by a weak currency firm. As a result, firms from countries with strong currencies have an advantage in the capital market in acquiring this income stream. Strong currency countries therefore tend to be sources of foreign direct investment, and weak currency countries tend to become host countries.

Most empirical studies have tested the currency area hypothesis by focusing on whether an overvaluation of a currency is associated with foreign direct investment outflows and undervaluation with foreign direct investment inflows. Studies of foreign direct investment in the United States, the United Kingdom, Germany, France, and Canada yielded results that were consistent with the currency area hypothesis (see Agarwal, 1980).

Despite this empirical support, the currency area theory cannot account for cross investment between currency areas, for direct investment in countries in the same currency area, and for the concentration of foreign direct investment in certain types of industries. Furthermore, it is not clear why hedging or a diversification advantage should accrue solely to the strong currency firms, or why investors show persistent ignorance or shortsightedness.

A more elaborate theory based on capital market imperfections, with similar implications to those of the currency area hypothesis, was developed by Froot and Stein (1989). They argued that a low real value of the domestic currency may be associated with foreign direct investment inflows owing to informational imperfections in the capital market that cause firms' external financing to be more expensive than their internal financing. Since the availability of internal funds depends on the level of net worth, a real depreciation of the domestic currency that lowers the wealth of domestic residents and raises that of foreign residents can lead to foreign acquisition of some domestic assets.

Their analysis of U.S. data indicates that foreign direct investment inflows into the United States are negatively correlated with the real value of the dollar. Moreover, other types of capital inflows have not shown a similar negative correlation, so that this relationship is a distinctive characteristic of foreign direct investment, as expected from the theory. However, this negative correlation between foreign direct investment inflows and the real value of currency was not evident in three out of the other four countries examined.

Additional evidence regarding the relationship between exchange rate levels and foreign direct investment was presented by Caves (1988). He argued that exchange rates have an impact on foreign direct investment inflows through two channels. First, changes in the real exchange rate modify the attractiveness of foreign investment in the United States by changing a firm's real costs and revenues. The net effect on foreign direct investment is ambiguous, depending on certain characteristics of the firm's activity, such as the share of imported inputs in total costs and the share of output that is exported. The second channel is associated with expected short-run exchange rate movements. A depreciation that is expected to be reversed will encourage foreign direct investment inflows to obtain a capital gain when the domestic currency appreciates.

Caves studied the behavior of foreign direct investment inflows into the United States using panel data from several source countries. The results showed a significant negative correlation between the level of the exchange rate, both nominal and real, and inflows of foreign direct investment. Despite these empirical results, the theory cannot satisfactorily explain why foreign residents would have an advantage over domestic residents at bidding for a given firm; nor is it clear why expected changes in the exchange rate would lead to direct investment inflows instead of portfolio inflows.

Either owing to the arguments used by the currency area theory, or by other theories with similar implications, there is some evidence that the decline in the real value of the domestic currency encourages inflows and discourages outflows of foreign direct investment. However, neither the theory nor the evidence about this relationship is completely satisfactory.

Diversification with Barriers to International Capital Flows

As noted earlier, there is no reason for firms to carry out diversification activities for their stockholders in perfect capital markets, since any desired diversification could be obtained directly by individual investors. Agmon and Lessard (1977) have argued that for international diversification to be carried out through corporations, two conditions must hold. First, barriers or costs to portfolio flows must exist that are greater than those to foreign direct investment. Second, investors must recognize that multinational firms provide a diversification opportunity that is otherwise not available. After providing some examples that justify assuming that the first condition holds, they postulate a simple model in which the rate of return of a security is a function both of a domestic market factor and of a rest-of-the-world market factor. They tested the proposition that securities prices of firms with relatively large international operations were more closely related to the rest-of-the-world market factor and less to the domestic market factors than shares of firms that are essentially domestic. They obtained favorable results for a sample of data applying to U.S. firms. However, as noted by Adler (1981) and Agmon and Lessard (1981), these results are consistent with the second condition mentioned above but do not support a fully developed theoretical model.

Errunza and Senbet (1981) developed a framework in which both firms and investors face barriers to international capital flows. As a result, individual investors have a demand for diversification services, and multinational firms are able to supply diversification services. In equilibrium, individual investors accept lower expected returns on multinational stocks than on domestic stocks in order to obtain diversification benefits. Since the diversification services provided by multinationals are reflected in the price of their stocks, Errunza and Senbet's empirical test is based on a market-value theoretical framework, which is applied to the U.S. capital market over subperiods characterized by differential government control. Their results suggest that a systematic relationship exists between the current degree of international involvement and excess market value. This relationship was stronger during the period characterized by barriers to capital flows in comparison with the period in which no substantial restrictions were in effect.[14]

---

[14]In Errunza and Senbet (1984), the authors further developed the theoretical basis for their view that indirect portfolio diversification by multinational firms helps complete international capital markets, and they expanded their empirical investigation. Some limitations of this paper are indicated in Bicksler (1984).

The Kojima Hypothesis

Kojima (1973, 1975, 1985) was concerned with explaining the differences in the patterns of U.S. and Japanese foreign direct investment in developing countries and the consequences of those differences for the expansion of international trade and global welfare.[15] Foreign direct investment was viewed as providing a means of transferring capital, technology, and managerial skills from the source country to the host country. However, it was argued that there were two types of foreign direct investment: trade-oriented and anti-trade-oriented. Foreign direct investment is trade oriented if it generates an excess demand for imports and an excess supply of exports at the original terms of trade. The opposite occurs if foreign direct investment is anti-trade-oriented.

Kojima also proposed that trade-oriented foreign direct investment was welfare improving in both source and host countries, while anti-trade-oriented foreign direct investment was welfare reducing. Since trade-oriented foreign direct investment implied investment in industries in which the source country has a comparative disadvantage, it would accelerate trade between the two nations, and promote a beneficial industrial restructuring in both countries. In contrast, anti-trade-oriented foreign direct investment would imply investment in industries in which the source country has a comparative advantage. Thus, international trade would be reduced, and industry would be restructured in a direction opposite to that recommended by comparative advantage considerations. This would reduce welfare in both countries, creating balance of payments problems, the export of jobs, and incentives for trade protectionism in the source country.

It was also argued that Japanese foreign direct investment has been trade oriented, while U.S. foreign direct investment has been anti-trade-oriented. This reflected the fact that Japanese foreign direct investment was mainly directed toward development of natural resources in which Japan has a comparative disadvantage, and toward some manufacturing sectors in which Japan had been losing its comparative advantage. Japanese investment was also viewed as being more export oriented, occurring in less sophisticated industries with smaller firms being more labor intensive, and with a higher share of local ownership. In contrast,

Kojima suggested that the United States has transferred abroad those industries in which it had a comparative advantage. The reason for this was found in the dualistic structure of the U.S. economy, with a group of innovative and oligopolistic new industries coexisting alongside a group of traditional price-competitive stagnant industries. Only the innovative and oligopolistic industries undertook foreign direct investment, since their rate of return on foreign investment was higher owing to their oligopolistic advantages. Since these were the industries in which the United States had a comparative advantage, such foreign direct investment was anti-trade-oriented.

Kojima therefore concluded that while U.S. foreign direct investment was rational from the multinational firms' point of view, it was damaging to national welfare and economic development. As a result, some policies were needed to modify the characteristics of these investments. These policies could potentially involve selecting the types of industries in which foreign direct investment would be allowed, requiring the use of licensing arrangements instead of foreign direct investment, allowing only joint ventures with local capital instead of wholly owned subsidiaries, and requiring a progressive transfer of ownership to local residents. Kojima viewed his proposed code of behavior for international investment as consistent with comparative advantage and as resulting in a higher level of international welfare.

This hypothesis has been evaluated at two levels. At the empirical level, there is the issue of whether significant differences exist in the patterns of U.S. and Japanese foreign direct investment as implied by the hypothesis. On this score, the evidence is not conclusive. While favorable evidence was presented in Kojima (1985) for investment in a group of Asian developing countries, Lee's (1983) analysis of the Korean experience, and Chou's (1988) discussion of Taiwan Province of China yielded mixed results. In addition, Mason (1980) argued that the existing differences in the pattern of foreign direct investment mainly reflected different stages in the evolution of U.S. and Japanese multinational firms.

At the theoretical level, there is the issue of whether the neoclassical framework adopted by Kojima is appropriate for studying foreign direct investment. According to Dunning (1988), Kojima's approach can neither explain nor evaluate the welfare implications of foreign direct investment prompted by the desire to rationalize international production, since it ignores the essential characteristic of foreign direct investment, that is, the internalization of intermediate product markets. The neoclassical framework of perfect compe-

---

[15]Kojima's hypothesis is mainly concerned with international economic relationships between industrial and developing countries. This is clear from several passages in his papers and is explicitly stated in Kojima (1975), where he speculates that two-way direct foreign investment between advanced industrial countries may be explained by other theories.

tition used by Kojima does not allow for the possibility of market failure. Furthermore, Lee (1984) argued that Kojima did not succeed in establishing a plausible microeconomic basis for his theory. In summary, although the Kojima hypothesis is consistent with some characteristics of U.S. and Japanese foreign direct investment behavior, the welfare implications and the policy recommendations derived from this approach have not been widely endorsed.

Other Variables

Although political instability, tax policy, and government regulations have in some circumstances been incorporated into the theories reviewed above, their importance justifies a more explicit consideration.

Political Instability

An unstable political and social environment is not conducive to inflows of foreign capital. The fear is that large and unexpected modifications of the legal and fiscal frameworks may drastically change the economic outcome of a given investment. However, empirical tests of this proposition have yielded rather mixed results.

The role of political instability has been examined empirically using both survey data and econometric analysis. Survey studies have employed data collected by contacting multinational firms and inquiring how their investment policies in foreign countries are affected by political risk. Almost all of these studies have concluded that political risk is an important factor in the decisions regarding foreign direct investment. The other type of study has used traditional econometric techniques, such as regression analysis, to test for the effect of political risk on foreign direct investment. While some studies have found a negative relationship between political risk and inflows of foreign direct investment, others fail to find any statistically significant relationship.[16]

These mixed results may reflect a variety of factors. First, it is difficult to measure political risk or political instability. Second, a given political event may give rise to different levels of risk depending on the country of origin of the investment or the type of industry in which the investment was made. Furthermore, some cross-country econometric studies did not allow for lags between the time when a change in risk is perceived and the time when the change in foreign direct investment takes

place. Finally, some of the early studies did not include factors, other than political risk, as explanatory variables of foreign direct investment.

More recent studies have addressed some of those problems and offered new evidence on the effects of political risk on foreign direct investment. Nigh (1985) uses pooled, time-series, cross-sectional estimation to examine the role of political risk in affecting foreign direct investment of U.S. multinationals in manufacturing. He distinguishes between industrial and developing host countries, and includes economic as well as political variables. Among the political variables, he distinguishes between intracountry and intercountry conflict and cooperation variables. His empirical results suggested that U.S. multinational firms reacted to both intracountry and intercountry variables when the host country was a developing country, but that they only responded to intercountry variables when the host country was an industrial country. Schneider and Frey (1985) compared the predictive power of four different models in explaining inflows of foreign direct investment for a sample of developing countries. The analyses included (1) a model with only political variables; (2) a model with only economic variables; (3) a model with an explanatory variable that incorporated political and economic factors in a single index; and (4) a model that included in a desegregated fashion both economic and political variables. They conclude that the fourth model provided the best forecasts, indicating that economic variables should also be included in the estimation, and that indices that try to capture simultaneously political and economic effects do not perform well.

Two recent papers have taken a different look at the problem. While the usual approach is to consider the effect of host-country political risk on inflows of foreign direct investment, Tallman (1988) examined whether political risk in the home country had an effect on outward foreign direct investment. Using the United States as the host country and a number of industrial countries as home countries, he examined the effects of international and domestic political and economic events on foreign direct investment. His results indicated that reducing domestic political risk reduced outward foreign direct investment, while improved political relations between countries increased outward foreign direct investment. Chase, Kuhle, and Walther (1988) also examined whether countries with relatively high political risk, as measured by available indices reported in commercial publications, provide higher returns on foreign direct investment. However, their empirical tests did not provide support for this hypothesis. The reasons may be that commercially available indices are not

---

[16]Surveys of the two types of studies mentioned above are presented in Agarwal (1980) and in Fatehi-Sedeh and Safizadeh (1989).

good representations of political risk, that reported returns are different from actual returns owing to intracompany transfer pricing, or that expected returns are not well represented by actual returns.

Tax Policy

Since the net return on foreign direct investment is affected by the tax system of both the home and the host country, tax policies affect the incentives to engage in foreign investment, as well as in the way in which that investment is financed.

There are two alternative approaches to avoiding the double taxation of income earned abroad if both the home and the host countries tax a multinational's earnings. Both approaches recognize the primary right of the host country to tax income generated within its jurisdiction, but differ on the portion of tax revenue that accrues to the home country. Under the territorial approach, the home country does not tax income earned abroad. Under the more common residence approach, the home country does tax income earned abroad, but allows for a tax credit on taxes paid to host governments. Furthermore, the home country tax payments can usually be deferred until the income earned abroad is repatriated to the domestic parent. Most analyses of tax effects focus on the residence approach.

A comprehensive theoretical treatment of the effects of taxes on direct investment capital flows has been developed by Jun (1989).[17] In this study, the author identifies three channels through which tax policy affects firms' decisions on foreign direct investment. First, the tax treatment of income generated abroad has a direct effect on the net return on foreign direct investment, which will be influenced by such instruments as the corporate tax rate, the foreign tax credit, and the deferral of home country taxes on unrepatriated income. Second, the tax treatment of income generated at home affects the net profitability of domestic investment, and thus the relative net profitability between domestic and foreign investment. Finally, tax policy can affect the relative net cost of external funds in different countries.

Jun uses an intertemporal optimizing model incorporating these three channels to discuss the effects on foreign direct investment of changes in tax policy. For example, an increase in the domestic corporate tax rate was shown to increase the outflow of foreign direct investment, although the magnitude of the effect depended on whether the marginal source of funds for the subsidiary is retained earnings, transfers from the parent firm, or external funds, and on whether the payment of taxes on unrepatriated income can be deferred. A reduction in the foreign tax credit would reduce foreign direct investment outflows unless the marginal source of financing of the subsidiary is retained earnings. An increase in the domestic investment tax credit, or the elimination of the deferral of tax payments on unrepatriated earnings, would reduce the outflow of foreign direct investment.

The limited empirical literature on this subject has recently been expanded by various studies of U.S. foreign direct investment inflows and outflows, starting with Hartman (1984).[18] This paper examines inflows of foreign direct investment into the United States by first separating investment financed by retained earnings from investment financed by transfer from abroad. For both categories, the paper studies the response of investment to the after-tax rate of return obtained by foreign investors in the United States (as a proxy for expected rate of return for firms considering expansion of current operations), and the overall after-tax rate of return on capital in the United States (as a proxy for expected returns for firms considering acquisition of existing assets). The estimated coefficients had the expected positive sign for both rates of return. However, the model did not explain investments financed by transfers from abroad very satisfactorily. The same type of equations were estimated by Boskin and Gale (1987) and by Young (1988), using expanded samples, revised data, alternative functional forms, and some additional explanatory variables. Although the estimated coefficients differ from those of Hartman (1984), the qualitative results were similar.

Slemrod (1989) examined the effect of host country and home country tax policy on foreign direct investment in the United States. The estimation results were generally supportive of a negative impact of the U.S. effective rate of taxation on total foreign direct investment, and on transfers of funds, but not on retained earnings. The paper then disaggregated the data by seven major investing countries to test for the effect of home country tax policy on foreign direct investment and did not find it had a significant impact. A different conclusion, however, was reached by Jun (1990), who found that U.S. tax policy toward domestic investment had a significant effect on U.S. direct investment outflows by influencing the relative net rate of return between the United States and abroad. The overall conclusion based on the evidence examined above is that both home country and host country tax policies seem to have an effect on foreign direct investment flows. However, the ability of present

---

[17]Other discussions of theoretical issues may be found in Gersovitz (1987) and in Alworth (1988).

[18]A summary of previous results can be found in Caves (1982).

models to capture those effects is not completely satisfactory.

Government Regulations

A number of factors, in addition to those included in the theories examined above, may have an impact on foreign direct investment decisions. They generally originate from government regulations that modify the risk and expected returns from a given investment project. Those regulations are sometimes implemented to counteract foreign firms' practices that are perceived to be harmful to the host country, such as intrafirm pricing and discriminatory input purchases. In other cases, they are implemented for other policy objectives, such as to favor the development of a particular industrial sector, to reduce regional disparities, or to reduce unemployment. Independent of their specific policy purpose, however, those regulations are likely to affect decisions on the size, timing, location, and sectoral allocation of foreign direct investment.

The various government regulations can be classified into incentives and disincentives to foreign direct investment, according to whether they tend to increase or to reduce the flow of investment to a given country. Incentives include, in addition to fiscal benefits such as tax credits and tax exemptions, some financial benefits such as grants and subsidized loans. Some countries provide nonfinancial benefits, such as public sector investment on infrastructure aimed at enhancing the profitability of a given foreign investment project, public sector purchasing contracts, and the establishment of free trade zones.

Disincentives include a number of impediments to foreign direct investment which may range from the slow processing of authorizations for foreign investment to the outright prohibition of foreign investment in specified regions or sectors. Most impediments, however, lie between those extremes and take the form of conditions attached to the authorization of foreign direct investment in general, or for certain regions and sectors. Those conditions may include setting a lower limit on the portion of inputs purchased from local sources and on export levels, or a specified relationship between the value of exported output and the value of imported inputs. Other conditions may include requirements regarding levels of employment, transfer of technology, expenditure on research and development, or investment in unrelated areas. In addition, there may be some upper limit on foreign ownership of equity and restrictions on foreign exchange transactions, especially those associated with profit remittances, and repatriation of capital. These regulations are particularly prevalent in developing countries.

The empirical effect of the various incentives and disincentives on the level of foreign direct investment has been examined by a number of authors. The results of those studies are documented in Agarwal (1980) and Organization for Economic Cooperation and Development (1989), which provide similar conclusions. In general, the incentives mentioned above appear to have a limited effect on the level of foreign direct investment. Investors seem to base their decisions on risk and return considerations that are only marginally affected by those incentives. However, this result may be partly due to difficulties that exist in isolating the effect of a given factor when various factors are operating simultaneously. Incentives are seldom granted without conditions; instead, they are usually subject to the compliance of requirements that constitute disincentives to foreign direct investment. Therefore, the empirical results may be capturing the net effect of incentives coupled with disincentives, which in principle can be positive or negative, depending on the strength of each component. If this is so, the weak response to incentives shown by foreign direct investment implies that the benefits of incentives serve primarily to compensate for the additional costs arising from the performance requirements usually attached to those incentives.

Disincentive regulations seem to have a more definite impact on foreign investment than incentive regulations. This is clearly true when a certain type of foreign direct investment is directly prohibited. Also, specific requirements are sometimes imposed as a condition for authorizing the investment, rather than as a condition for receiving special benefits. In this situation, in which disincentives are not accompanied by matching incentives, those requirements may be too costly, and thus prevent the investment project from being undertaken. Furthermore, the existence of a wide range of disincentives may have a negative effect on foreign direct investment beyond the one originating from the additional costs of present regulations. If investors interpret those regulations as an indication of an environment hostile to foreign investment, they may decide against investing because of possible future regulations that would reduce their profits even further.

Conclusions

At present there is no unique widely accepted theory of foreign direct investment. Instead, there are various hypotheses emphasizing different microeconomic and macroeconomic factors that are likely to affect it. While most of those hypotheses have some empirical support, no single hypothesis is sufficiently supported to cause the others to be rejected.

Theories derived from the industrial organization approach have probably gained the widest acceptance. They seem to provide a better explanation for cross-country, intra-industry investment, and for the uneven concentration of foreign direct investment across industries than do alternative models.

Regardless of the specific ranking of the various theories according to their explanatory power, it is clear from a review of the literature that in explaining the determination of international capital movements direct investment flows must be distinguished from portfolio flows. The basis for this distinction is that direct investment implies control of the foreign firm, and therefore the usual arguments regarding expected returns and diversification do not provide a satisfactory explanation. Other factors, usually associated with industrial organization and the theory of the firm, become crucial in explaining why residents of a given country would want to keep control of a foreign firm. The different reasons motivating direct investment flows and portfolio flows also imply that those flows do not necessarily move together. As a result, a given pattern of foreign direct investment flows does not necessarily have to be associated with a particular pattern of overall capital flows.

References

Adler, Michael, "Investor Recognition of Corporation International Diversification: Comment," *Journal of Finance*, Vol. 36 (March 1981).

Agarwal, Jamuna P., "Determinants of Foreign Direct Investment: A Survey," *Weltwirtschaftliches Archiv*, Vol. 116, Heft 4 (1980).

Agmon, Tamir, and Donald R. Lessard, "Investor Recognition of Corporate International Diversification," *Journal of Finance*, Vol. 32 (September 1977).

————, "Investor Recognition of Corporate International Diversification: Reply," *Journal of Finance*, Vol. 36 (March 1981).

Aliber, R.Z., "A Theory of Direct Foreign Investment," in *The International Corporation: A Symposium*, ed. by C.P. Kindleberger (Cambridge, Massachusetts: MIT Press, 1970).

————, "The Multinational Enterprise in a Multiple Currency World," in *The Multinational Enterprise*, ed. by John H. Dunning (London: Allen & Unwin, 1971).

Alworth, Julian, *The Finance, Investment and Taxation Decisions of Multinationals* (Oxford; New York: Basil Blackwell, 1988).

Bicksler, James L., "Discussion," *Journal of Finance*, Vol. 39 (July 1984).

Boddewyn, J.J., "Theories of Foreign Direct Investment and Divestment: A Classificatory Note," *Management International Review*, Vol. 25, No. 1 (1985).

Boskin, M., and W. Gale, "New Results on the Effects of Tax Policy on the International Location of Investment," in *The Effects of Taxation on Capital Accumulation*, ed. by Martin S. Feldstein (Chicago: University of Chicago Press, 1987).

Buckley, Peter J., "The Limits of Explanation: Testing the Internalization Theory of the Multinational Enterprise," *Journal of International Business Studies*, Vol. 19 (Summer 1988).

————, and Mark Casson, *The Future of the Multinational Enterprise* (London: Macmillan, 1976).

Caves, Richard E., *Multinational Enterprise and Economic Analysis* (Cambridge; New York: Cambridge University Press, 1982).

————, "Exchange-Rate Movements and Foreign Direct Investment in the United States," Harvard Institute of Economic Research, Discussion Papers Series No. 1383 (May 1988).

Chase, C.D., J.L. Kuhle, and C.H. Walther, "The Relevance of Political Risk in Direct Foreign Investment," *Management International Review*, Vol. 28 (3rd Quarter 1988).

Chou, Tein-Chen, "American and Japanese Direct Foreign Investment in Taiwan: A Comparative Study," *Hitotsubashi Journal of Economics*, Vol. 29 (December 1988).

Coase, R.H., "The Nature of the Firm," *Economica*, Vol. 4 (November 1937).

DeAnne, Julius, and Stephen E. Thomsen (1989a), "Explosion of Foreign Direct Investment Among the G-5," Royal Institute of International Affairs, RIIA Discussion Papers, No. 8 (1989).

———— (1989b), "Inward Investment and Foreign-Owned Firms in the G-5," Royal Institute of International Affairs, RIIA Discussion Papers, No. 12 (1989).

Dunning, John H., "Trade, Location of Economic Activity and the MNE: A Search for an Eclectic Approach," in *The International Allocation of Economic Activity*, ed. by Bertil Ohlin, P.O. Hesselborn, and P.J. Wijkman (London: Macmillan, 1977).

————, "Explaining Changing Patterns of International Production: In Defence of the Eclectic Theory," *Oxford Bulletin of Economics and Statistics*, Vol. 41 (November 1979).

————, "Toward an Eclectic Theory of International Production," *Journal of International Business Studies*, Vol. 11 (1980).

————, *International Production and the Multinational Enterprise* (London: Allen & Unwin, 1981).

————, "The Eclectic Paradigm of International Production: A Restatement and Some Possible Extensions," *Journal of International Business Studies*, Vol. 19 (Spring 1988).

————, and Alan M. Rugman, "The Influence of Hymer's Dissertation on the Theory of Foreign Direct Investment," *American Economic Review, Papers and Proceedings*, Vol. 75 (May 1985).

Errunza, Vihang R., and Lemma W. Senbet, "The Effects of International Operations on the Market Value of the Firm: Theory and Evidence," *Journal of Finance*, Vol. 36 (May 1981).

————, "International Corporate Diversification, Market Valuation, and Size-Adjusted Evidence," *Journal of Finance*, Vol. 39 (July 1984).

Fatehi-Sedeh, K., and M.H. Safizadeh, "Association Between Political Instability and Flow of Foreign Direct Investment," *Management International Review*, Vol. 29, No. 4 (1989).

Flowers, Edward B., "Oligopolistic Reactions in European and Canadian Investment in the United States," *Journal of International Business Studies*, Vol. 7 (Fall/Winter 1976).

Froot, Kenneth A., and Jeremy C. Stein, *Exchange Rates and Foreign Direct Investment: An Imperfect Capital Markets Approach*, NBER Working Paper No. 2914 (Cambridge, Massachusetts: National Bureau of Economic Research, March 1989).

Gersovitz, M., "The Effect of Domestic Taxes on Foreign Private Investment," in *The Theory of Taxation for Developing Countries*, ed. by David Newbery and Nicholas Stern (New York; Oxford: Oxford University Press, 1987).

Graham, Edward M., "Transatlantic Investment by Multinational Firms: A Rivalistic Phenomenon?" *Journal of Post Keynesian Economics*, Vol. 1 (Fall 1978).

————, and Paul R. Krugman, *Foreign Direct Investment in the United States* (Washington: Institute for International Economics, 1989).

Hartman, David G., "Tax Policy and Foreign Direct Investment in the United States," *National Tax Journal*, Vol. 37 (December 1984).

Hufbauer, G.C., "The Multinational Corporation and Direct Investment," in *International Trade and Finance: Frontiers for Research*, ed. by Peter B. Kenen (Cambridge, England: Cambridge University Press, 1975).

Hymer, S.H., "The International Operations of National Firms: A Study of Direct Foreign Investment," Ph.D. dissertation, 1960, Massachusetts Institute of Technology (Cambridge, MIT Press, 1976).

Jun, Joosung, *Tax Policy and International Direct Investment*, NBER Working Paper No. 3048 (Cambridge, Massachusetts: National Bureau of Economic Research, July 1989).

————, "U.S. Tax Policy and Direct Investment Abroad," in *Taxation in the Global Economy*, ed. by Assaf Razin and Joel Slemrod (Chicago; London: University of Chicago Press, 1990).

Knickerbocker, Frederick T., *Oligopolistic Reaction and Multinational Enterprise* (Boston: Division of Research, Harvard University Graduate School of Business Administration, 1973).

Kojima, Kiyoshi, "A Macroeconomic Approach to Foreign Direct Investment," *Hitotsubashi Journal of Economics*, Vol. 14 (June 1973).

————, "International Trade and Foreign Investment: Substitutes or Complements," *Hitotsubashi Journal of Economics*, Vol. 16 (June 1975).

————, "Japanese and American Direct Investment in Asia: A Comparative Analysis," *Hitotsubashi Journal of Economics*, Vol. 26 (June 1985).

————, and Terutomo Ozawa, "Micro- and Macroeconomic Models of Direct Foreign Investment: Toward a Synthesis," *Hitotsubashi Journal of Economics*, Vol. 25 (June 1984).

Lee, Chung H., "International Production of the United States and Japan in Korean Manufacturing Industries: A Comparative Study," *Weltwirtschaftliches Archiv*, Vol. 119, Heft 4 (1983).

————, "On Japanese Macroeconomic Theories of Direct Foreign Investment," *Economic Development and Cultural Change*, Vol. 32 (July 1984).

Lipsey, Robert E., *The Internationalization of Production*, NBER Working Paper No. 2923 (Cambridge, Massachusetts: National Bureau of Economic Research, April 1989).

Mason, R. Hal, "A Comment on Professor Kojima's 'Japanese Type versus American Type of Technology Transfer'," *Hitotsubashi Journal of Economics*, Vol. 20 (February 1980).

Nigh, Douglas, "The Effect of Political Events on United States Direct Foreign Investment: A Pooled Time-Series Cross-Sectional Analysis," *Journal of International Business Studies*, Vol. 16 (Spring 1985).

Organization for Economic Cooperation and Development, *Investment Incentives and Disincentives: Effects on International Direct Investment* (Paris, 1989).

Rugman, Alan M. "Internalization as a General Theory of Foreign Direct Investment: A Re-Appraisal of the Literature," *Weltwirtschaftliches Archiv*, Vol. 116, Heft 2 (1980).

————, "New Theories of the Multinational Enterprise: An Assessment of Internalization Theory," *Bulletin of Economic Research*, Vol. 38 (May 1986).

Schneider, Friedrich, and Bruno S. Frey, "Economic and Political Determinants of Foreign Direct Investment," *World Development*, Vol. 13 (February 1985).

Slemrod, Joel, "Tax Effects on Foreign Direct Investment in the U.S.: Evidence from a Cross-Country Comparison," NBER Working Paper No. 3042 (Cambridge, Massachusetts: National Bureau of Economic Research, July 1989).

Tallman, Stephen B., "Home Country Political Risk and Foreign Direct Investment in the United States," *Journal of International Business Studies*, Vol. 19 (Summer 1988).

Teece, D., "Multinational Enterprise, Internal Governance, and Industrial Organization," *American Economic Review, Papers and Proceedings*, Vol. 75 (May 1985).

Thomsen, Stephen E., "The Growth of American, British, and Japanese Direct Investment in the 1980s," Royal Institute of International Affairs, RIIA Discussion Papers, No. 2 (1989).

Vernon, Raymond, "International Investment and International Trade in the Product Cycle," *Quarterly Journal of Economics*, Vol. 80 (May 1966).

————, "The Product Cycle Hypothesis in a New International Environment," *Oxford Bulletin of Economics and Statistics*, Vol. 41 (November 1979).

Williamson, Oliver E., *Markets and Hierarchies, Analysis and Antitrust Implications: A Study in the Economics of Internal Organization* (New York: Free Press, 1975).

Young, Kan H., "Effects of Taxes and Rates of Return on Foreign Direct Investment in the United States," *National Tax Journal*, Vol. 41 (March 1988).

Yu, Chwo-Ming J., and Kiyohiko Ito, "Oligopolistic Reaction and Foreign Direct Investment: The Case of the U.S. Tire and Textiles Industries," *Journal of International Business Studies*, Vol. 19 (Fall 1988).

IV

Risk and Capital Flight in Developing Countries

Liliana Rojas-Suárez

Private capital flight from developing countries has been of concern to policymakers, especially since the emergence of the debt crisis and the associated drastic decline in capital inflows from industrialized countries. Capital flight has been viewed as a constraint on economic growth because it implies a loss of resources that could be used for domestic investment. Moreover, it is often argued that a reversal of these capital outflows could significantly contribute to the solution of the debt crisis, and thereby to renewed access by developing countries to international capital markets. These considerations have led the authorities to consider policies that encourage the repatriation of capital flight or at least to stop such outflows. However, identifying the policies that can be most effective in achieving these objectives depends crucially on what factors initiated the capital outflows in the first place.

This study reviews the factors that have been identified as stimulating capital flight from developing countries. In this analysis, capital flight is associated with the fraction of a country's stock of external claims that does not generate *recorded* investment income. Such external claims therefore do not generate a stream of income that can be used to service foreign debts or to finance domestic investment. Capital flight is thus distinguished from "normal" outflows of capital that would be undertaken to achieve portfolio diversification and that would yield a recorded flow of income. The analysis in this study suggests that increased risks in the domestic economic environment are likely to be key factors generating capital flight. In particular, two types of risk may have been particularly important: (1) default risk associated with the expropriation of domestic assets; and (2) the risk of large losses in the real value of domestic assets as a result of economic policies that lead to rapid inflation or to large exchange rate depreciations. Indeed, it is argued that the pattern of foreign capital inflows and capital flight from developing countries in the 1970s and 1980s can be associated with changing perceptions by domestic residents and foreign lenders of the risks of holding the domestic and external debt of indebted developing countries. While different perceptions of the risk of holding domestic assets can explain the simultaneous occurrence of large inflows of foreign capital and of large capital flight from developing countries during the 1970s and early 1980s, the emergence of the debt crisis and the accompanying policy responses reduced such differences and resulted in a decline of foreign capital inflows coupled with a continuation of capital flight.

This study first provides estimates of capital flight for a group of developing countries with recent debt-servicing problems, and then discusses the determinants of capital flight and examines measures of the risk of default associated with holding domestic financial instruments. It considers alternative policies for reducing capital flight, and finally the main conclusions are summarized.

Estimation of Capital Flight

Previous empirical studies have employed a broad range of definitions of capital flight. Some authors[1] have adopted a "narrow" approach that identifies capital flight with short-term speculative capital outflows. Others[2] have adopted a "broad" definition that identifies capital flight with total private capital outflows. An alternative approach based on a "derived measure" identifies capital flight with the fraction of a country's stock of external claims that does not yield recorded investment income.[3] This latter definition implies that a capital outflow should be considered capital flight only if it limits the resources available for either servicing the country's external debt or financing development programs. Numerous studies have compared and critically evaluated these alternative

---

[1]See Cuddington (1986).
[2]See, for example, World Bank (1985), Morgan Guaranty Trust Company (1986), and Duwendag (1987).
[3]See Dooley (1986).

measures,[4] and no general agreement has been reached on the relative superiority of each.[5] This study uses the "derived" measure to provide updated estimates of capital flight in developing countries that have faced debt-servicing problems, since this measure provides the most direct estimate of the economy's loss of resources that could potentially be used for domestic investment.

Empirical estimates suggest that during 1978–88 the stock of flight capital increased for a group of developing countries that had faced debt-servicing problems (see Table 1).[6] The aggregate stock of

capital flight for this group of countries, which amounted to $47 billion at the end of 1978, increased continuously during the period and reached $184 billion at the end of 1988 (Table 1).[7]

Although the stock of capital flight showed a sustained increase over the period, the rate of change of capital flight did not follow a stable pattern. As is further discussed below, expansionary fiscal and monetary policies coupled with an increasing overvaluation of the exchange rate resulted in high rates of increase in the stock of capital flight during the period 1978–83.[8] The adoption of stabilization programs in some of these countries reduced somewhat the rate of increase of capital flight during 1984–86, particularly in some Latin American countries which undertook comprehensive adjustment programs in 1985 and 1986. These programs, which included strong contractions of the fiscal deficits and major devaluations of the exchange rate, resulted in

---

[4]See, for example, Deppler and Williamson (1987), Gordon and Levine (1989), and Cumby and Levich (1987).

[5]Perhaps the most severe criticism of *all* the proposed measurements is contained in Gordon and Levine (1989). They argue that severe statistical problems prevent the proposed measurements from adequately capturing the scale of capital flight.

[6]The methodology for estimating capital flight involves computing the stock of external claims that would generate the income recorded in the balance of payments statistics and subtracting this stock from an estimate of total external claims (see Dooley (1986)). Total external claims are estimated by adding the cumulative capital outflows, or increases in gross claims, from balance of payments data (which consist of the cumulative outflows of capital recorded in the balance of payments plus the cumulated stock of errors and omissions) to an estimate of the unrecorded component of external claims. This last estimate is

generated by subtracting the stock of external debt implied by the flows reported in the balance of payments from the stock of external debt reported by the World Bank.

[7]The countries included in this group and in Tables 1 and 2 are Argentina, Bolivia, Chile, Colombia, Ecuador, Gabon, Jamaica, Mexico, Nigeria, Peru, the Philippines, Venezuela, and Yugoslavia.

[8]In fact, for this group of countries, the rate of increase in the stock of capital flight reached 24 percent in 1983.

Table 1. Capital Flight in Ratio to Total External Debt and Total External Claims for a Group of Highly Indebted Developing Countries
(In billions of U.S. dollars)

	Capital Flight[1] (1)	External Debt (2)	Ratio of Capital Flight to Total External Debt (1) ÷ (2)	External Claims[2] (3)	Ratio of Capital Flight to Total External Claims (1) ÷ (3)
1978	47.30	113.70	0.42	71.62	0.66
1979	64.14	141.76	0.45	92.17	0.70
1980	75.41	179.06	0.42	119.41	0.63
1981	85.16	224.26	0.38	134.16	0.63
1982	99.95	261.30	0.38	142.57	0.70
1983	123.77	285.70	0.43	164.13	0.75
1984	136.43	301.05	0.45	182.52	0.75
1985	147.54	311.60	0.47	199.70	0.74
1986	152.67	326.39	0.47	210.30	0.73
1987	180.62	349.75	0.52	233.73	0.77
1988	184.01	360.43	0.51	239.14	0.77

Sources: World Bank, *World Debt Tables*, various issues; International Monetary Fund, *Balance of Payments Yearbook*, various issues; and IMF staff estimates.

[1]Data refer to *net* capital flight, that is, the unrecorded stock of capital outflows less the unrecorded stock of capital inflows. For methodology used, see fn. 6 in text.

[2]The stock of external claims is defined as the net stock of recorded claims on nonresidents other than direct investment plus the net stock on unrecorded claims of residents.

a sharp decline in the rate of growth of capital flight, which reached only 3 percent during 1986.

However, many of these programs were abandoned in 1987; fiscal deficits expanded once more, and inflation accelerated. As a result, the rate of growth of capital flight increased again and reached 18 percent during 1987. It decelerated in 1988 as some major countries initiated new adjustment programs.

It has been argued that given the magnitude of capital flight, repatriation of those capital outflows, or at least of the investment income that they generate, could significantly contribute to solving the external debt problems faced by these countries. A better understanding of the importance of capital flight relative to the countries' external financial positions can be gained by analyzing the ratios of capital flight to total external debt and total external claims (Table 1).

During 1978–82, the ratio of capital flight to total external debt declined from 42 percent in 1978 to 38 percent in 1982, as the large inflows of foreign capital to this group of developing countries more than offset the increase in capital flight. This trend reversed during 1983–88, as the ratio of capital flight to total external debt increased from 43 percent in 1983 to 51 percent in 1988. This increase was the result of both a continuous increase in the stock of capital flight and a reduction in the amount of new private foreign lending available to developing countries.

The ratio of the stock of capital flight to total external claims increased from 66 percent in 1978 to 70 percent in 1982, consistent with the acceleration of capital flight during this period. Except for some temporary declines in 1985 and 1986, when comprehensive adjustment programs were successful in reducing the rate of expansion of capital flight, the ratio of capital flight to total external claims continued to increase during 1983–88, reaching 77 percent in 1988.

Despite the size of these estimates of the private holdings of external assets, it has been argued that this capital flight will have a highly adverse effect on an economy only if it generates a substantial transfer of real resources.[9] For example, in periods when capital flight was offset by an inflow of foreign loans, the proceeds from exports and other external inflows were still used to finance imports, and therefore the impact of capital flight on growth was not necessarily severe. However, when access to external credit became limited after the emergence of the debt crisis in 1982, greater capital flight had to be "financed" either through a reduc-

---

[9]See, for example, Deppler and Williamson (1987).

Table 2. External Debt and Resource Transfer as Financing Components of Capital Flight for a Group of Highly Indebted Developing Countries, 1979–88

(In billions of U.S. dollars—annual averages)

	Change in Stock of Capital Flight	Change in Total External Debt	Resource Balance[1]
1979–82	13.16	36.90	–4.50
1983–85	15.86	16.77	25.50
1986–88	12.16	16.28	11.90

Sources: World Bank, *World Debt Tables*, Appendix I, various issues; International Monetary Fund, *Balance of Payments Yearbook*, various issues; and IMF staff estimates.

[1]Defined as net exports of goods and nonfactor services.

tion in the country's stock of international reserves or through an increase in net exports, thereby reducing the resources available to sustain economic growth. Data available support this hypothesis. During 1979–82, for example, a large inflow of foreign private capital to the indebted developing countries occurred, and their total external debt rose faster than the estimated stock of flight capital (Table 2). As a result, the aggregate for this group of countries showed a negative resource balance, implying that at least some of the external inflows were used to finance imports.[10] This picture changed drastically after 1982: although the total external debt of these countries continued to increase (primarily because of inflows of official funds), capital flight resulted in net transfers of resources in most of the countries. This result implies that the continuation of capital flight after 1982 coupled with the deceleration of external loans led to a net decline in imports, which imposed an important constraint on growth.[11]

---

[10]Important exceptions are Argentina and Venezuela. Rodriguez (1987) argued that in Venezuela the increase in external debt nearly matched the increase in the stock of flight capital.

[11]Although the resource balance for most of these countries became positive after 1982, they experienced current account deficits in part because of interest payments on their external debt.

Table 3. Capital Importing Developing Countries with Recent Debt-Servicing Problems: Macroeconomic Variables Affecting Capital Flight as Suggested in Literature, 1978–88

	1978	1979	1980	1981	1982	1983	1984	1985	1986	1987	1988
Inflation rate[1]	28.26	31.54	35.94	41.80	46.51	64.93	80.35	83.16	61.05	85.66	163.91
Real GDP growth[1]	3.85	5.31	3.80	–0.98	0.14	–1.79	2.59	3.32	3.48	2.39	1.71
Central government fiscal deficits[2] (in percent of GDP)	2.03	1.14	2.25	4.94	4.43	3.90	3.06	2.50	3.86	4.50	3.89
Real effective exchange rate[2] (1980 = 100)	81.80	89.25	100.00	107.87	94.20	86.78	93.66	90.76	67.48	55.26	56.14
Total of current account[1] balances (in billions of U.S. dollars)	–29.62	–23.38	–27.93	–82.26	–83.28	–31.76	–15.50	–10.96	–33.38	–15.99	–18.28
Disbursements of foreign loans as ratio to foreign debt[2]	26.48	28.40	21.93	23.49	17.45	11.93	8.06	7.24	7.68	6.80	6.63
Domestic real interest rate[2]	–4.57	–7.32	–15.52	–22.97	–24.08	–15.47	21.17	26.24	–27.96	–16.00	26.53
Interest rate differential in favor of foreign assets[2,3]	–3.09	0.23	13.53	32.93	27.99	12.37	8.48	2.31	20.61	5.26	8.41

Sources: International Monetary Fund, *International Financial Statistics*, and *World Economic Outlook*.
[1] Countries included are those classified, for purposes of the World Economic Outlook, as capital importing developing countries with recent debt-servicing problems.
[2] For countries included, see footnote 7 in the text.
[3] Defined as the six-month U.S. Treasury bill rate adjusted for the observed exchange rate change minus the domestic deposit rate.

Risk and Capital Flight

The recent literature explaining the causes of capital flight can, in general, be divided into two groups. The first (see, for example, Cuddington (1987), Dornbusch (1985), and Duwendag (1987)) has typically based its analysis on standard portfolio models where agents are assumed to allocate their wealth to maximize the overall risk-adjusted return on their portfolios. In this context, capital flight has been explained in terms of the effects of domestic macroeconomic variables on the relative returns between domestic and foreign assets. Since domestic interest rates in a number of the indebted developing countries that experienced capital flight were subject to controls,[12] an overvaluation of the exchange rate, rapid inflation, and inconsistent and unsustainable fiscal and monetary policies have been identified as the major causes of capital flight. For example, if expansionary monetary and fiscal policies created an overvalued exchange rate, domestic agents would expect devaluation of the exchange rate to occur eventually, leading them to shift out of domestic assets into foreign assets. Moreover, a large fiscal deficit financed by monetary creation would create both inflation and incentives for capital flight as agents attempted to prevent losses in the real value of their domestic asset holdings.

Econometric studies relating capital flight to the macroeconomic variables, which have been suggested by the first group as being responsible for capital flight, have yielded divergent results.[13] For instance, Cuddington (1986) found that currency

[12] In recent years, several countries, including Mexico and Bolivia, have undertaken financial liberalization.

[13] Table 3 summarizes the behavior of some of these variables during 1978–88.

overvaluation (measured as the deviation of the actual real exchange rate from its equilibrium level) was a significant variable explaining capital flight in Argentina, Mexico, Uruguay, and Venezuela during 1974–84, while Meyer and Bastos-Márques (1989) concluded that the inflation rate and the real return on domestic assets were the major determinants of capital flight in Brazil during 1971–88. However, one "identification" problem in these studies is that macroeconomic policies are likely to influence both "normal" capital outflows and capital flight. In addition, while this approach can basically explain the outflows of capital from developing countries, it cannot explain the simultaneous occurrence of capital flight and the increased inflow of foreign loans during the 1970s and early 1980s.

A second approach has taken the view that the residents and nonresidents of indebted developing countries have at times had differing views on the perceived risks of holding the domestic and external financial instruments of the indebted developing countries. In particular, such differences in perceived risks have been regarded as explaining the simultaneous decision of domestic agents to finance investment with foreign borrowing and to hold their wealth in the form of foreign assets. As pointed out by Lessard and Williamson (1987), while the portfolio-based approach concentrates on risk and return differences between domestic and foreign assets that can be held by domestic residents, the "risk differential" approach emphasizes the differences in the perceived risks to residents and nonresidents of holding capital in a developing country. While both approaches emphasize domestic policies as a major factor influencing capital flight, the risk differential approach also emphasizes the role of rigidities in the legal and institutional frameworks of developing countries as a channel through which adverse shocks to the economy will result in capital flight.

Several empirical studies have found considerable support for this risk differential hypothesis. For example, Khan and Haque (1985) argued that the perceived risks of investment in developing countries were larger than those of investment in industrial countries because of the "expropriation" risk. This expropriation risk reflected institutional and legal arrangements for protecting private property that were weaker in developing countries than in industrial countries. Facing this expropriation risk, domestic residents prefer to hold their assets abroad (where they earn a more secure rate of return) and to borrow external funds to finance domestic investment. With this strategy, domestic agents make their portfolios less accessible to taxation or expropriation. Eaton (1987) extended the

Khan-Haque hypothesis of capital flight by linking the risk of expropriation (which in his model is identified with high taxation) of domestically owned assets to the existence of public and publicly guaranteed private foreign debt. Eaton argued that as the stock of publicly guaranteed private foreign debt increases, the emergence of any factors that increase the probability of a private borrower defaulting would also lead other residents to expect higher future taxes as the government assumed the obligations of the insolvent borrower. Domestic residents would therefore have an incentive to place their funds abroad.

The role of fiscal rigidities in creating risks was emphasized by Ize and Ortiz (1987), who examined capital flight using a fiscal framework where domestic government debt was perceived as "junior" relative to external government debt. They argued that fiscal rigidities prevent governments in developing countries from adjusting quickly to shocks that reduce their debt-servicing capacity. As a result, a major economic shock could increase the perceived risk that the government would be unable to service its obligations fully. Moreover, in this situation, the risk that the authorities would not fully service their domestic debt would generally be perceived to be higher than the corresponding risk of servicing foreign obligations because the cost of a default on foreign obligations (which could lead to a reduction in trade credits) would be higher. These differences in perceived risks stimulate capital flight by reducing the risk-adjusted return on domestic debt,[14] and can explain the joint occurrence of increasing external debt and capital flight in developing countries during the late 1970s and early 1980s.

As the previous section has shown, capital flight continued to be a feature of developing countries during the rest of the 1980s, but since 1982 it has been accompanied by a drastic reduction in the inflow of new private external credit available to these countries. This study advances an hypothesis that aims to explain the recent joint behavior of capital flight and foreign lending.

It has been argued that the difficulties of dealing with structural fiscal deficits and rising inflation, as

---

[14]In contrast, Diwan (1989) argued that there are circumstances when domestic borrowers would prefer to default on foreign debt. For example, a sharp decline in the price of exports would reduce the cost of defaulting on foreign debt because the penalty associated with such a default (exclusion from foreign trade) would fall as export prices declined. As a result, domestic residents would prefer to finance domestic investment in the export goods sector with foreign (as opposed to domestic) loans. Moreover, given the total volume of savings, the availability of additional foreign resources would just crowd out the domestic component of total savings, leading to capital flight.

well as the limited access of many indebted developing countries to international capital markets, have reduced the costs of not fully servicing foreign obligations relative to the corresponding costs of not servicing domestic obligations.[15] The increase in the perceived probability of default on foreign debt has been viewed as being reflected in the decline of the secondary market price for external bank debt issued by many heavily indebted developing countries. As the perceived difference of default risk between domestic and external debt declined, domestic debt would no longer be considered junior relative to external debt.[16]

Although differences in perceived risk between domestic and external debt declined after 1982, the *total* default risk of holding debt (either domestic or external) issued by these countries has increased as a result of the adverse developments and policies affecting the capacity of these countries to service their debt. Therefore, the continuation of capital flight coupled with the decline in foreign lending after 1982 can be explained by a "generalized" perception of an increase in the default risk of holding debt issued by these countries. If this increase in risk perception has occurred, the lack of external creditworthiness (that prevents countries from borrowing in the international capital markets) and the continuation of capital flight are both reflections of the same fundamental phenomena.[17] As a result, policies oriented toward improving the attractiveness of holding domestic financial instruments of indebted developing countries would also help restore creditworthiness.

If the perceived differences in the default risk of holding domestic and external debt have been practically eliminated, then the default risk of holding external debt would be a good proxy for the corresponding risk on domestic debt. This hypothesis suggests, therefore, that the level of capital flight since the emergence of the debt crisis should be positively related to increases in the probability of default on external debt. If heavily indebted developing countries still had normal access to international capital markets, the spread between their borrowing costs and the London interbank offer rate (LIBOR) could potentially provide a measure

of default risk. However, since the emergence of the debt crisis little or no spontaneous lending to these countries has taken place and therefore no representative interest rates exist. An alternative measure of the default risk can nonetheless be obtained from the secondary market price of external debt by subtracting the LIBOR rate from the implicit yield evident in the international secondary market price for external debt.[18]

Owing to the lack of data, it is not possible to use regression analysis to test directly the hypothesis that capital flight has responded positively to increases in the default risk on external obligations since the emergence of the debt crisis. However, for those countries for which sufficient data were available to estimate default risk, the correlation between capital flight and default risk on external debt is positive and very high (Table 4).[19]

Policies to Prevent or Reverse Capital Flight

Macroeconomic and Structural Policies

As already noted, many analyses of capital flight have emphasized the role of expansionary monetary and fiscal policies and institutional and legal

---

[15]For example, see Diwan (1989).

[16]Some have even argued that domestic debt should now be considered "senior" relative to external debt. This argument is intended to rationalize the simultaneous decline in private external lending and the continuous increase in domestic debt.

Although the differences in the perceived default risks of domestic and external debt have been reduced, the risks of a loss in the real value of domestic assets as a result of a discrete devaluation or an increase in inflation still remain a concern for holders of domestic debt.

[17]Gajdeczka and Oks (1990) attribute capital flight after 1986 to the loss of creditworthiness of these countries.

[18]The implicit yield to maturity for external debt (i^s) was obtained from the observed secondary market price on the country's external debt (P) and the application of the following present value formula:

$$P = \sum_{k=1}^{n} \frac{C}{(1+i^s)^k} + \frac{FV}{(1+i^s)^n},$$

where the face value (FV) is set at 100 since the discount quoted in the secondary markets applies to $100 worth of contractual debt; the contractual coupon payment (C) is the interest rate on six-month U.S. Treasury bills (as a measure of the risk-free interest rate) plus the average interest rate spread agreed to by the country on signature of the contract; and n is the average maturity of the contract.

The risk of default on external obligations during 1985–88 was estimated by subtracting the six-month LIBOR rate from the calculated implicit yield on external debt.

The risk of default on external obligations during 1982–84 was approximated by using data on spreads between the loan rates charged to indebted developing countries on external bank loans and LIBOR provided by the Deutsche Bundesbank (spreads between public sector deutsche mark bonds issued by nonresidents and LIBOR) and the Bank of England.

Notice, however, that the implicit yield evident in the international secondary market price for external debt cannot fully represent the cost of borrowing, since it is derived under conditions of credit rationing.

[19]However, as mentioned above, the lack of international creditworthiness and the continuation of capital flight appear to be two aspects of the same problem. Therefore, the risk of default on external debt is also an endogenous variable that should be simultaneously explained with the behavior of capital flight.

Table 4. Selected Highly Indebted Developing Countries Facing Debt-Service Problems: Correlation Between Capital Flight and Default Risk[1]

Country	Correlation
Argentina	0.640
Brazil[2]	0.826
Chile	0.044
Colombia	0.892
Ecuador	0.718
Jamaica	0.824
Mexico	0.821
Nigeria	0.992
Peru	0.954
Philippines	0.604
Venezuela	0.067
Yugoslavia	0.960

Sources: Salomon Brothers, New York; Data Resources, Inc.; and Deutsche Bundesbank.

[1] Countries shown are those for which the default risk could be calculated during 1982–88.

[2] Data correspond to 1982–87.

arrangements as key factors increasing the risks of holding domestic assets. Sound macroeconomic policies and appropriate structural reforms are thus likely to be important elements in solving the problem of capital flight. In many countries, a sustained reduction of the fiscal deficit is typically an important first step in reducing the perceived risks of holding domestic debt. Large fiscal deficits financed with nonindexed domestic debt are likely to generate the expectation that the government will eventually use the inflation tax and/or a devaluation of the currency to reduce the outstanding real value of the debt.[20]

The consistency of exchange rate, monetary, and fiscal policies is another crucial element in stemming capital flight. While many countries have used a fixed exchange rate to provide an anchor for the domestic price level, problems have at times arisen when adverse shocks suddenly lead to a sharp fall in the stock of international reserves and thereby create the expectation of a devaluation and of possible abandonment of the adjustment program. Such expectations, which can lead to increasing capital flight and additional losses of reserves, arise

because of rigidities that inhibit the government's ability to adjust quickly to adverse shocks. In particular, rigidities induced by wage indexation schemes, minimum wages, laws preventing layoffs, controls on the prices of public goods, and inefficient tax systems often prevent a government from adjusting its fiscal deficit quickly to offset the impact of an adverse shock.

The role of appropriate structural and macroeconomic policies in reducing (and reversing) capital flight is evident from the recent experience of several Latin American countries. The stock of flight capital in Argentina declined in 1986 (implying repatriation) following the adoption in June 1985 of a comprehensive adjustment program that was initially successful in reducing inflation and in fostering an economic recovery. However, sustained fiscal deficits led to renewed inflation, and capital flight apparently accelerated again. In Brazil, the introduction of the Cruzado plan in early 1986 was also followed by a decline in the net outflow of capital. However, inflation accelerated in 1987 and estimated capital flight increased sharply during that year. In December 1987, the Mexican authorities introduced a comprehensive economic program based on a social pact with labor and business that encompassed front-loaded fiscal and monetary corrections as well as a strong devaluation of the Mexican peso. As a result of the successful implementation of this program, empirical estimates suggest that Mexico experienced a net repatriation of capital flight in 1988, the first in the 1980s.

Many countries have also used a variety of other policies to stem or reverse capital flight. The effectiveness of these policies is now examined in terms of recent country experiences of implementing such policies.[21]

Capital Controls

It has often been argued that externalities and policy distortions imply that the social rate of return on domestic investment in developing countries is higher than the private rate of return. As a result, capital controls have been viewed as a means of ensuring that domestic savings are invested domestically. As noted in Gordon and Levine (1989), however, a fundamental problem with this argument is that it assumes that capital not invested abroad would be invested domestically; it therefore ignores the possible substitution between savings and consumption. In particular, the announcement of capital controls might bring

---

[20] For further discussion of these issues see Calvo (1988).

[21] The experiences reported here are largely based on previous studies undertaken by the staff of the International Monetary Fund.

expectations of further government intervention that would discourage domestic investment in favor of increased consumption. In addition, savings may be held in various inflation "hedges" (such as real estate or inventories) that have little impact on productive capacity.

Although capital controls are ineffective in promoting domestic investment, the experiences of some countries suggest that such controls have had a short-run effect on capital flight. For example, Brazil experienced a much lower ratio of capital flight to total external debt than Mexico although Brazil's average inflation rate during the late 1970s and early 1980s was higher than Mexico's. This could potentially reflect the more restrictive capital controls in Brazil. However, when capital controls are effective in stemming capital flight in the short run, the removal of such controls can be accompanied by large-scale capital flight, especially when expansionary macroeconomic policies lead to rising inflation and expectations of devaluation. As documented by Cuddington (1986), Argentina is a good example of sharp increases in capital flight following the removal of capital controls, which in turn increased the Government's incentive to reimpose them.

Overall, experience suggests that although capital controls have sometimes helped in the short run to stem capital flight, the problems associated with them may be larger than the benefits. As capital controls by themselves constitute a distortion, they may lower domestic savings because domestic residents have been constrained to hold less diversified portfolios. Moreover, when capital controls are perceived as a policy instrument used on a discretionary basis, expectations that such controls will be imposed encourage capital flight. In the long run, therefore, they may decrease the real resources available for investment.

Debt-Equity Swaps

Debt-equity swaps can be attractive to investors because assets can be purchased in the debtor countries with external claims on those countries purchased at a discount in the secondary market. While this mechanism has sometimes been effective in reversing capital flight, its ability to increase *net* capital inflows may be limited for two reasons. First, the profitability of debt-equity swaps depends on the discount in the secondary market; and, if this market is very thin, increases in the demand for claims on debtor countries would raise the prices of those claims and reduce the profitability of debt-equity swaps. In this situation, only a limited amount of swaps could be undertaken. Moreover, even if commercial banks were willing to sell

additional claims on debtor countries at a discount, the net inflow of funds to the countries would not necessarily increase significantly, since foreign commercial banks would still have no incentive to engage in additional voluntary loans.

Second, since some debt-equity swap schemes have involved reselling discounted paper for domestic currency at preannounced exchange rates, the money supply can increase as the swap occurs, thereby generating inflationary pressures. If more rapid inflation occurred, it would increase the risks of holding domestic assets and encourage additional capital flight, which might offset the initial inflow originated by the debt-equity swap. The Mexican debt-equity swap program initiated in May 1986 was suspended in late 1987 in part because the authorities wanted to limit the monetary expansion produced by these operations. In contrast, the Chilean program, introduced in 1985, allowed domestic residents to convert external claims on Chile into tradable domestic bonds, and this effectively sterilized the monetary impact of these operations.[22] These experiences suggest that one of the key factors determining whether debt-equity swaps can be successful in repatriating capital flight is whether they are conducted in the context of an appropriate monetary policy.

Foreign Currency Deposits

Local deposits denominated in foreign currencies have been used as a mechanism to prevent capital flight in several countries (India, Mexico, Uruguay, and Turkey).[23] While offering depositors some potential protection from exchange risk, they will not be viewed as carrying much lower risk than other domestic deposits if the authorities have in the past frozen or limited withdrawals or returns on these deposits. The freezing of the dollar-denominated accounts in Mexico in 1982 provides an example of such risk.[24] However, these accounts, as well as some other financial instruments indexed to foreign exchange, may usefully contribute to stemming capital flight when the government is pursuing appropriate macroeconomic and struc-

---

[22]Even if those operations can be made noninflationary, subsidized swap arrangements, such as those in Chile in 1983–84, can generate large operating deficits in the central bank.

[23]As reported in previous studies undertaken by the staff of the International Monetary Fund, in Turkey the Dresdner Bank collected deposits from Turkish workers in Germany and transferred these deposits to the Central Bank of Turkey where they were kept as foreign currency deposits. As a result, workers' remittances rose sharply and the stock of these foreign currency deposits reached $5.9 billion by the end of 1988.

[24]During this freeze, withdrawals from dollar-denominated accounts were paid in Mexican pesos using the controlled exchange rate.

tural policies but faces a credibility problem.[25] If successful in eliminating exchange rate risk, indexed assets may stimulate domestic saving and contribute to lower domestic real interest rates and, thereby, lower the government's costs of financing its domestic debt. However, while foreign currency-denominated deposits can potentially help stem capital flight with good policies, they can create additional difficulties when policies are inadequate. Rising inflation can lead to a rapid shift from deposits denominated in the domestic currency to those denominated in foreign currencies, thereby destabilizing domestic monetary relationships.

In Peru, for example, accelerating inflation and balance of payments deficits during the early 1980s led domestic residents to increase their holdings of bank deposits denominated in dollars, and by the end of 1984 these deposits, which amounted to $1.7 billion, were equivalent to more than 50 percent of broad money. Convertibility of these deposits into foreign currency was suspended in 1985.

Other Policies

Several other policies have been suggested to encourage the repatriation of flight capital. For example, tax treaties that would allow countries to tax assets held abroad by domestic residents were considered one alternative.[26] However, as noted by Gordon and Levine (1989), it may be difficult to enforce such treaties unless they are implemented globally.[27] Tax amnesty programs have also been used,[28] but expectations of future tax amnesties might reduce the normal collection of taxes and might, paradoxically, motivate increases in capital flight at times when amnesties are not in place.

Another policy has been to tighten domestic credit to generate liquidity shortages sufficient to induce some liquidation of foreign asset holdings for financing domestic investments or firms' working capital needs. However, repeated liquidity shortages might decrease the expected returns from domestic investments and might instead induce greater capital flight.

Conclusions

Capital flight implies a loss of resources that could have been used to increase domestic invest-

ment and that could in turn have significantly increased countries' debt-servicing capacity. This study has argued that two forms of risk have been major causes of capital flight: the risk of direct default or repudiation associated with the fear of expropriation of domestic assets and the risk of large losses in the real value of domestic assets arising from inflation or large exchange rate devaluations. Moreover, the simultaneous occurrence of large inflows of foreign capital and large capital flight from developing countries during the 1970s and early 1980s reflected the different perceptions of foreign lenders and domestic residents of developing countries about the risks of holding domestic claims. In particular, for a variety of institutional reasons, foreign lenders perceived a lower default risk than did domestic residents. However, since the emergence of the debt crisis in 1982 the differences in perceived risks have been reduced and have resulted in a decline of foreign capital inflows coupled with continuation of capital flight.

Indeed, the adverse developments that accompanied the emergence of the debt crisis may have increased the perceived default risk of holding either the domestic or external debt of highly indebted developing countries. If this is true, the continuation of capital flight in the mid- and late 1980s, coupled with the decline in private foreign lending, can be explained by a generalized perception of an increase in the default risk of holding debt issued by highly indebted developing countries.

If concerns about default risks have played a major role in the portfolio decisions of the domestic residents of heavily indebted developing countries, the policies with the greatest chance of stemming capital flight are those that decrease the risks of holding domestic assets. In this situation, sound macroeconomic policies complemented by appropriate structural reforms would have to be key elements in stemming or reversing capital flight.

Once these core macroeconomic and structural policies are in place, other policies such as debt-equity swaps or foreign currency deposits—although insufficient by themselves to solve the problem of capital flight—can potentially contribute to reducing it. Capital controls are likely to be at best a short-run deterrent to capital flight and, by introducing additional distortions, could even accentuate the problem in the long run.

---

[25]For a further elaboration on these issues, see Calvo and Guidotti (1990).

[26]From 1967 to 1981, Brazil was negotiating a treaty with the United States, but no final agreement took place.

[27]Moreover, if those treaties involve a symmetric treatment of taxes between countries, the total tax base of the domestic country may be reduced if holdings of domestic assets by foreigners are excluded from the tax base.

[28]In 1986 Colombia introduced a tax amnesty on previously undeclared income and wealth.

References

Calvo, Guillermo, "Controlling Inflation: The Problem of Non-Indexed Debt," IMF Working Paper No. 88/29 (Washington: International Monetary Fund, March 1988).

————, and Pablo E. Guidotti, "Indexation and Maturity of Government Bonds: An Exploratory Model," in *Public Debt Management: Theory and History,* ed. by Rudiger Dornbusch and Mario Draghi (Cambridge; New York: Cambridge University Press, 1990).

Cuddington, John T., *Capital Flight: Estimates, Issues, and Explanations,* Princeton Studies in International Finance, No. 58 (Princeton, New Jersey: International Finance Section, Princeton University, 1986).

————, "Macroeconomic Determinants of Capital Flight: An Econometric Investigation," in *Capital Flight and Third World Debt,* ed. by Donald R. Lessard and John Williamson (Washington: Institute for International Economics, 1987).

Cumby, Robert, and Richard Levich, "On the Definition and Magnitude of Recent Capital Flight," in *Capital Flight and Third World Debt,* ed. by Donald R. Lessard and John Williamson (Washington: . Institute for International Economics, 1987).

Deppler, Michael, and Martin Williamson, "Capital Flight: Concepts, Measurement, and Issues," in *Staff Studies for the World Economic Outlook,* By the Research Department of the International Monetary Fund (Washington: International Monetary Fund, August 1987).

Diwan, Ishac, "Foreign Debt, Crowding Out and Capital Flight," *Journal of International Money and Finance,* Vol. 8 (March 1989).

Dooley, Michael, "Country-Specific Risk Premiums, Capital Flight and Net Investment Income Payments in Selected Developing Countries" (Washington: International Monetary Fund; unpublished, March 1986).

Dornbusch, Rudiger, "External Debt, Budget Deficits, and Disequilibrium Exchange Rates," in *International Debt and the Developing Countries,* ed. by Gordon W. Smith and John T. Cuddington (Washington: World Bank, 1985).

Duwendag, Dieter, "Capital Flight from Developing Countries: Estimates and Determinants for 25 Major Borrowers," Société Universitaire Européenne de Recherches Financières, SUERF Series No. 52A, 1987.

Eaton, Jonathan, "Public Debt Guarantees and Private Capital Flight," NBER Working Paper No. 2172 (National Bureau of Economic Research, March 1987).

Gajdeczka, P., and Daniel Oks, "Domestic Deficits, Debt Overhang, and Capital Outflows in Developing Countries," *AMEX Bank Review,* annual series entitled *Finance and the International Economy: 3* (1990).

Gordon, David B., and Ross Levine, "The 'Problem' of Capital Flight: A Cautionary Note," *World Economy,* Vol. 12 (June 1989).

International Monetary Fund, *Balance of Payments Statistics Yearbook* (Washington: International Monetary Fund), various issues.

————, *International Financial Statistics Yearbook* (Washington: International Monetary Fund), various issues.

————, *World Economic Outlook* (Washington: International Monetary Fund, May 1990).

Ize, Alain, and Guillermo Ortiz, "Fiscal Rigidities, Public Debt and Capital Flight," *Staff Papers,* International Monetary Fund, Vol. 34 (June 1987).

Khan, Mohsin S., and Nadeem Ul Haque, "Foreign Borrowing and Capital Flight: A Formal Analysis," *Staff Papers,* International Monetary Fund, Vol. 32 (December 1985).

Lessard, Donald R., and Williamson, John, "The Problem and Policy Responses," in *Capital Flight and Third World Debt,* ed. by Donald R. Lessard and John Williamson (Washington: Institute for International Economics, 1987).

Meyer A., and M.S. Bastos-Márques, "A Fuga de Capital no Brasil," Fundaçao Getulio Vargas, Instituto Brasileiro de Economia, Centro de Estudios Monetarios e de Economia Internacional, No. 06/89 (August 1989).

Morgan Guaranty Trust Company, "LDC Capital Flight," *World Financial Markets* (March 1986).

Rodriguez, Miguel A., "Consequences of Capital Flight for Latin American Debtor Countries," in *Capital Flight and Third World Debt,* ed. by Donald R. Lessard and John Williamson (Washington: Institute for International Economics, 1987).

World Bank, *World Development Report* (New York: Oxford University Press, 1985).

Occasional Papers of the International Monetary Fund

77. Determinants and Systemic Consequences of International Capital Flows: A Study by the Research Department of the International Monetary Fund. 1991.

76. China: Economic Reform and Macroeconomic Management, by Mario Blejer, David Burton, Steven Dunaway, and Gyorgy Szapary. 1991.

75. German Unification: Economic Issues, edited by Leslie Lipschitz and Donogh McDonald. 1990.

74. The Impact of the European Community's Internal Market on the EFTA, by Richard K. Abrams, Peter K. Cornelius, Per L. Hedfors, and Gunnar Tersman. 1990.

73. The European Monetary System: Developments and Perspectives, by Horst Ungerer, Jouko J. Hauvonen, Augusto Lopez-Claros, and Thomas Mayer. 1990.

72. The Czech and Slovak Federal Republic: An Economy in Transition, by Jim Prust and an IMF Staff Team. 1990.

71. MULTIMOD Mark II: A Revised and Extended Model, by Paul Masson, Steven Symansky, and Guy Meredith. 1990.

70. The Conduct of Monetary Policy in the Major Industrial Countries: Instruments and Operating Procedures, by Dallas S. Batten, Michael P. Blackwell, In-Su Kim, Simon E. Nocera, and Yuzuru Ozeki. 1990.

69. International Comparisons of Government Expenditure Revisited: The Developing Countries, 1975–86, by Peter S. Heller and Jack Diamond. 1990.

68. Debt Reduction and Economic Activity, by Michael P. Dooley, David Folkerts-Landau, Richard D. Haas, Steven A. Symansky, and Ralph W. Tryon. 1990.

67. The Role of National Saving in the World Economy: Recent Trends and Prospects, by Bijan B. Aghevli, James M. Boughton, Peter J. Montiel, Delano Villanueva, and Geoffrey Woglom. 1990.

66. The European Monetary System in the Context of the Integration of European Financial Markets, by David Folkerts-Landau and Donald J. Mathieson. 1989.

65. Managing Financial Risks in Indebted Developing Countries, by Donald J. Mathieson, David Folkerts-Landau, Timothy Lane, and Iqbal Zaidi. 1989.

64. The Federal Republic of Germany: Adjustment in a Surplus Country, by Leslie Lipschitz, Jeroen Kremers, Thomas Mayer, and Donogh McDonald. 1989.

63. Issues and Developments in International Trade Policy, by Margaret Kelly, Naheed Kirmani, Miranda Xafa, Clemens Boonekamp, and Peter Winglee. 1988.

62. The Common Agricultural Policy of the European Community: Principles and Consequences, by Julius Rosenblatt, Thomas Mayer, Kasper Bartholdy, Dimitrios Demekas, Sanjeev Gupta, and Leslie Lipschitz. 1988.

61. Policy Coordination in the European Monetary System. Part I: The European Monetary System: A Balance Between Rules and Discretion, by Manuel Guitián. Part II: Monetary Coordination Within the European Monetary System: Is There a Rule? by Massimo Russo and Giuseppe Tullio. 1988.

60. Policies for Developing Forward Foreign Exchange Markets, by Peter J. Quirk, Graham Hacche, Viktor Schoofs, and Lothar Weniger. 1988.

59. Measurement of Fiscal Impact: Methodological Issues, edited by Mario I. Blejer and Ke-Young Chu. 1988.

58. The Implications of Fund-Supported Adjustment Programs for Poverty: Experiences in Selected Countries, by Peter S. Heller, A. Lans Bovenberg, Thanos Catsambas, Ke-Young Chu, and Parthasarathi Shome. 1988.

57. The Search for Efficiency in the Adjustment Process: Spain in the 1980s, by Augusto Lopez-Claros. 1988.

56. Privatization and Public Enterprises, by Richard Hemming and Ali M. Mansoor. 1988.

55. Theoretical Aspects of the Design of Fund-Supported Adjustment Programs: A Study by the Research Department of the International Monetary Fund. 1987.

54. Protection and Liberalization: A Review of Analytical Issues, by W. Max Corden. 1987.

53. Floating Exchange Rates in Developing Countries: Experience with Auction and Interbank Markets, by Peter J. Quirk, Benedicte Vibe Christensen, Kyung-Mo Huh, and Toshihiko Sasaki. 1987.

52. Structural Reform, Stabilization, and Growth in Turkey, by George Kopits. 1987.

51. The Role of the SDR in the International Monetary System: Studies by the Research and Treasurer's Departments of the International Monetary Fund. 1987.

50. Strengthening the International Monetary System: Exchange Rates, Surveillance, and Objective Indicators, by Andrew Crockett and Morris Goldstein. 1987.

49. Islamic Banking, by Zubair Iqbal and Abbas Mirakhor. 1987.

48. The European Monetary System: Recent Developments, by Horst Ungerer, Owen Evans, Thomas Mayer, and Philip Young. 1986.

47. Aging and Social Expenditure in the Major Industrial Countries, 1980–2025, by Peter S. Heller, Richard Hemming, Peter W. Kohnert, and a Staff Team from the Fiscal Affairs Department. 1986.

46. Fund-Supported Programs, Fiscal Policy, and Income Distribution: A Study by the Fiscal Affairs Department of the International Monetary Fund. 1986.

45. Switzerland's Role as an International Financial Center, by Benedicte Vibe Christensen. 1986.

44. A Review of the Fiscal Impulse Measure, by Peter S. Heller, Richard D. Haas, and Ahsan H. Mansur. 1986.

42. Global Effects of Fund-Supported Adjustment Programs, by Morris Goldstein. 1986.

41. Fund-Supported Adjustment Programs and Economic Growth, by Mohsin S. Kahn and Malcolm D. Knight. 1985.

39. A Case of Successful Adjustment: Korea's Experience During 1980–84, by Bijan B. Aghevli and Jorge Márquez-Ruarte. 1985.

38. Trade Policy Issues and Developments, by Shailendra J. Anjaria, Naheed Kirmani, and Arne B. Petersen. 1985.

36. Formulation of Exchange Rate Policies in Adjustment Programs, by a Staff Team Headed by G.G. Johnson. 1985.

35. The West African Monetary Union: An Analytical Review, by Rattan J. Bhatia. 1985.

34. Adjustment Programs in Africa: The Recent Experience, by Justin B. Zulu and Saleh M. Nsouli. 1985.

33. Foreign Private Investment in Developing Countries: A Study by the Research Department of the International Monetary Fund. 1985.

30. The Exchange Rate System—Lessons of the Past and Options for the Future: A Study by the Research Department of the International Monetary Fund. 1984.

29. Issues in the Assessment of the Exchange Rates of Industrial Countries: A Study by the Research Department of the International Monetary Fund. 1984.

Note: For information on the title and availability of Occasional Papers not listed, please consult the IMF *Publications Catalog* or contact IMF Publication Services. Occasional Papers Nos. 5–26 are $5.00 a copy (academic rate: $3.00); Nos. 27–64 are $7.50 a copy (academic rate: $4.50); and from No. 65 on, the price is $10.00 a copy (academic rate: $7.50).